The Information Retrieval Series   Volume 31

Efthimis Efthimiadis • Juan M. Fernández-Luna •
Juan F. Huete • Andrew MacFarlane

Editors

Teaching and Learning in Information Retrieval

 Springer

Editors

Efthimis Efthimiadis
University of Washington
PO Box 352840
Seattle, WA 98195-2840
USA
efthimis@u.washington.edu

Andrew MacFarlane
City University London
Department of Information Science
Northampton Square
London EC1V 0HB
United Kingdom
andym@soi.city.ac.uk

Juan F. Huete
Juan M. Fernández-Luna
Universidad de Granada
Departamento de Ciencias de la
Computación eInteligencia Artificial
C/ Periodista Daniel Saucedo Aranda, s/n.
18071 Granada
Spain
jhg@decsai.ugr.es
jmfluna@decsai.ugr.es

ISSN 1387-5264
ISBN 978-3-662-50677-6   e-ISBN 978-3-642-22511-6
DOI 10.1007/978-3-642-22511-6
Springer Heidelberg Dordrecht London New York

ACM Computing Classification (1998): H.3, K.3.2

Springer is part of Springer Science+Business Media (www.springer.com)

To Efthimis

Acknowledgements

The editors are very grateful to Rachel Woodbrook for her hard working in assembling and formatting the book from the different submissions – a very arduous task!

Andrew MacFarlane would like to thank the committee of the Information Retrieval Specialist group of the BCS for their continued support in the area of Teaching and Learning in IR.

Each chapter was reviewed by at least two referees looking at the subject matter, coverage, appropriateness and clarity of expression. We are very grateful for the referees for taking the time to produce thorough reviews for the chapters presented in this book. The referees were as follows:

David Bawden, City University London, UK
Suzanne Bell, University of Rochester, USA
Daniel Blank, University of Bamberg, Germany
Fidel Cacheda, University of A Coruña, Spain
Fazli Can, Bilkent University, Turkey
Pablo Castells, Autonomous University of Madrid, Spain
Anne Diekema, Utah State University, USA
Ayse Goker, City University London, UK
Kai Halttunen, University of Tampere, Finland
Dick Hartley, Manchester Metropolitan University, UK
Frances Johnson, Manchester Metropolitan University, UK
Diane Kelly, University of North Carolina, USA
Donald Kraft, Louisiana State University, USA
Monica Landoni, University of Lugano, Switzerland
Ray Larson, University of California, Berkeley, USA
Fotis Lazarinis, TEI of Mesolonghi, Greece
Rafael López García, University of A Coruña, Spain
Juan-Antonio Martínez-Comeche, University Complutense Madrid, Spain
Xiannong Meng, Bucknell University, USA
Stefano Mizzaro, University of Udine, Italy

Uma Murthy, Virginia Tech, USA
Pauline Rafferty, Abersystwyth University, UK
Edie Rassmussen, University of British Columbia, Canada
Ian Ruthven, University of Strathclyde, UK
Mark Sanderson, RMIT University, Australia
Anabela Serrano, ESEIG/Instituto Politécnico do Porto, Portugal
Debora Shaw, Indiana University Bloomington, USA
Jesús Tramullas, Universidad de Zaragoza, Spain
Clare Thornley, University College Dublin, Ireland
Jesús Vegas, Universidad de Valladolid, Spain
José Luis Vicedo, University of Alicante, Spain
Seungwon Yang, Virginia Tech, USA

Contents

Contributors

Suzanne Bell University of Rochester, Rochester, NY, USA

Daniel Blank University of Bamberg, Bamberg, Germany

Fidel Cacheda University of A Coruña, A Coruña, Spain

Juan-Antonio Martínez-Comeche University Complutense Madrid, Madrid, Spain

Efthimis N. Efthimiadis University of Washington, PO Box 35284098195-2840 Seattle, WA, USA

Juan M. Fernández-Luna Departamento de Ciencias de la Computación eInteligencia Artificial C/ Periodista Daniel Saucedo, Universidad de Granada, Aranda, s/n. 18071, Granada, Spain

Edward Fox Virginia Tech, Blacksburg, VA, USA

Norbert Fuhr University of Duisburg-Essen, Duisburg-Essen, Germany

Rafael López García University of A Coruña, A Coruña, Spain

Kai Halttunen University of Tampere, Tampere, Finland

Andreas Henrich University of Bamberg, Bamberg, Germany

Juan F. Huete Departamento de Ciencias de la Computación eInteligencia Artificial C/ Periodista Daniel Saucedo, Universidad de Granada, Aranda, s/n. 18071, Granada, Spain

Frances Johnson Manchester Metropolitan University, Manchester, UK

Andrew MacFarlane City University London, London, UK

Thomas Mandl University of Hildesheim, Hildesheim, Germany

Gary Marchionini University of North Carolina-Chapel Hill, Chapel Hill, NC, USA

Stefano Mizzaro University of Udine, Udine, Italy

Josiane Mothe Université de Toulouse/IRIT, Toulouse, France

Uma Murthy Virginia Tech, Blacksburg, VA, USA

Sanghee Oh University of North Carolina-Chapel Hill, Chapel Hill, NC, USA

Jeffrey P. Pomerantz University of North Carolina-Chapel Hill, Chapel Hill, NC, USA

Thomas Rolleke Queen Mary University of London, London, UK

Gilles Sahut Institut Universitaire de Formation des Maîtres, Ecole Interne de l'Université de Toulouse le Mirail, Université de Toulouse, CNRS-UMR5505, Cedex 9, France

Mark Sanderson RMIT University, Melbourne, VIC, Australia

Hinrich Schütze University of Stuttgart, Stuttgart, Germany

Benno Stein Bauhaus-Universitat Weimar, Weimar, Germany

Clare Thornley University College Dublin, Dublin, Ireland

Ricardo da S. Torres University of Campinas, Campinas, Sao paulo, Brazil

Javier Velasco-Martin University of North Carolina-Chapel Hill, Chapel Hill, NC, USA

Amy Warner The National Archives, London, UK

Barbara M. Wildemuth University of North Carolina-Chapel Hill, Chapel Hill, NC, USA

Seungwon Yang Virginia Tech, Blacksburg, VA, USA

About the Editors

Efthimis N. Efthimiadis obtained his PhD in Information Science from City University London in 1992. His research focused on the design of front-end interfaces that improve access to databases, and on the evaluation of information retrieval systems. Further interests included the application of probabilistic techniques to information retrieval and in methods that incorporate user preferences and user interaction in the retrieval techniques. Efthimiadis' research in the area of query expansion was concerned with the evaluation of ranking algorithms and the study of the searching behaviour of end users. Prof. Efthimiadis taught courses on the principles of information retrieval, database design, online search techniques, Internet access, introduction to information science, business information and medical informatics.

Juan M. Fernández-Luna obtained his Computer Science degree in 1994 from the University of Granada, Spain. In 2001, he got his PhD from the same institution, working on a thesis in which several retrieval models based on Bayesian networks for Information Retrieval were designed. Currently, his main research area is XML retrieval, although he is also working in collaboration with Juan F. Huete in collaborative IR, recommender systems, learning to rank and heterogeneous data source integration. He has experience in organizing international conferences and workshops, e.g., I and II International Workshops on Teaching and Learning of Information Retrieval. He has been a co-editor of several journal special issues, highlighting the special Information Retrieval issue on Teaching and Learning of Information Retrieval. He also belongs to the programme committee of the main IR conferences.

Juan F. Huete is an assistant professor at the Department of Computer Science and Artificial Intelligence at the University of Granada. He got his Ph.D. in 1995, researching on the uncertainty treatment in Artificial Intelligence under the formalism of Bayesian networks. From 1998, his research interest is Information Retrieval, designing retrieval models based on these graphical models. He is also currently working in the Recommender System field, although other fields like collaborative IR or learning to rank. He has been a co-editor of a special

Information and Processing Management issue on Bayesian Networks and Information Retrieval. He has co-organized several international conferences, as well as workshops. Among these last types of events, the following three could be highlighted: I and II International Workshop on Teaching and Learning of Information Retrieval and the SIGIR'07 Workshop on Information Retrieval and Graphical Models.

Andrew MacFarlane is a senior lecturer in the Department of Information Science at City University, and currently co-directs the Centre of Interactive Systems Research with Prof. Stephen Robertson of Microsoft Research Cambridge. He got his PhD Information Science from the same department under the supervision of Prof. Robertson and Dr. J.A. McCann (now at Imperial College London) in 2000. His research interests currently focus on a number of areas including parallel computing for information retrieval, disabilities and Information Retrieval (dyslexia in particular), AI techniques for Information Retrieval and Filtering, and Open Source Software Development. He is the Chair of the BCS Information Retrieval Specialist Group and is a long standing member of that SG.

Efthimis Efthimiadis: An Appreciation

Efthimis Efthimiadis passed away on Thursday, 28 April 2011 at the age of 54 after a courageous battle with pancreatic cancer. Efthi was born in Athens, Greece, and received a Bachelor of Arts degree in Economics from the University of Athens and Master and Doctoral degrees from City University, London. In London, he met and married the love of his life, Jagoda. Efthi went to the USA to teach at UCLA and he and Jagoda lived in Los Angeles where their son Nicholas was born, before moving to Seattle to work for the University of Washington. Efthi was a professor in the Information Science School at the University of Washington for 14 years. Efthi is remembered by his colleagues for his intellectual curiosity and enthusiasm for research, as well as his kindness, sense of humour and infectious smile. Efthi was an active person and he loved to travel and spend time with his family. Efthi is survived by Jagoda, his son Nicholas, and his mother Veta and brother Agapios, both of Athens, Greece. Efthi's family and friends will remember Efthi for his courage, his joy in life, and his selfless commitment and loyalty to those he loved.

Andy, Juan and Juanma pay tribute to Efthi's drive and enthusiasm without which it would have been very difficult to produce this book. We dedicate it to his memory.

Chapter 1
Introduction to Teaching and Learning in Information Retrieval

Efthimis N. Efthimiadis[†], Juan M. Fernández-Luna, Juan F. Huete, and Andrew MacFarlane

1.1 Introduction

For a number of years, the editors of this volume have attempted to provide a higher profile for teaching and learning as applied to information retrieval (IR), either by organizing workshops such as the Teaching and Learning in IR workshops run in 2007 (Huete et al. 2007) and 2008 (MacFarlane et al. 2008), or editing special issues on the subject in learned journals (Fernández-Luna et al. 2009b). This book continues this effort and addresses a number of significant issues in the discipline, which had been identified either by us or by colleagues who have written papers to be presented at the workshops we organized or published in journals.

It was felt by us, when first starting out this journey, that insufficient attention was given to an important aspect of academics' lives – teaching. There has been very little work done on pedagogical research in IR, apart from the notable effort of Edward Fox and colleagues to address the issue of what should be in the curricula for various types of students at the tertiary level – undergraduate, masters, and Ph.D. (Fox 1996).

The objective of this book is to provide ideas and practical experience of teaching and learning for IR, for those whose job requires them to teach in one form or another, and delivering IR courses is a major part of their working lives. In doing this we hope to share best practice and encourage the dissemination of ideas which are known to work well with real students, and in doing so provide a better profile for the field as a whole. We also where necessary tackle the theoretical ideas in teaching and learning which need to be addressed by any practitioner.

J.M. Fernández-Luna (✉)
Departamento de Ciencias de la Computación eInteligencia Artificial C/ Periodista Daniel Saucedo, Universidad de Granada, Aranda, s/n. 18071, Granada, Spain
e-mail: jmfluna@decsai.ugr.es

E. Efthimiadis et al. (eds.), *Teaching and Learning in Information Retrieval*,
The Information Retrieval Series 31, DOI 10.1007/978-3-642-22511-6_1,
© Springer-Verlag Berlin Heidelberg 2011

In this introduction, we briefly introduce a taxonomy of teaching and learning in IR, and show how this taxonomy is applied to the structure and organization of the main themes addressed in this book. A conclusion is given at the end.

1.2   A Taxonomy of Teaching and Learning

While undertaking a large-scale review of the literature in teaching and learning in IR (Fernández-Luna et al. 2009a), a taxonomy was derived which reflects the main aspects of the activities addressed in this book (see Fig. 1.1).

The taxonomy has two levels: one is more subject focused and provides a classification for the various fields in which IR can be applied, as well as the technical levels (Level 1); one focuses on the pedagogical aspects of teaching and learning as applied to IR, such as teaching and learning methods, assessment and student feedback and curricula design (Level 2). As there are clear overlaps between the two levels and for the sake of brevity, we focus on Level 2 in this chapter to explain the books' overall purpose and organization in Sect. 1.3. Level 1 issues are tackled explicitly where necessary.

1.3   Book Structure and Organization

1.3.1   Teaching and Learning Methods 1: Classroom

A number of different classroom techniques can be used for delivering material to students including lectures. Mizzaro provides a brief overview of presentations used to get students to engage in the material by providing an overview of a

> Level 1
>> [A] Technical Levels (non-technical to highly technical)
>> [B] Educational Goals:
>>> [b1] Library and information Science
>>> [b2] Computer Science
>
> Level 2
>> [1] Teaching and Learning methods:
>>> [1a] classroom
>>> [1b] e-learning (distance learning)
>>> [1c] use of IR systems for teaching
>> [2] Assessment and feedback
>> [3] Curricula

Fig. 1.1 A taxonomy of teaching and learning

research paper or a key technology (such as ranking techniques). Using an analogy with building methods, Halttunen describes a "scaffolding" method in which the teacher provides the overall framework for the student to learn, gradually taking away the "support" from the student who can then engage with the material without any help. This has the advantage of allowing students to learn at their own pace. Weekly Web exercises are used in this framework. Students are "anchored" into the material and tutorial support "fades" as they demonstrate they can engage with the ideas independently. Similarly, a problem-based learning approach can be used as advocated by Thornley, which starts with a given problem and leads to some solution or solutions. Thornley's educational philosophy is to start with the educational objectives, giving them conceptual frameworks to tackle problems, understanding that some problems are difficult, and being comfortable with that fact. The author then provides frameworks for students to work through problems independently. Sanderson also advocates a problem lead approach to teach Web search. A particular issue in IR is the need for understanding of relevance and the evaluation of sources in this context. Mothe and Sahut describe a method whereby examples of different sources are used to get students to think about the information quality issue, both as a consumer and providers of information. This allows the student to gain an understanding of the skills required to evaluate documents and judge relevance while searching.

1.3.2   Teaching and Learning Methods 2: Online Learning

The Internet and Web provides other opportunities to use different techniques in order to instruct students. Online learning, E-Learning, or Distance learning is a very clear example, and is now widely used in teaching for both remote and face-to-face students. Popular online learning systems are WebCT and Moodle. Martinez-Comeche and Cacheda-Seijo describe the use of a number of online tools in order to support student learning including forums and Wikis. Forums are used by encouraging the students to share problems, thereby identifying issues in the cohort. Questions are also posed in order to gauge the understanding of a particular topic, e.g., an understanding of recall. Wikis are used to disseminate information among students, and they are engaged to write for the Wiki, in the context of group work. Fox and colleagues describe the use of Second Life – a shared virtual environment – as a teaching for learning in such activities as project meetings. Bell presents her experiences in designing an entirely online IR course, her successes, failures, modifications, and planned changes. It is of particular interest how she uses screen capture software for the creation of demonstrations and tutorials. The course management system is Desire2Learn which is similar to other well-established systems, such as Blackboard including content areas, a discussion board, survey and quizzing functions, an electronic dropbox and grading system, and detailed tracking functions (who has looked at what, how many times, and for how long).

1.3.3 Teaching and Learning Methods 3: Use of Software/IR Systems

General Web tools are very useful for any subject being taught (see Sect. 1.3.2); however, the teaching of IR has particular problems which must be addressed by the use of various types of search tools. Lopez-Garcia and Cacheda-Seijo describe a set of software libraries which allow students to build IR components such as crawlers and searchers and how these are used to support the learning of Computer Science (CS) students. Johnson and Fox et al. point to a number of open source tools which can be used for the same purpose. Halttunen by contrast shows how search tools are used to support learning for Library and Information Science (LIS) students, including the examination of the output from these tools to examine issues such as evaluation. Similarly, Johnson describes different types of Web tools used to support understanding of how to design search in the context of visualization techniques. Sanderson and Warner also describe the use of Web tools for learning.

1.3.4 Assessment and Feedback

After delivery of material it is normal to test the student to assess their learning, and to what degree they have absorbed the material. In order to assist student learning, feedback is given to further help the student with their learning. This can be formative (unmarked to assist learning with certain issues for example) or summative (marked which goes towards the qualification which the student is undertaking). There are many forms of assessment methods such as exams, courseworks, online tests, etc. Mizzaro briefly describes the use of term projects as an optional assessment, together with a final mandatory oral examination. Halttunen conducts a survey at the beginning of the module delivered, and then uses a variety of methods to assess students' learning, including a reflective essay and practical search, collecting quantitative data in the later. Martinez-Comeche and Cacheda-Seijo use formative online assessments to assist student learning, and then use a class exam to provide a final mark for the student. Results on two different types of delivery are examined and conclusions drawn. Thornley advocates the use of traditional forms of assessment including essays, group work, and class tests. MacFarlane focuses on the use of Multiple Choice Questions (MCQs) to support the learning of students unfamiliar with the underlying mathematics needed for search, such as Boolean logic and evaluation measures (e.g., precision/recall). The use of this method for formative assessment is advocated, and a strategy is provided which provides the reader as to how to construct a set of questions to support student learning. Blank and colleagues describe a number of different practical assessments which can be used to assess student learning including searching online systems and the use of programming problems, e.g., either a project or implementing a component such as ranking. Sanderson and Warner focus on

Web search and the different components in such activities such as querying and evaluation, making flaws a feature of the exercise which students could reflect on and learn from these flaws. They describe an in-class feedback session where the results of searches were discussed in the context of conducting scientific experiments. Since the course of Bell is entirely online the use of prompt feedback is essential. The email has proved to be an effective tool to get both regular and immediate feedback. The students appreciate the friendly and enthusiastic tone of the communications. In order to engage the students, detailed and personalized feedback on assignments was provided.

Teaching and learning is not just about assessing the performance of students – a good teacher will try and reflect on what they have done and attempt to improve their methods to help students who will take the module in the future. In order to do this, it is desirable to get feedback from students on their experience of learning. The use of anonymous feedback is very common, and work described in this book is no exception. Lopez-Garcia and Cacheda-Seijo describe feedback which allows the students to provide information on the difficulties they faced while implementing components for the coursework as well as teaching materials made available. This information can be used by a reflective teacher to improve the delivery of their subject. Mizzaro also uses feedback to collect not only the students' experience of the course, but also prior experience to undertaking the module. The latter can be used to tailor the course to student needs. Mizzaro uses a highly structured questionnaire which gathers quantitative data using the Likert scale, as well as qualitative data (an example questionnaire is provided in the appendix). Yang and colleagues describe the use of feedback from graduate students to develop IR curricula. Bell gathered formal feedback on the course through two online surveys each semester: a standard one, fourteen Likert scale statements and three open-ended questions, and a survey she designed using SurveyMonkey to ask questions specifically about the content of this course. The input from both surveys has proved valuable and informative, and provided guidance for changes.

1.3.5 Curricular

A key question is – given the breadth and depth of knowledge gained on information over the past 50 years – what material do we deliver to the students. This will often start with educational goals or learning outcomes, which can drive our thoughts on what knowledge we want our students to have on completion of our modules. Johnson focuses on educational goals for different types of students including CS and LIS. Mizzaro focuses on the issue of teaching Web IR and traditional IR techniques to CS students. Blank and colleagues take account of knowledge from LIS, but focus on more technical issues such as understanding of data structures for CS students. Fox and colleagues also focus on more technical issues, but for graduate students. Mothe's and Sahuts' educational goals are more focused on assessing the quality of sources, useful for any student at any level of education. Sanderson focuses more on LIS students, and the needs of users and using Web search to meet those needs. Yang and colleagues give an example of educational goals derived for curricula using the example of "image retrieval" module, which can be used by the reader to think about how to write their own learning objectives. Bell presents an entirely online course focused on LIS students, with the objective of understanding the basics of using electronic IR systems in order to obtain information, emphasizing Internet and commercial services.

Once the educations goals have been derived, teachers can think about curricula for their modules. All the papers in this book give reference to the material which can be delivered either implicitly or explicitly. For example, Blank et al. and Mizzaro take their educational goals and show what is delivered on their modules. A key chapter in the development of curricula and other educational resources is Yang et al.'s chapter, which focuses on the development of such for IR courses, but in a digital library context. They take important aspects of both LIS and CS disciplines to build a set of topics which can be tailored to students, in the context of a generic digital library curricula previously defined. This is an important effort in bringing together ideas from the various disciplines in order to address both system- and service-oriented issues, which many types of student can benefit from. A method or process to continually update the syllabuses of IR courses is described – evaluation of what is being delivered is a hallmark of a reflective teacher. Resources developed by this resource are made publicly available.

1.4 Conclusion

The chapters in this book provide an excellent overview of teaching and learning in IR, for all types of teacher, whether they are new to the field, new to teaching, or looking to incorporate new ideas into their current teaching has a lot to gain from reading them. The overview we provide earlier allows the reader to identify particular interests in the various chapters, but there is much to be gained by reading all the chapters in the book and thinking about how the techniques and ideas outlined could help in improving teaching. We hope that this volume will become a valuable source of information for those who undertake the delivery of ideas to students – a handbook of teaching and learning in IR.

References

Fernández-Luna JM, Huete JF, MacFarlane A, Efthimiadis EN (2009a) Teaching and learning information retrieval. Inf Retr 12(2):201–226

Fernández-Luna JM, Huete JF, MacFarlane A (2009b) Introduction to the special issue on teaching and learning in information retrieval. Inf Retr 12:99–101

Fox E (1996) Courseware, training and curriculum in information retrieval. In: Frei HP, Harman D, Schauble P, Wilkinson R (eds) Proceedings of the 19th annual ACM SIGIR conference and research and development in information retrieval, Zurich, Switzerland. doi:10.1145/243199.243321

Huete J, Fernández-Luna JM, MacFarlane A, Ounis I (eds) (2007) First international workshop on teaching and learning of information retrieval (TLIR 2007), London, UK. http://www.bcs.org/server.php?show=nav.8704. Accessed 27 Oct 2010

MacFarlane A, Fernández-Luna JM, Huete JF, Efthimiadis E (eds) (2008) Second international workshop on teaching and learning in information retrieval (TLIR 2008), London, UK. http://www.bcs.org/ewic/tlir2008. Accessed 27 Oct 2010

Chapter 2
Fostering Student Engagement in an Online IR Course

Suzanne Bell

2.1 Introduction

The benefits of student engagement in the learning process, sometimes referred to as active learning, are the subject of considerable research in the education literature, particularly as they apply to K-12 students.[1] The topic of creating learning situations that encourage and inspire students to become actively involved in the learning process is appropriate for teaching and learning at any level, of course, and it is encouraging to see it being increasingly addressed in the context of higher education.[2] The case of the entirely online course, however, presents special challenges as well as opportunities.[3] In an in-person class engagement starts at a face-to-face personal level and is more easily perpetuated by a regular meeting schedule. How can an online course move beyond the passive presentation of readings and assignments to engage the students and inspire them to become active, contributing members of a classroom community?

This chapter explores the topic of creating student engagement in the online class environment, both at a broad level applying to any discipline, and more specifically as the topic applies to teaching information retrieval. The core of the chapter describes my experience with an undergraduate information retrieval course, LIS 330 (see Sect. 2.3). The course includes some students planning to

---

[1] Dunlap et al. (2007) provides an excellent list of such references.

[2] Examples of works looking at engagement in the higher education classroom may be found in Smith et al. (2005), Steele and Fullagar (2009); works looking at engagement in online courses are noted in Sect. 2.4.1.

[3] Newlands and Coldwell (2005) provides an accessible discussion of the differences, challenges, and advantages of online vs. classroom instruction by looking at student and faculty expectations, crucial factors in successful teaching and learning.

S. Bell (✉)
River Campus Libraries, University of Rochester, Rochester, NY 14627, USA
e-mail: sbell@library.rochester.edu

E. Efthimiadis et al. (eds.), *Teaching and Learning in Information Retrieval*,
The Information Retrieval Series 31, DOI 10.1007/978-3-642-22511-6_2,
© Springer-Verlag Berlin Heidelberg 2011

pursue a master's in library science, but many who are not. The latter students are headed for careers in information technology and computer support across the spectrum of the business world. The students are a fairly diverse population and are taking the course because it is required. All of these factors can create special challenges for fostering engagement, especially in an all-online environment. Using various active learning techniques, however, I believe I have created a successful course, and one that others can learn from and emulate.

Courses are always an evolving process and this one is no different. Some things I tried fell flat; feedback on other activities, such as the use of real-life questions, indicated the students wanted more, and some activities were far more successful than I anticipated. The successes, failures, modifications, and planned changes are described. The use of screen capture software for the creation of demonstrations and tutorials for information retrieval resources is of particular interest. IR resources – databases, Web search engines – cry out for visual, active demonstration, and then imitation and repetition by learners to achieve mastery. In an in-person class, half the time might be spent on live demonstrations and student imitation and practice. Luckily, screen capture software allows us to imitate that experience to a reasonable extent.

2.2 Teaching and Learning Information Retrieval

There is a strong and growing body of literature about pedagogy for the specific topic of "information retrieval," including both classroom and e-learning environments. Much of the work comes out of the first and second International Workshops on Teaching and Learning of Information Retrieval (Huete et al. 2007; MacFarlane et al. 2008), the special issue of *Information Retrieval* devoted to this topic (Information Retrieval 2009), and most recently, this book. Other sources also contribute to the discussion, e.g., methods for establishing a curriculum for information retrieval (Blank et al. 2009). Much of the work just mentioned [for example, Henrich and Sieber (2009)] approaches the topic of IR courses from a computer science rather than a library science point of view, with exceptions such as Bawden et al. (2007). This chapter approaches information retrieval from a library science perspective.

2.2.1 Need for Engagement in an Online IR Class

Electronic information retrieval is actually a subject well suited for online instruction; indeed, the very act of participating in the class is a form of information retrieval. However, the lack of face time in a classroom situation means that the amount that students must absorb by reading is perforce much greater (instructions, explanations, feedback, lecture notes), and the burden of responsibility for putting in the hours of practice and experimentation required to develop good IR skills is totally dependent on the students' own initiative. There are no labs, no artificially set aside times wherein the students are obliged to grapple with the online resources, and no one to provide a personal, guiding hand. As Newlands and Coldwell (2005) notes:

> "The responsibility for learning rests squarely on the students' own shoulders. . . . the online learning environment is a *pull* technology as opposed to the face-to-face classroom situation which is more congruent with *push* technology. . . . in the online environment, the best that the teacher can achieve is to make available the information that they require the student to access. It is then up to the student to access and read that information."

An even greater challenge in an IR class is that the students then have to *leave* the structure and relative handholding of the course management system and go off on their own into databases or the Web. They are constantly obliged to forge their own new trails into virgin, unknown territory without the immediacy of an instructor, or even classmates, present. While I felt that the content of an information retrieval course could lend itself well to an online environment, I was concerned that the self-discipline required of the students was likely to be a stumbling block for many of them. Despite the successful engagement shown in other studies of online learners (Chen et al. 2008), I was anxious about keeping my students motivated and on task in the asynchronous online environment. Getting the students engaged in their learning process would be crucial.

2.2.2   Fostering Student Engagement Online

Quite a number of articles and books have been written providing advice and the best practices for online teaching (Artino 2008; Bangert 2006; Dawley 2007; Downing and Holtz 2008; Kao et al. 2008; Koontz et al. 2006; Tallent-Runnels et al. 2006; Van Keuren 2006; Yang and Huang 2003). Many trace their roots to Chickering and Gamson's seminal work, "Seven principles of good practice in undergraduate education." These principles state that good teaching (and thus, good learning):

1. Encourages contact between students and faculty
2. Develops reciprocity and cooperation among students
3. Encourages active learning
4. Gives prompt feedback
5. Emphasizes time on task
6. Communicates high expectations
7. Respects diverse talents and ways of learning (Chickering and Gamson 1987)

A study from the student perspective also identifies seven items that students most often mention as contributing to effective online teaching, including: adapting to student needs, using meaningful examples, motivating students to do their best, facilitating the course effectively, and showing concern for student learning (Young 2006).

I wish I had approached the design of my course having read all of this material, but have to admit that time pressures forced me to resort to the resources closest to hand: my "college of colleagues" and my own intuition. Thus, my first step in preparation for teaching online was to gather both student and faculty perspectives on the process. I talked to members of the staff at the University of Rochester Libraries who were currently working on their MLS degrees and taking online courses, as well as to faculty friends or friends of friends who had experience teaching online; all were very helpful. From that groundwork I proceeded to adjust material that had worked in the classroom, and to invent new material specifically for the online environment.

2.3   About LIS 330

The School of Information Studies (SOIS) at the University of Wisconsin, Milwaukee (UWM) offers both an undergraduate degree and a graduate program in Library and Information Science. LIS 330, Electronic Information Retrieval Systems, is a required course in the Bachelor of Science in Information Resources (BSIR) curriculum. There are two prerequisites: LIS 110, Introduction to Information Science and LIS 210, Information Resources for Research. A core course, LIS 330 is offered in both the fall and spring semesters and has a long history of being offered on-campus in alternating day and evening time slots. Students in LIS 330 are usually in their junior or senior year, and many of them are nontraditional students: somewhat older than college age and juggling full- or part-time employment, families, and coursework. Offering LIS 330 as an online, distance education course provides obvious advantages for both the School and the students.

From 2003 to 2005, I taught a very similar course in the traditional classroom for the graduate LIS program at the University of Buffalo, NY. The experience inspired me to write a textbook for the course based on the curriculum I developed (Bell 2006, 2009). When UWM approached me to teach their course I was eager for the opportunity to apply my methodologies and teach again. The course would need updating and changing in a number of ways, but principally it would need to be reconfigured for entirely online delivery, as I am based far from Wisconsin in Rochester, NY. The students and I never meet in person.

2.3.1   *Educational Objectives and Goals of LIS 330*

The description of LIS 330 in the UWM Undergraduate Catalog says simply: "Basics of using electronic information retrieval systems, emphasizing Internet and commercial services, in order to obtain information" (School of Information Studies 2010). In choosing and designing content for LIS 330, my objectives are to enable students to:

- Understand basic information retrieval terminology and techniques
- Understand the interface structures of information retrieval systems from a variety of vendors
- Quickly adapt to and interpret new interfaces on known or new information retrieval systems
- Analyze information requests and then:
- Select appropriate resource(s) from the available commercial or free Web databases or search engines
- Formulate and employ appropriate search strategies to retrieve relevant information
- Evaluate search outcomes
- Demonstrate knowledge of a range of commercially and publicly available information retrieval systems
- Gain an understanding of human information seeking behaviors, in order to assist others more effectively in their query formation and searching
- List and discuss evaluation criteria for commercial and Internet-based search systems
- Identify and discuss problems, issues, and future developments in information retrieval and online searching

Overall, my educational goals are to produce students who are knowledgeable and informed about information retrieval issues, and, very importantly, who are *flexible* and able to adapt to an ever-changing IR environment. I do this by providing the students with certain basic, universal tools (such as Boolean logic), and then exposing them to a wide variety of resources and information retrieval problems. I was able to achieve these goals in the classroom; could they be attained as well in an entirely online, asynchronous environment?

2.3.2   The Online Course Environment at UWM

UWM uses the course management system Desire2Learn, or D2L, for its online course offerings. D2L is similar to other well-established, sophisticated online course systems (such as Blackboard), in that it includes content areas, a discussion board, survey and quizzing functions, an electronic dropbox and grading system, and detailed tracking functions (who has looked at what, how many times, and for how long).

2.4   What Worked

2.4.1   A Welcoming Tone

One of the first things I wanted to do was establish a relaxed, friendly atmosphere, and to try to create some semblance of an "in-class" experience. It was important to me to prevent "the emotional and cognitive disconnection experienced by many students taking Web-based courses" (Lewis and Abdul-Hamid 2006). To that end, I repurposed an activity I'd used in the in-person version of this class to work online: the first thing students are asked to do is post an introduction for themselves to a discussion board set up for the purpose. They are asked to provide responses to seven questions:

- Name you go by (e.g., if your name is James and you prefer James, not Jim; or Beth Ellen but you go by Ellen, let us know)
- What year you are (sophomore, junior, senior, other?)
- Where you work, if you do
- Are you thinking of going for an MLS (library degree?)
- If yes, what kind of library do you think you'd like to work in someday?
- What you hope to get out of this class?
- Something fun/unique/special about you

Most of the questions are for my benefit, obviously, but the whole exercise, and the last question in particular, have proved very useful in engaging the students right from the beginning of the class. They discover former coworkers, people they have taken classes with before, people who have similar interests, and people who impress them. All of it sparks a camaraderie that seems to be beneficial. Others have also found this kind of activity useful, describing it as "the first step in nurturing a dynamic online interaction" (Lewis and Abdul-Hamid 2006).

To introduce myself, I post my introduction after all the students have posted theirs, and add to the course content a very short (1.5 min) movie of me welcoming them to the class. This gives the students a face and voice to associate with the abstract concept of "instructor" for the class. At the conclusion of this initial movie introduction I urge students to "surprise and delight me," an echo of Chickering and Gamson's Principle 6, high expectations. The movie has the same cheerful, "let's get the work done but have some fun, too" attitude that I try to convey in all my posts, emails, and weekly messages. I thoroughly concur with David James on the need for humor in online courses (James 2004).

2.4.2 Good Communication

2.4.2.1 Email

I quickly discovered that it helps to start each week with a class email, something others have found effective as well (Lewis and Abdul-Hamid 2006). The email includes highlights from the previous week, what the current week covers, and reminders about current assignments or prompts to start thinking about upcoming assignments. I then post the text of the email as an announcement on the homepage of the course. Sending it first as email, however, is a proactive way of reminding the students every week that I am still there and that the class is actively progressing; it seems to help the students manage their "time on task" (Chickering and Gamson's Principle 2). My tone is friendly and enthusiastic, and always ends with a reminder that if they were having any problems at all to get in touch. Since almost all of my interaction with the students is written (despite offering my phone numbers and Skype name, only two students have ever contacted me by phone), I try to ensure that my written "tone" is as close to my spoken tone as possible, to reduce the distance and inherent impersonal feel of the online environment. I also try to send the weekly email on the same day, even at about the same time, to provide a bit of the sense of regularity one gets with attending classes in person.

In teaching an online course, it helps to be an email addict. Experienced faculty warned me that online courses take a great deal of time, and advised including statements in the syllabus along the lines of "allow 24 h for responses to email." I did not include any limiting statements, because I knew I could not help checking in, and if a message were waiting, I would answer. Which is exactly what happened, and I never regretted giving free rein to my email addiction: there were never that many emails, and those who did write really appreciated the immediate feedback. As one student wrote on the UWM course evaluation: "I loved that the teacher was always available, even at crazy times of the night once in a while. It is always nice to have teachers who really care and want to help the students do their work correctly." Chickering and Gamson recognized "prompt feedback" in their Principle 4, and subsequent studies have found that having their interpersonal communication needs met by prompt, individualized responses is very important to student satisfaction (Dennen et al. 2007; Jung et al. 2002; Woods 2002), to the point of affecting their overall persistence in the course (Anonymous 2004). Students appreciate instructors who communicate in a "consistent, thoughtful, and personal way" (Young 2006), and who convey their enthusiasm and "persona" (Lewis and Abdul-Hamid 2006).

Feedback from the surveys conducted at the end of the semesters (see Sect. 2.6.2) indicates that the students appreciate both the tone and frequency of the communication. Some of the comments from the surveys: "I have often had the feeling with online courses that the teacher is absent and I'm doing everything on my own. I never got this feeling with 330." "Very enthusiastic about the subject matter, which makes it so much easier for students to enjoy it, too. She also was very easy to understand and communicate with." "Excellent, clear way of communicating and a great sense of humor, which definitely made me enjoy the class that much more." "The commentaries were also funny which was encouraging in the assignments."

2.4.2.2 Detailed Assignment Write-Ups

One is constantly aware in the online world that material that could be quickly explained and understood in person requires additional work to be accurately conveyed and correctly understood when it is being transmitted in purely written form. To that end, my assignments tend to start with more than the usual amount of detailed instructions. I worry constantly about the tradeoff between turning students off by being too wordy and forcing them to write for clarification because I have not been clear enough; thus wasting (their) valuable time while we negotiate answers back and forth. I do not get very many questions, though, and the students have not complained about the level of detail in the assignment write-ups. In the official SOIS course survey, 100% of respondents in both semesters "strongly agreed" with the statement: "The instructor clearly communicated the class assignment/activity expectations" (Table 2.2).

2.4.2.3   Detailed, Personalized Feedback

The other type of communication that I feel is important in engaging the students and keeping them feeling like they are making progress is providing detailed feedback on assignments. Artino (2008) also notes the importance of clear, challenging yet "proximal goals," along with "timely, honest, and explicit task feedback." I have experimented with several ways of doing this: for simpler assignments or ones that require no corrections, the comments function in the D2L dropbox may suffice. For all of the search assignments, the student turns in a Word file that I mark up using Track Changes. I then either upload the new file to the dropbox, or email it directly to the student. When I know the assignments will take me several days to grade, I prepare an "Answer Key" document and email it to everyone, and follow up with individually marked up papers. According to my surveys, the students liked all of these methods (Table 2.1). As one commented: "I seriously thought it was fantastic that you did all of these."

When I mark up papers, every question gets some kind of response from me. If the answer is correct, a simple "yes!" or "you got it" or "great job" and the points awarded is enough; if the answer is incorrect I provide a full explanation of why and where I think the student may have gone wrong, using screen snaps myself if I think it will help. Yes, it takes a considerable amount of time, and no, my classes are not very large: I request that enrollment be capped at 20 people, specifically so I *can* provide this level of personalized feedback. (Such a limit is also advocated by others, see Stevens-Long and Crowell 2002.) I feel that this feedback is crucial in demonstrating to the students that I care about their learning – which tends, I believe, to make them care more about their learning as well. Student comments from the course surveys support this idea: "I felt like you cared and that made me care." "It made it look like you really care. And for that matter, it also made it clear that you remembered who I was from one assignment to the next." In the SOIS survey, 100% of respondents in both semesters "strongly agreed" with the statement: "The instructor's comments on assignments, papers, and/or exams were helpful and constructive" (Table 2.2), and one noted: "she provided EXCELLENT feedback."

2.4.3 Organization and "Chunking" of Material

The D2L course system allows the instructor to structure the course content like an outline: within each outline level, the student sees a list of files, links, and subfolders of files. Folders can be visible or hidden. In my discussions with students during my planning stages, they told me they appreciated good organization and "chunking" of material: clearly defined packets of information with clear educational goals. While Dunlap et al. (2007) sees content chunking and sequencing as reflecting a "didactic, transmission" approach to instruction, she still appreciates "manageable units of instruction" – and so do students. I organize each week's material into a folder, and within the folders, put materials in the same order each time: lecture notes, movie demos, readings, and assignments.

That approach was definitely right: 100% of respondents to my survey said that this was helpful (Table 2.1). Comments included: "Yes! The consistency was very helpful and I knew what to expect each week." "This was one of the most organized online courses I have ever taken. There was so much content provided, and I feel the instructor did a great job going over the content." Organization was a recurring theme in the official School of Information Science course evaluation as well: 100% of respondents in both semesters "strongly agreed" with the statements: "The course was well organized" and "The instructor was organized and prepared for class" (Table 2.2). The terms "organized," "organization," and other synonyms also appear multiple times in the comments on the course "strengths." Organization is obviously important to students, and it is easy to understand why. An organized presentation of material helps relieve some of the cognitive load and need for self-direction for students, a responsibility that is difficult for many (Artino 2008).

2.4.3.1 Visible Organization

In an attempt to "chunk" the course content visibly as well as intellectually, I experimented with the visible/invisible feature in D2L. In the first semester, I only revealed 1 week of material at a time, and rotated the order of the folders so that the current week was always on top. At the end of that semester, responses to my question about this approach were decidedly mixed; only 40% of respondents were in favor of that approach (Table 2.1). Comments included "Sometimes it is nice to get an idea as to what to expect in future weeks so I could plan accordingly with work and outside class commitments." On the other hand: "I liked to have only the current week visible . . . It was easier to stay focused on one thing at a time." Based on this feedback, in the next semester I tried revealing the current week and one week ahead, still rotating the folders so that the current week was always at the top, minimizing the amount of scrolling needed.

The students appreciated the effort put into this somewhat mechanical aspect of the course: in my survey at the end of the second semester, 100% of the respondents were in favor of this approach (Table 2.1). Comments included: "I really liked being able to work ahead. Some teachers do not allow students to do that, and its [*sic*] frustrating" and simply "clap... clap... clap..." (indicating applause). Removing any potential area of frustration seems to help promote students' engagement with the course.

2.4.3.2 Clear Weekly Objectives

I try to address what I have been told about students' desire for clearly stated educational objectives and outcomes by starting each weekly set of PowerPoint lecture notes with the same set of slides: What this lecture will cover, Learning Objectives, and Learning Outcomes. It may sound somewhat artificial and not very scholarly, but I find the exercise of having to put what I want to happen that week into words – and then consulting it from time to time in the creation of the material for that week – really keeps me on track. I have no explicit reactions from the students about the material in these slides, but I hope it helps them feel like they know where they are going for the week, and that it provides realistic goals for all of us.

2.4.4 Student Choice in Assignments

It seems obvious: people are likely to work harder when the task or topic interests them. At the same time, any course has curriculum goals to be met, which is tricky to accomplish without a certain amount of structured instruction. While some students would respond well to an entirely freeform, "here's the general idea – go learn something" approach, as noted earlier, most students prefer *not* to have to shoulder all the responsibility for their own learning. A required course is a special problem, since students may go into it having, they think, little or no interest in the material. They need to be persuaded that there are elements of the topic with the potential to interest them, to be given the tools to enable them to successfully explore, and then to be unleashed to pursue their interests. Teachers of information retrieval have a decided advantage here; human nature's natural curiosity seldom fails to be drawn into the interesting puzzle solving of information seeking. As one student commented on the course survey: "I was not excited to take this class, but think it will prove to be one of the more useful courses in my studies with SOIS."

I find that giving the students a controlled, steadily increasing amount of personal choice in the assignments is a powerful engagement method. Early assignments almost all include a question towards the end of the activity that allows the student to make a choice of how to proceed, and asks them to describe the outcome and to justify their choice. At that stage the level of freedom is minimal, but manageable: the material is still new to them and they are more comfortable with a sense of structure. But even at this level, I am regularly surprised at the quality of the answers. Their remarks show that the students stopped and thought before answering: demonstrating a moment of real engagement with the material.

Later in the course I try to open up the assignments more and more. The students are equipped to make informed choices and employ appropriate strategies by then, and these assignments almost invariably produce some of the students' best work. These assignments include developing search strategies for an historical topic of their choice in the *America: History and Life* database, an interview assignment, the final search assignment (see Sect. 2.6.1.1), and the major project. For the major project they choose any database from the hundreds offered by UWM, or a freely available online resource, and create a teaching module or sales pitch for the resource. (The database or resource cannot be one covered in the class.) There is some structure to the assignment: the students need to define the audience for their presentation, and justify all the subsequent choices they make, e.g., delivery method, points included, etc. But all the big choices and decisions are theirs – whatever they want to do, backed up by justifications. The results are almost always outstanding, and the whole class gets to enjoy them: the students post their projects to a discussion board so that everyone can see them and learn something about another resource. PowerPoint presentations are common, but students also come up with ingenious ways to convey their work online: links to Web pages or to their own screen capture videos, PowerPoint with voiceover, scripts and handouts for theoretical in-person, hands on sessions. The students are encouraged to work with a partner on the major project, which also usually works well: some of the most innovative projects have been the team-created ones. The "greater success" of collaborative projects is also noted in other case studies (Artino 2008).

Overall, the assignments are designed to engage the students at any and every opportunity, and give them steadily increasing latitude for choice in topic or both topic and execution. This supports two more of Chickering and Gamson's best practices: making the students active participants in their learning (Principle 3), and respecting diverse talents and ways of learning (Principle 7).

2.4.5 Incorporating Multimedia

The positive effects of incorporating multimedia into online learning have been documented by Lewis and Abdul-Hamid (2006), Chen and Williams (2009), and Zhang (2005) among others. In the case of Scarnati and Garcia (2007), the redesign of a music history course by putting it entirely online, richly enhanced with multimedia, resulted in a much more effective class overall. Though my creations are much simpler than the ones described in these studies, the effect on student satisfaction has been similar. The screen capture software Camtasia™ is probably the single most effective teaching tool I use, and one that is ideal for the content of this course.[4]

---

[4] Oud (2009) provides an excellent discussion of the cognitive research that explains why media can be so effective in teaching, as well as guidelines for the creation of such screencasts.

Camtasia allows me to record demos of the databases being covered each week, capturing the action on the screen along with voiceover narration. The result is about as close as it is possible to get to presenting the demo live in class. Although I carefully plan what I am going to do (especially to keep each video fairly brief: 7–8 min at most), and rehearse it before recording, these movies are not polished by any means. My recordings are usually one-shot takes complete with the occasional misstep, with very little – if any – editing afterward. The "bloopers" give the movies a sense of immediacy and real life that I think makes them rather more engaging than a slick, polished production. The textbook (Bell 2009) includes many screen shots, but there is no substitute for seeing the process of information retrieval in action. Indeed, "[o]nly if the teacher can record problem solving activities and make it available as a video, [can] the complete information be made available to learners" (Schroeder and Spannagel 2006). In fact, the video format may in some ways be more helpful than a live demo, since it can be played over and over, stopped, backed up, fast-forwarded – whatever the student needs.

The most important thing is that the students find them useful, and the end-of-semester surveys definitely show they do. In my survey, in both semesters 80% or more of the respondents "strongly agreed" with the statement "The 'movies' were helpful." The remaining 20% "agreed" (Table 2.1). Survey comments on the movies were very positive: "Great portion of the learning. Learned a lot by the hands on viewing of the movies. Really worked nice." "[T]hey were very helpful and appreciated! Seeing and hearing something demonstrated 'live' is a good thing as people have varied learning styles and may not pick up on written instructions as easily." "This was probably the only course content I looked at in depth." "It always makes more sense when someone shows you exactly what to do than to try to explain it with words." "Lectures were very good and easy to follow with the use of movies."

2.5   What Did Not Work: Discussion Boards

The importance of discussion boards as a means to fostering engagement and active learning in online courses appears repeatedly in the literature (Jewell 2005; Persell 2004; Schellens and Valcke 2006; Wilson et al. 2007). The validity of what these authors are describing is provided by a reverse example, a case study of a less-than-effective class wherein the instructor did not participate in the online discussions (Shieh et al. 2008). Various case studies have found that while great emphasis is put on use of the discussion boards in online classes, the students' interactions there "are often quite shallow," and it is important for the instructor to "scaffold" the discussion (Artino 2008). Mazzolini and Maddison (2003) provide a detailed study of how the posting patterns of instructors affect how students use online discussion forums. A study by Dennen (2008) indicated that even if students do more reading than posting on the discussion boards ("lurking"), they are likely to feel that they learned more. Posting for the sake of posting does not contribute to student engagement.

Some of my discussion board activities work well: as noted in Sect. 5.1, the initial "introduction" post evokes very interesting, honest responses, and initiates more back-and-forth comments than any other "discussion." Responding to question prompts about a reading early in the semester works surprisingly well. Not nearly as surprising, the discussion board assignment for the week we address issues of image retrieval works well. The students make up a talk title and find an image to go on the first slide of their imaginary PowerPoint, and post both to a discussion board. This generally evokes creative, funny responses and commentary. Overall, however, my use of the discussion boards is the most problematic area in my online teaching.

2.5.1 More Instructor Involvement

The majority of my students' responses on the discussion boards are just that: responses to the initial question, without any further commentary on each other's posts. They are answering *me*, not talking amongst themselves, and the fault is probably mine. For one thing, I was trying so hard to stay out of the way that I seldom commented on any of their posts – I did not want them to think I was hovering and interfering in their discussion – but I think that approach backfired. Rather than not interfering, they may have interpreted my absence as not caring and not paying attention. This suspicion is borne out by comments on the student survey: "By interjecting more you end up spurring on ideas and comments. If you look at the boards, where you've commented there is a flurry of activity BECAUSE everyone thinks you're watching . . . it is nice to see your comments." On the other hand, another student noted: "I think in a class like this, tons of discussion board usage is not really necessary."

2.5.2 Better Questions

I think my questions also need work: if I want to foster *discussion*, I need to ask questions that do not have obvious, set answers, e.g., questions that foster higher level, critical thinking. In the current situation, if the first person to post provides the answer, what is there left for the others to say except to reiterate that answer in various forms? As one student put it: "a simple question will just get regurgitated over and over and create a giant circle-jerk that does not go anywhere or do anything." The questions "have to be interesting enough that people can come at [them] in a little different way and have a little different interpretation" (Lewis and Abdul-Hamid 2006). If not, the students are only posting because they must, in order to get the 2 points for that week's post. This is not useful to the students, as one noted: "I tend to do really poorly in classes that require a certain amount of discussion board posts every week because I feel like I'm just writing because I have to."

Questions about the discussion board or "class participation" in the course surveys were the only ones to elicit decidedly mixed responses. In the SOIS survey, the statement "The instructor encouraged class participation" elicited responses from "neither agree nor disagree" to "strongly agree" in each semester (Table 2.2). In my survey of the first semester's class, all of the respondents thought that the use of the discussion boards was "about right," but one added a cautionary note: "I feel like there was not a lot of student-to-student discussion unless the assignment particularly demanded it – something to keep in mind." I should have paid better attention; the next semester I added more discussion board questions, without spending enough time on the quality, with the result that some students now found use of the discussion boards to be "too much," along with some of the comments already noted (Table 2.1). The discussion boards provide a major opportunity for student engagement that I have yet to use as effectively as I would wish.

2.6   Assessments and Feedback

2.6.1   Assessing the Students

I feel that learning to do information retrieval well (in the library science sense of searching for information) is something like learning a language: building skills and knowledge incrementally combined with frequent practice are usually most effective. This idea guides how I present the material, and my assessment of the students: we start with basic concepts presented incrementally. The search assessments ask the students to apply those concepts in situations that are increasingly less well defined (but more like real life), and thus more difficult.

The students' final grades are based on a number of activities: the weekly search assignments, two other written assignments, the major project, and discussion board participation; a total of 20 grade elements in all. Everyone has individual strengths and weaknesses; the number and variety of the assignments tries to ensure that each student has opportunities to do well, and the overwhelming majority does do very well. A final grade of B or less is unusual, and even those students usually have several pieces of work that are excellent (they simply are not able, or chose not, to be consistent).

2.6.1.1   Search Assignments

Appropriately for a library science information retrieval course, the primary emphasis in the assessment activities is on searching. We start by learning about a small set of basic concepts (what I call the "Searcher's Toolkit"): Boolean logic, field searching, controlled vocabulary, truncation, etc. The weekly assignments then require the students to apply these "tools" in many different databases and search engines, so they are constantly practicing their skill set in situations of increasing complexity. Early assignments are fairly literal (find some piece of information and record it, with an exact description of how to find it), while later ones require more judgment, self-instruction, or problem solving. Structuring the activity in this way is intended to instill qualities of flexibility, adaptability, and independence in the students. The regularity of the assignments keeps me constantly apprised of their progress and alert to any need for intervention.

The final search assignment is a strong example of an "authentic instructional task" that requires students to engage in active learning (Partlow and Gibbs 2003). Students select any five questions from a list of 20 reference encounters drawn from my daily work over the years. They must decide what resource(s) to use from the entire universe of databases available at UWM or the Web, and as with all the other search assignments, describe in detail their thought processes, strategies used, results, and why they feel the results are appropriate for the question or situation. It is a challenging assignment, but again, the students generally do "surprise and delight" me with their results: by demonstrating mastery of the original concepts, choosing appropriate or interesting resources, creating excellent search queries, providing thoughtful analysis of a question, relentlessly pursuing an answer, or in some way displaying the combination of inspiration and organized problem solving that distinguishes a skilled information professional. Comments from some of the students indicate a certain delight in the challenge and pride at their successful results.

2.6.1.2 End Results

While not all of the students emerge from the class as information retrieval experts, they certainly leave much more aware and knowledgeable than when they entered. When they enter the course, they can do a Google search and look something up in Wikipedia like anyone else. By the end of the course, at a minimum they understand Boolean logic, they know that the University subscribes to hundreds of databases, they are aware that databases offer searching in specific fields, and they know they have been exposed to a wealth of searching beyond Google. Again, at a minimum, this may translate into a student choosing Google Scholar over Google for her next search, and perhaps to using the Advanced search screen in Scholar. At the other end of the spectrum, some students come out of the course with all of the basic searching concepts ready in their minds, knowing how to evaluate the resources they have at hand and how to select appropriate ones for the information need, able to execute efficient, intelligent searches in those resources, and able to learn from the initial results so as to refine and improve the search. They can go into a database they've never seen before and interpret the interface well enough to do a basic search, and again, learn from those results and refine the initial search. In short, they have the skills of an entry-level information professional: my skills, without my years of experience. At both ends of the spectrum I feel I have achieved success: the students who are not pursuing a career as an information professional have still had an intense learning experience, and are aware of the possibilities. Those students who are going to pursue an MLS are very well prepared, and will be able the use the skills they have gained throughout their academic and professional careers.

The students, as ever, have the last word. In the SOIS survey, 100% of respondents "strongly agreed" with the statements "The course assignments/ activities promoted my skills and knowledge of the subject matter" and "The course met its objectives" (Table 2.2).

2.6.2 Gathering Feedback from the Students

Formal feedback on the course is gathered through two online surveys each semester: a standard instrument used by the School of Information Science (14 Likert scale statements and three open-ended questions), administered via the course management system D2L, and a survey I designed using SurveyMonkey to ask questions specifically about the content of this course,[5] and to invite comments. The surveys are not required, and the response rate on both is about 50%. Comments and results from both surveys appear with their associated topics in the body of this chapter. Tables 2.1 and 2.2 provide a complete list of all the questions, response values, and results (for the rating scale questions) from both semesters. Comments from the open-ended questions and comments fields are included at appropriate points in the text of this chapter. The input from both surveys has proved extremely valuable and informative, and provided guidance for changes already made as well as plans for future changes, discussed below.

2.7 Future Work

The most pressing issue is to change how I use the discussion boards. My next approach will be to assign fewer, but more thought provoking, discussions, and to participate more myself: to "scaffold" the discussion. It would be extremely satisfying for me to see real "discussion" going on between the students, and from what the literature reports, the students would find that more satisfying and engaging as well.

Another immediate term goal is to evolve the scoring sheet currently used for the major project into a true rubric. The major project scoring sheet is currently a table

---

[5] A review of the literature on evaluations for online courses is provided by Achetemeier et al. (2003). For additional work on assessment of online teaching and learning, including an example of a survey created specifically for online courses, see Bangert (2004, Appendix A) and Herron and Wright (2006).

that appears in the description of the project, which is accessible to the students from the beginning of the course. This table provides a list of all the elements that I am looking for, and the number of points associated with each one. To turn this table into a rubric will require the additional specification of what represents high, medium, or low achievement for each element, and the associated point ranges. The descriptive material for each level of work gives the students much more information about how their work will be judged, and provides a rationalization for the number of points awarded in a "$0 - n$" points possible situation. For more on rubrics and their development, see Allen and Tanner (2006) and Schmitt et al. (2008).

A more long-term goal is to experiment with software that supports creation of *interactive* screencasts. It would be a much stronger and more engaging learning experience to have the students actively participating rather than passively watching as I demonstrate concepts. Deciding how to incorporate interactivity will take a good deal of planning, however, as will determining the most appropriate software to use, not to mention climbing another learning curve to master a new program. Although demanding in terms of time and effort, it will be an excellent investment in supporting student learning.

2.8 Conclusion

As we have seen from the literature and the example of LIS 330, Electronic Information Retrieval Systems, a required class in the BS in Information Retrieval degree at the University of Wisconsin, Milwaukee, it is fully possible to engage students even in a totally asynchronous online class. Frequent, personal communications that convey a sense of personality and humor, detailed assignment instructions as well as prompt, detailed feedback, providing latitude for student choice in the assignments, careful organization and structuring ("chunking") of material, and the use of multimedia in the form of screencast videos, all contribute to strong student engagement in LIS 330. The very nature of the material is an advantage, since it involves puzzle solving and information seeking, activities that many people find intrinsically interesting. One key element, the discussion board, has not been used as effectively as it could have been, but is fixable in the near term. Assigning fewer but more carefully chosen questions, and more frequent posts by the instructor, should address the problem. Converting the current scoring sheet for the major project to a rubric is also possible in the immediate future. A major goal for the future is to develop interactive screencast tutorials. This work will make an already successful online information retrieval course even more engaging and pedagogically effective.

Appendix Tables

Table 2.1 Author's SurveyMonkey survey of LIS 330 students

Question	Response values[a]	Spring 08/09	Fall 09/10
How much of the material in this class was new to you?	Very little	0%	33%
	About half	20%	33%
	Almost all	80%	33%
Was the total amount of work required by this class:	Too little	0%	0%
	About right	80%	100%
	Too much	20%	0%
In general, was the weekly workload:	Too little	0%	0%
	About right	80%	100%
	Too much	20%	0%
The order and timing of the assignments gave me enough time to complete them comfortably	Agree[b]	40%	50%
	Agree strongly	60%	50%
The weekly lecture notes (summarizing the chapter, providing learning objectives and outcomes, additional searches, etc.) were useful	Neutral	0%	33%
	Agree	40%	17%
	Agree strongly	60%	50%
The screen capture "movies" were useful	Agree	20%	17%
	Agree strongly	80%	83%
Did you find having each week's material in the same order, with the same labeling scheme, helpful?	Yes	100%	100%
	No	0%	0%
	Not sure	0%	0%
S08/09: The weekly course material was unveiled one week at a time. Would you have preferred to have everything visible from the start, so you could work ahead?	No: way it was worked ok	40%	
	Yes: everything should have been visible	40%	
	Not sure	20%	
F09/10: Did revealing the current week plus one week ahead, with the current material at the top, work for you?	Yes		100%
	No		0%
	Not sure		0%
S08/09: Was the use of the Discussion Boards:	Too little	0%	
	About right	100%	
	Too much	0%	
F09/10: I tried adding more use of the Discussion Boards this semester. Was the use of the Discussion Boards:	Too little		0%
	About right		67%
	Too much		33%
Which feedback methods did you find useful? (check all that apply)	Brief comments in the dropbox	40%	67%
	Uploading marked-up assignments to the dropbox	0%	83%
	Emailing "answer key" document to everyone	20%	83%
	Marking up your assignment and emailing it back	20%	83%

[a]Every question included the option to comment; comments are quoted at appropriate places in the text

[b]Only response values with content are listed for this question and the two following. The full set of response values was: Disagree strongly, Disagree, Neutral, Agree, Agree strongly

Table 2.2 University of Wisconsin-Milwaukee School of Information Science Standard Survey

Question	Response values[a]	Spring 08/09	Fall 09/10
The course was well organized	Strongly agree	100%	100%
The reading materials were helpful in furthering my	Strongly agree	100%	83%
understanding of the subject matter	Agree	0%	17%
The course assignments/activities promoted my skills and the	Strongly agree	100%	100%
knowledge of the subject matter			
My performance on assignments/activities and/or tests	Strongly agree	86%	100%
reflected what I learned in the course	Agree	14%	0%
The course met its objectives	Strongly agree	100%	100%
I was satisfied with the overall quality of this course	Strongly agree	100%	100%
The instructor clearly communicated the class assignments/	Strongly agree	100%	100%
activity expectations			
The instructor graded and returned papers, tests, and/or	Strongly agree	100%	100%
written assignments in a timely manner			
The instructor's comments on assignments, papers, and/or	Strongly agree	100%	100%
exams were helpful and constructive			
The instructor was organized and prepared for class	Strongly agree	100%	100%
The instructor encouraged class participation	Strongly agree	57%	67%
	Agree	29%	17%
	Neither agree nordisagree	14%	17%
The instructor was accessible in person, by phone, or by	Strongly agree	100%	100%
email outside of class			
The instructor demonstrated a thorough knowledge of the	Strongly agree	100%	100%
subject matter			
I was satisfied with the instructor's overall teaching	Strongly agree	100%	100%
effectiveness			
Open-ended questions[b]			
What were the major strengths of the course and/or the instructor?			
What suggestions do you have to improve the course or the instructor's teaching?			
Other comments?			

[a]Response values on all questions were: Strongly agree, Agree, Neither agree nor disagree, Disagree, Strongly disagree. Only response values that were used are shown
[b]Responses to the open-ended questions are included at appropriate places in the text

References

Achetemeier SD, Morris LV, Finnegan CL (2003) Considerations for developing evaluations for online courses. J Asynchronous Learn Netw 7:1–13

Allen D, Tanner K (2006) Rubrics: tools for making learning goals and evaluation criteria explicit for both teachers and learners. CBE Life Sci Educ 5:197–203. doi:10.1187/cbe.06-06-0168

Anonymous (2004) Instructional interaction: key to student persistence? Distance Educ Rep 8:3

Artino AR Jr (2008) Promoting academic motivation and self-regulation: practical guidelines for online instructors. TechTrends 52:37–45

Bangert AW (2004) The seven principles of good practice: a framework for evaluating on-line teaching. Internet Higher Educ 7:217–232

Bangert AW (2006) Identifying factors underlying the quality of online teaching effectiveness: an exploratory study. J Comput Higher Educ 17:79–99

Bawden D, Bates J, Steinerov J et al (2007) Information retrieval curricula: contexts and perspectives. In: First international workshop on teaching and learning of information retrieval (TLIR 2007), London, UK. http://www.bcs.org/server.php?show=nav.8704

Bell SS (2006) Librarian's guide to online searching. Libraries Unlimited, Westport, CT

Bell SS (2009) Librarian's guide to online searching, 2nd edn. Libraries Unlimited, Westport, CT

Blank D, Fuhr N, Henrich A et al (2009) Information retrieval: concepts and practical considerations for teaching a rising topic. Datenbank-Spektrum 9:1–12

Chen H, Williams JP (2009) Use of multi-modal media and tools in an online information literacy course: college students' attitudes and perceptions. J Acad Libr 35:14–24

Chen PD, Gonyea R, Kuh G (2008) Learning at a distance: engaged or not? Innovate 4:3

Chickering AW, Gamson ZE (1987) Seven principles of good practice in undergraduate education. AAHE Bull 3–6

Dawley L (2007) The tools for successful online teaching. Information Science, Hershey, PA

Dennen VP (2008) Pedagogical lurking: student engagement in non-posting discussion behavior. Comput Hum Behav 24:1624–1633. doi:10.1016/j.chb.2007.06.003

Dennen VP, Darabi AA, Smith LJ (2007) Instructor-learner interaction in online courses: the relative perceived importance of particular instructor actions on performance and satisfaction. Distance Educ 28:65–79

Downing KF, Holtz JK (2008) Online science learning: best practices and technologies. Information Science, Hershey, PA

Dunlap JC, Sobel D, Sands DI (2007) Supporting students' cognitive processing in online courses: Designing for deep and meaningful student-to-content interactions. TechTrends 51:20–31

Henrich A, Sieber S (2009) Blended learning and pure e-learning concepts for information retrieval: experiences and future directions. Inf Retr 12:117–147. doi:10.1007/s10791-008-9079-3

Herron JF, Wright VH (2006) Assessment in online learning: are students really learning? In: Wright VH, Sunal CS, Wilson EK (eds) Research on enhancing the interactivity of online learning. Information Age, Greenwich, CT

Huete J, Fernández-Luna JM, MacFarlane A, Ounis I (eds) (2007) First international workshop on teaching and learning of information retrieval (TLIR 2007), London, UK. http://www.bcs.org/server.php?show=nav.8704

Information Retrieval (2009) Special issue on teaching and learning in information retrieval (2009) Inf Retr 12:99–226

James D (2004) A need for humor in online courses. College Teach 52:93–94

Jewell V (2005) Continuing the classroom community: suggestions for using online discussion boards. English J 94:83–87

Jung I, Choi S, Lim C et al (2002) Effects of different types of interaction on learning achievement, satisfaction and participation in Web-based instruction. Innov Educ Teach Int 39:153–162. doi:10.1080/13558000210121399

Kao GY, Lin SSJ, Sun C (2008) Beyond sharing: engaging students in cooperative and competitive active learning. Educ Technol Soc 11:82–96

Koontz FR, Li H, Compora DP (2006) Designing effective online instruction: a handbook for web-based courses. Rowman & Littlefield Education, Lanham, MD

Lewis CC, Abdul-Hamid H (2006) Implementing effective online teaching practices: voices of exemplary faculty. Innov Higher Educ 31:83–98. doi:10.1007/s10755-006-9010-z

MacFarlane A, Fernández-Luna JM, Huete JF, Efthimiadis E (eds) (2008) Second international workshop on teaching and learning in information retrieval (TLIR 2008), London, UK. http://www.bcs.org/ewic/tlir2008

Mazzolini M, Maddison S (2003) Sage, guide or ghost? The effect of instructor intervention on student participation in online discussion forums. Comput Educ 40:237–253

Newlands DA, Coldwell JM (2005) Managing student expectations online. Lect Notes Comput Sci 3583:355–363. doi:10.1007/11528043

Oud J (2009) Guidelines for effective online instruction using multimedia screencasts. RSR 37:164–177

Partlow KM, Gibbs WJ (2003) Indicators of constructivist principles in internet-based courses. J Comput Higher Educ 14:68–97

Persell CH (2004) Using focused web-based discussions to enhance student engagement and deep understanding. Teach Sociol 32:61–78

Scarnati B, Garcia P (2007) The fusion of learning theory and technology in an online music history course redesign. Innovate 4:2

Schellens T, Valcke M (2006) Fostering knowledge construction in university students through asynchronous discussion groups. Comput Educ 46:349–370. doi:10.1016/j.compedu.2004.07.010

Schmitt EM, Hu AC, Bachrach PS (2008) Course evaluation and assessment: examples of a learner-centered approach. Gerontol Geriatr Educ 29:290–300. doi:10.1080/02701960802359524

School of Information Studies (2010) UWM Undergraduate Catalog 2009–2010. http://www4.uwm.edu/ugcatalog/SC/C_540.html

Schroeder U, Spannagel C (2006) Supporting the active learning process. Int J E-Learn 5:245–264

Shieh RS, Gummer E, Niess M (2008) The quality of a Web-based course: perspectives of the instructor and the students. TechTrends 52:61–68

Smith KA, Sheppard SD, Johnson DW et al (2005) Pedagogies of engagement: classroom-based practices. J Eng Educ 94:87–101

Steele JP, Fullagar CJ (2009) Facilitators and outcomes of student engagement in a college setting. J Psychol 143:5–27

Stevens-Long J, Crowell C (2002) The design and delivery of interactive online graduate education. In: Rudestam KE, Schoenholtz-Read J (eds) Handbook of online learning. Sage, Thousand Oaks, CA

Tallent-Runnels MK, Thomas JA, Lan WY et al (2006) Teaching courses online: a review of the research. Rev Educ Res 76:93–135

Van Keuren J (2006) Web-based instruction: a practical guide for online courses. Rowman & Littlefield Education, Lanham, MD

Wilson BM, Pollock PH, Hamann K (2007) Does active learning enhance learner outcomes? Evidence from discussion participation in online classes. J Polit Sci Educ 3:131–142

Woods RH (2002) How much communication is enough in online courses? Exploring the relationship between frequency of instructor- initiated personal email and learners' perceptions of and participation in online learning. Int J Instr Media 29:377–394

Yang SC, Huang LJ (2003) Designing a web-based historical curriculum to support student engagement. J Comput Assist Learn 19:251–253

Young S (2006) Student views of effective online teaching in higher education. Am J Distance Educ 20:65–77

Zhang D (2005) Interactive multimedia-based e-learning: a study of effectiveness. Am J Distance Educ 19:149–162

Chapter 3
Teaching IR: Curricular Considerations

Daniel Blank, Norbert Fuhr, Andreas Henrich, Thomas Mandl,
Thomas Rölleke, Hinrich Schütze, and Benno Stein

3.1 Motivation

Data volumes have been growing since computers were invented, and powerful database and information retrieval technologies have been developed to manage and retrieve large volumes of data in order to turn data into information. Since the mid-1990s, not only the data volume, but in particular the number of people exposed and dependent on information supply and search also, has increased exponentially. Information (Web) search has become an inherent and frequent part in the life of billions of people, and information search is important in both professional and private contexts.

Although the preceding paragraph might seem to be the typical motivation for all texts addressing IR topics, it has important impacts on teaching IR. Whereas before the mid-1990s information search was a task mostly executed by trained and dedicated search professionals such as librarians and database administrators, the professionals, semi-professionals, and hurried end-users today share the same goal: to find relevant information quickly. Consequently, information retrieval (IR) is now part of various curricula for bachelor and master programs. These programs range from library science over information science to computer science; even programs in areas such as management science that used to regard IR as unimportant have now integrated this field as a key qualification. Basic knowledge in search engine usage and literature research is also part of curricular suggestions for school lessons.

Obviously, different target groups for teaching IR implicate different educational objectives. In the intended vocational field, IR systems might be *used*, *implemented*, *designed*, or *managed*. Fernández-Luna et al. (2009) express the variety of perspectives by a *technical continuum* ranging from nontechnical to highly technical. This continuum is spanned starting with the disciplines of

D. Blank (✉)
University of Bamberg, Bamberg, Germany
e-mail: daniel.blank@uni-bamberg.de

E. Efthimiadis et al. (eds.), *Teaching and Learning in Information Retrieval*,
The Information Retrieval Series 31, DOI 10.1007/978-3-642-22511-6_3,
© Springer-Verlag Berlin Heidelberg 2011

psychology and general linguistics over library and information science, human–computer interaction (HCI), and management information systems to computational linguistics and computer science. These perspectives have to be considered when developing teaching concepts for IR.

There is a long way to go if we try to achieve a well-established understanding of how to teach IR. Even the authors of this chapter do not agree on all aspects considered in this chapter. We see our contribution as a first step, and by no means as a final result. We hope to stimulate discussion and to provoke a fruitful exchange of ideas, and we welcome comments on all opinions expressed in this chapter.

3.2 Toward a Curriculum for IR

To compose a curriculum in IR, we merge suggestions from various text books (cf. Sect. 3.2.3), synoptic articles such as the ones given by Croft (1995), Melucci and Hawking (2006), or Bawden et al. (2007), and IR summer schools. In the following, we will first draw a closer look at the different target groups for teaching IR. Thereafter, we will outline our proposal for an IR curriculum. Finally, we will discuss the adequacy of different forms of teaching for the different aspects and address potential groupings of IR courses as well as educational levels.

3.2.1 Educational Goals

On the background of library and information science, Bawden et al. (2007) distinguish four related, but distinct subject areas: human information behavior (HIB), information seeking (IS), information retrieval (IR), and general topics (Gen). Although the curriculum presented by Bawden et al. (2007) has a strong focus on cognitive aspects, it is useful for our considerations. Even a curriculum for computer scientists should not ignore these aspects. Nevertheless, a more system- and implementation-oriented approach might be better suited for students with a computer science background. At this point, first, important differences between potential target groups become obvious. In an overstated way, one could say that teaching IR as an advanced algorithms and data structures course might be conceivable for computer scientists, whereas an approach starting with human information needs might be appropriate for psychologists. However, in each case, a profound knowledge of the other perspectives on IR is rewarding. An IR course should not restrict itself to one specific perspective on IR but elaborate the multi-disciplinary character.

Despite this multi-disciplinary character for the respective target groups, different aspects of IR will be interesting and – even more important – qualifying for the aimed-at profession. As a consequence, it is necessary to have an understanding that the students in an IR course will have, depending on their study course, different motivations, expectations, and personal prerequisites. To simplify things, we differentiate the audience with respect to their expected working relationship to IR systems:

1. *IR system user* (U): For students falling into this category, the efficient, goal-oriented use of IR systems is the main focus. Use often refers to research activities, which are in many cases domain specific.
2. *Management* (M): In the future working context of students falling into this category, we expect tasks regarding the supply of data and information in an organization. These professionals integrate IR into the broader picture of information and knowledge management. Consequently, there is a business-oriented view on IR, but with the need for a strong conceptual and technical background.
3. *Administration* (A): Here, the main focus is on the technical administration and optimization of search tools. Examples could be the maintenance for site search or intranet search in enterprises or domain specific Web search tools.
4. *Development* (D): This group comprises students who would like to be part of development projects in the field of IR. They may later develop and optimize systems or their components, and plan and implement innovative search technology applications.

3.2.2 Contents

Table 3.1 gives an overview of our proposed curriculum. For the different target groups, the appropriate depth of coverage is indicated. In the following, we will discuss the different topic groups – presented in bold face in Table 3.1 – in greater detail.

3.2.2.1 Introduction

Although today everybody is using search engines, the roots and the background of IR need some explanation. To this end, different concrete search situations can be considered and first naive-user experiments can be integrated into the concept.

At first, for all target groups (U, M, A, and D in Table 3.1), a detailed mission statement for IR should be given. The history of IR and its background in library science and information science should be outlined and important terms (e.g., *data*, *knowledge*, and *information*) should be introduced. To communicate the various facets of IR, different usage scenarios can be discussed, starting from Web search engines over search tasks in a digital library up to enterprise search scenarios or market investigation using IR techniques.

The knowledge of certain resources, the knowledge of necessary tools like thesauri, and the efficient use of such tools are sometimes the focus of entire courses. From a computer science perspective, awareness of professional search

Table 3.1 Topics for teaching IR along with their importance for different target groups

	U	M	A	D
Introduction				
Motivation and overview	•	•	•	•
History of IR	•	•	•	•
Terms and definitions	•	•	•	•
IR topics and usage scenarios	•	•	•	•
Efficient search: Search strategies	•	○	○	○
Efficient search: Knowledge of resources	•	○	○	○
IR versus DB-driven Retrieval	○	•	○	•
Language analysis				
Tokenization	○	○	•	•
Filtering (stop words, stemming, etc.)	•	•	•	•
Meta-data	○	•	•	•
Natural language processing		○	○	•
Text and indexing technology				
Pattern matching	○	○	•	•
Inverted files	○	○	•	•
Tree-based data structures		○	○	•
Hash-based indexing		○	•	•
Managing gigabytes	○	○	•	•
IR models				
Boolean model and its extensions	•	•	•	•
Vector space model and its generalization	•	•	•	•
Probabilistic retrieval		○	○	•
Logical approach to IR		○	○	•
BM25 (Okapi)	○	•	•	•
Latent variable models (e.g., LSA)		○	○	•
Language modeling		○	○	•

	U	M	A	D
IR evaluation				
Performance factors and criteria	•	•	•	•
IR performance measures	○	•	•	•
Test collections	○	•	•	
System vs. user oriented		•	○	•
Cognitive models and user interfaces				
Information seeking	•	•	•	○
Information searching	•	•	•	○
Strategic support	•	•	•	○
HCI aspects	•	•	•	•
Input modes and visualizations	○	•	•	•
Agent-based and mixed-initative interfaces	○	○	○	•
Data mining and machine learning for IR				
Clustering	○	○	•	•
Classification	○	•	•	•
Mining of heterogenous data	○	○	•	•
Special topics (application oriented)				
Web retrieval	○	•	•	•
Semantic Web	○	•	•	•
Multimedia retrieval	○	○	•	•
Social netwoks/media	○	•	○	•
Opinion mining and sentiment analysis		○	○	•
Geographic IR		○	○	•
Information filtering	○	•	•	•
Question answering	○	○	○	•
Special topics (Technological)				
Cross-language IR		○	○	•
Distributed IR	○	•	•	•
IR and ranking in databases		○	•	•
Learning to rank		○	○	•
Summarization		○	○	•
XML retrieval	○	•	•	•

• = mandatory
○ = overview only
blank = dispensable

should be created and examples – maybe in a specific domain – should be presented. To this end, we have integrated the topics *search strategies* and *knowledge of resources* into the curriculum (mandatory for target group U and overview for target groups M, A, and D). For instance, the chapter *Models of the Information Seeking Process* in Hearst (2009) gives a compact overview on these aspects.

Finally, in order to sharpen the students' understanding, a discussion of the relationship between databases and IR should be given together with a consideration of the overlap (text extensions for relational databases, metadata search in IR systems, semi-structured data, and the like).

3.2.2.2 Language Analysis

First, students should be introduced to the basic problems of free text search. As a partial solution, traditional IR takes a rather simple approach to compositional semantics: under most IR models, the interpretation of a document is based on the (multi) set of the words it contains; these bag-of-words models ignore the grammatical concepts that govern sentence construction and text composition (Jurafsky and Martin 2008). Students should understand this difference and be able to argue about the loss in the representational power, the analytical simplification, and the algorithmic consequences. In particular, the basic steps to construct a bag-of-words model should be introduced, such as tokenization, term normalization, and term selection.

Tokenization is the first step in IR language analysis, where the raw character stream of a document is transformed into a stream of units, which will be used as terms later on. The subsequent steps can be grouped into the categories term normalization and term selection. Term normalization aims at the formation of term equivalence classes and includes case-folding, expanding of abbreviations, word conflation, and normalization of dates and numbers. Term selection, on the contrary, aims at extracting the content carrying words from a unit of text. Highly frequent and uniformly distributed terms such as stop words are not well suited to discriminate between relevant and nonrelevant documents, and hence are usually removed. However, students should be aware that for the analysis of a document's genre, sentiment, or authorship, stop words play an important role. Other forms of term selection include collocation analysis or key phrase extraction. Tokenization, term normalization, and term selection are language dependent, thus language identification is mandatory for language analysis. Robust language analysis is crucial to the effectiveness of an IR system. Users (target group U in Table 3.1) should understand the consequences of common language analysis techniques such as stop wording and stemming. Administrators and Developers (target groups A and D) should be aware of the challenges of and the technology for language analysis and should be able to maintain and develop a robust language analysis processing pipeline.

Natural language processing (NLP) is a large research field on its own (Manning and Schütze 1999). Students should learn that, currently, the application of NLP techniques in IR is limited to shallow techniques, but that from a technological viewpoint IR and NLP are growing together. Reasons for the latter are (1) advanced IR tasks such as plagiarism analysis, fact retrieval, or opinion mining; (2) the increased computing power; and (3) the recent advances in NLP owing to the use of machine learning techniques. Because of this development, selected NLP technologies such as part-of-speech tagging and language modeling (LM) should be considered in the curriculum for advanced student groups (cf. Table 3.1: overview for target group M and A, mandatory for target group D).

3.2.2.3   Text and Indexing Technology

From a computer science perspective, this field is the most traditional one, covering pattern matching, efficient data storage, hashing, and text compression. Besides learning about the various methods, students also should understand their tradeoff between expressiveness and efficiency.

Patterns can be of different types, ranging from simple to complex: terms, substrings, prefixes, regular expressions, and patterns that employ a fuzzy or error-tolerant similarity measure. Consider the phonological similarity between two words as an example for a tolerant measure. Technology for pattern matching comprises classical string searching algorithms and heuristic search algorithms, but requires also sophisticated data structures, such as n-gram inverted files, suffix trees and suffix arrays, signature files, or tries.

The central data structure for efficient document retrieval from a large document collection is the inverted file. Specialized variants and advanced improvements exploit certain retrieval constraints and optimization potential – for example, memory size, distribution of queries, proximity and co-occurrence queries, knowledge about the update frequency of a collection, presorted lists, meta-indices, and caching strategies (Witten et al. 1999). Students in target groups A and D should gain hands-on experience with inverted indices, either by implementing a simple indexing component or by using state-of-the-art IR libraries such as Apache Lucene or Terrier.

Another retrieval technology is hashing (Stein 2007). One distinguishes exact hashing, applied for exact search (e.g., with MD5), and fuzzy hashing, also called hash-based similarity search. Students should know about these techniques and typical application areas such as near-duplicate detection and plagiarism analysis.

Text compression is employed to reduce the memory footprint of index components, or to alleviate the bottleneck when loading posting lists into main memory. It is of particular interest to students of types A and D as a means to increase retrieval efficiency and to scale IR systems to large text corpora or a high query load.

3.2.2.4   IR Models

IR models can be viewed as – mostly mathematical – frameworks to define scores of documents. The scores allow us to rank documents, and the ranking is expected to reflect the notion of relevance. Ranking is today standard, whereas the first retrieval model, namely, the Boolean model, did not provide ranking. Models such as coordination level match, extended Boolean (weighting of query terms), and fuzzy retrieval helped to add ranking to Boolean expressions. A main breakthrough for retrieval was the usage of vector-space algebra, leading to what is referred to as the vector-space model [VSM, promoted by the SMART system (Salton et al. 1975)]. All Students (target groups U, M, A, and D) should know this model not only as a milestone in IR but also as a model delivering a retrieval quality that – until today – is a strong baseline when evaluating IR systems.

The 1970s saw the development of what became known as the probabilistic retrieval model, or more precisely, the binary independence retrieval (BIR) model, by Robertson and Sparck Jones (1976). Foundations such as the probability of relevance and the probabilistic ranking principle should be covered by all IR courses.

The 1980s brought the logical approach to IR. The probability of a logical implication between document and query is viewed to constitute the score. This "model" is mainly theoretical. It is useful to explain other IR models (Wong and Yao 1995).

The 1990s brought the retrieval model BM25 (Robertson et al. 1994). BM25 can be viewed as a successful mix of TF-IDF, BIR, and pivoted document length normalization. At least students in advanced courses (target groups M, A, and D) should not only know BM25 but also understand its background.

The late 1990s saw the paradigm of language modeling to be used in IR (Croft and Lafferty 2003). With some respect, LM is more probabilistic than the previously mentioned BIR model.

The theory and contributions of IR models are covered in extensive literature background including Wong and Yao (1995) (logical framework to explain IR models), Rölleke et al. (2006) (matrix framework to explain IR models), Robertson (2004) (understanding IDF), and a number of textbooks (Rijsbergen 1979; Belew 2000; Grossman and Frieder 2004; Manning et al. 2008; Croft et al. 2009). Overall, students should understand the necessity for ranking, the different theoretic foundations of the various models, and the parameters involved in these.

3.2.2.5   IR Evaluation

The empirical evaluation of the performance of IR systems is of central importance because the quality of a system cannot be predicted based on its components. Since an IR system ultimately needs to support the users in fulfilling their information needs, a holistic evaluation needs to set the satisfaction of the user and his or her work task as the yardstick. In addition to user studies, there is a large tradition of system-oriented evaluations following the Cranfield paradigm. All students should be aware of the different levels of evaluations that can be carried out, their potential results, and their disadvantages.

IR user studies typically provide test users with hypothetical search tasks in order to allow for a comparison. In such experiments, the user is asked to report his satisfaction with the system or its components. If the curriculum also includes classes in HCI, students might already have studied empirical evaluation and usability tests. That knowledge can be reviewed in the class. Otherwise, it should be integrated into the IR class. Students should at least be aware of some of the difficulties involved in designing user experiments. Optimally, students of types M, A, and D should be asked to design and conduct a small user study within class themselves. They should be aware of tools that can support such a test.

Evaluations based on the Cranfield paradigm need to be the main focus of a lecture on evaluation in IR. Research has adopted this scheme, which tries to ignore subjective differences between users in order to be able to compare systems and algorithms (Buckley and Voorhees 2005). The most important measures based on relevance judgments are recall and precision. All students need to be able to know about recall and precision and should be able to interpret them.

Students of types A and D need to be able to calculate values and should know some other evaluation measure like binary preference (bpref) and cumulative gain (Järvelin and Kekäläinen 2002). In a laboratory class, these students could experiment with different measures to see whether they lead to different results.

Students need to know the main evaluation initiatives TREC[1] (Buckley and Voorhees 2005; Robertson 2008), CLEF,[2] and NTCIR[3] and should know some typical results. New tasks (Mandl 2008) and critical aspects (Al-Maskari et al. 2007) of these initiatives should be addressed for students of types A and D, as well. An advanced course for student type D could deal with the limitations of evaluation resources and the problems of their reusability and might also include the conduction of a small evaluation. Students of type D should learn about alternative approaches to evaluate enterprise or site search systems.

3.2.2.6 Cognitive models and user interfaces

Whereas database systems are mostly accessed from application programs, queries to IR systems are typically entered via a user interface. Thus, students should learn that in order to achieve a high retrieval quality for the user, cognitive aspects of interactive information access and the related problems of HCI have to be addressed.

Cognitive IR models distinguish between information seeking and searching. The former regard all activities related to information acquisition, starting from the point where the user becomes aware of an information need, until the information is found and can be applied. Popular models in this area have been developed by Ellis (1989) and Kuhlthau (1988). In contrast, information searching focuses only on the interaction of the user with an information system. Starting from Belkin's concept of "Anomalous state of knowledge" 1980 or Ingwersen's cognitive model 1992 regarding the broad context of the search, more specific approaches include the berry-picking model (Bates 1989), the concept of polyrepresentation, or Belkin's episodic model. In all these models, the classical view of a static information need is

---

[1] http://trec.nist.gov/, last accessed: 2010-10-26.

[2] http://www.clef-campaign.org/, last accessed: 2010-10-26.

[3] http://research.nii.ac.jp/ntcir/, last accessed: 2010-10-26.

replaced by a more dynamic view of interaction. For guiding the user in the search process, an IR system should provide strategic support; for this purpose, Bates (1990) identified four levels of search activities that are applied by experienced searchers, for which a concrete system can provide different degrees of system support.

The design of the *user interface* to an IR system also is a crucial topic (Hearst 2009). First, HCI aspects like Shneiderman's design principles 1998 and interaction styles should be introduced. Classical input interfaces include command languages, forms, and menus. A large number of visualizations for IR have been developed (Hearst 2009; Mann 2002), either as static views or allowing for direct manipulation. In order to free the user from routine tasks in search, agent-based interfaces (Lieberman 1995; Shneiderman and Maes 1997) have been proposed, but more recent developments favor mixed-initiative interfaces (Schaefer et al. 2005).

3.2.2.7 Data Mining and Machine Learning for IR

Classification methods and data mining techniques like clustering – which we will jointly refer to as "machine learning" – were originally a neglected part of the information retrieval curriculum. However, in recent years, the importance of machine learning for IR has increased significantly, both in research and in practical IR systems. This is partly due to the fact that documents are closely integrated with other data types, in particular with links and clicks on the Web; and exploiting data types such as links and clicks often necessitates the use of machine learning. Closely connected to the heterogeneity of data types in large IR systems is the fact that documents in today's typical collections are extremely diverse in quality and origin. Classification is often needed to classify documents according to their expected utility to the user. Spam detection is perhaps the most important example for this. Finally, many recent improvements in core information retrieval have come from classification and clustering, e.g., viewing document retrieval as a text classification problem (Manning et al. 2008, Chaps. 11 and 12) or improving retrieval performance using clustering (Liu and Croft 2004). These uses of machine learning in IR theory and applications should guide the selection of machine learning topics for IR courses. Machine learning methods frequently used in the context of IR include Naive Bayes, Rocchio, and Support Vector Machines (SVMs).

For clustering, the classical hierarchical clustering methods such as single-link and complete-link clustering offer students who are new to the subject easy access to the basic ideas and problems of clustering. It is important to present clustering in the context of its applications in IR such as search results clustering (Manning et al. 2008, Chap. 16) and news clustering,[4] because it is sometimes not immediately obvious to students how clustering contributes to the core goal of information finding.

---

[4] See, e.g. http://news.google.com/, last accessed: 2010-10-26.

PageRank (Brin and Page 1998) should be considered as a data mining technique other than clustering, since it exemplifies the interaction of textual documents with complex metadata such as links and clicks. In our experience, students show great interest in link analysis algorithms because they would like to understand how the search engines they use every day rank documents.

Much work in machine learning requires a deeper knowledge of mathematical foundations in analysis and algebra. It is, therefore, important to avoid machine learning methods that are beyond the capabilities of most students. Naive Bayes, Rocchio, hierarchical clustering, and PageRank are examples of algorithms that all students should be able to understand and are, therefore, good choices for every IR course. More advanced topics should be included in courses for target groups A and D.

3.2.2.8 Special Topics

There are many active research fields in information retrieval. Some of them are already of great commercial importance and others will have to show their potential in the future or have found their niche. One indication for which topics are currently hot is given by the sessions and workshops organized at the bigger IR conferences such as the Annual International ACM SIGIR Conference or the European Conference on IR Research (ECIR). Another indication might be seen in the evaluation tracks considered at TREC, CLEF, or the INitiative for the Evaluation of XML-Retrieval (INEX).[5]

In Table 3.1, a selection of topics is given together with a rough assessment of their importance for the target groups. In our perception, even IR users at an academic level should be aware of Web search topics such as the PageRank algorithm, problems of crawling, or the basics of search engine optimization. Semantic Web technology (Shadbolt et al. 2006), multimedia objects, and structured documents – especially XML documents – have had a strong influence on IR research, and basic knowledge in these areas will be important to assess innovations in IR in the next years. Since IR systems themselves and the collections they have to cover are becoming more and more distributed, a basic understanding of related aspects such as source selection strategies or schema integration methods seems essential. Furthermore, we have added *question answering* and *information filtering* to the topics that should be covered at least in a cursory manner for IR users because they represent specialized perspectives demonstrating the broader applicability of IR techniques.

Other topics such as *social media IR*, *cross language IR*, *geographic IR*, or *opinion mining* might also be of interest to IR users (target group U), but seem more dispensable for this target group if there is not enough time to cover these topics.

---

[5] http://www.inex.otago.ac.nz/about.html, last accessed: 2010-10-26.

3.2.3 Literature and Forms of Teaching

The more stable aspects of the topics listed in Table 3.1 are covered in IR textbooks (Grossman and Frieder 2004; Baeza-Yates and Ribeiro-Neto 1999; Manning et al. 2008; Croft et al. 2009). The more advanced topics currently discussed in research are addressed in IR conferences and journals such as SIGIR or ECIR.

For the different topics, different forms of teaching might be adequate. First of all, there is the *classical lecture* with the professor giving a talk and trying to engage students by interspersing questions and short discussions. Obviously, the extent to which meaningful interaction is possible depends on the number of students in the class. Another concept is the *reading club or seminar-style class*. Here, chapters of a book, research papers, or research topics are given to the students. The students have to work through these topics till the next meeting and then the contents are discussed. Obviously, this concept is more appropriate for small groups and advanced topics. However, in such situations, the dialog-oriented style of a reading club can motivate the students and foster autonomous learning. Besides lectures, there are tutorials, lab classes with hands-on training (usually performed on one's own), and projects (usually performed in groups). We will discuss the latter three in Sect. 3.3.

3.2.4 Packages and Levels

One problem with curricular considerations is that in the end, a course or a group of courses has to fit into the framework of bachelor or master programs. In this context, the available workload is usually predefined – in Europe, frequently measured in ECTS (European Credit Transfer and Accumulation System) credit points. Assuming that one ECTS credit point corresponds to a workload of 30 h for the average student, a group of comprehensive IR modules including lectures, exercises, and projects could easily comprise 20 or more ECTS credits. However, in many programs only a smaller portion will be available.

Another problem comes from the fact that at least three types of students have to be distinguished. There are *bachelor* and *master* students in programs where IR should be a part of the core curriculum. Such programs will usually be computer science, applied computer science, or information science programs. Obviously, there should be courses for both groups and, therefore, in many cases, there will be the need for an IR course for bachelor students and an (advanced) IR course for master students. With respect to the topics listed in Table 3.1, a course for bachelor students could, for example, be restricted to the extent indicated for "IR system users" in the left column. If considered useful, basic implementation techniques and additional IR models can be added if the available credit points permit. In any case, exercises and small projects should be included already in bachelor level courses to facilitate the learning success. For master students, the remaining topics together with more comprehensive projects can be offered.

Finally, there is a growing need to provide IR courses as a *secondary subject* for students in more loosely related programs. In fact, basic IR competence can be seen as a domain-spanning key qualification. If enough teaching capacity is available and the potential audience is big enough, specialized courses for IR as a secondary subject can be beneficial in this respect, because otherwise there is the danger that the expectations of the students and the previous knowledge are too diverse. On the contrary, one could argue that such a mixed audience is beneficial for the students, since it is a good preparation for working in interdisciplinary teams. Although this argument has some truth, the challenge for the lecturer is high.

3.3   Tutorials, Exercises, and IR Projects

Each IR course has to integrate practical exercises in order to improve the problem understanding and the problem-solving competence. When teaching IR in tutorials, exercises, and IR projects, various software tools can be used (e.g., search engines, catalogs, tagging systems, digital libraries, and existing research prototypes in the Web). For many algorithms in the context of IR, applets and animations can be inspected by students. The following tasks are possible even if the students do not have any programming skills:

- *Using retrieval systems to find documents relevant for given information needs*: Such exercises can help students understand why search is a hard problem and what typical capabilities of today's search systems are.
- *Evaluating and comparing the quality of retrieval results*: Given an information need, students can use search engines and compare their performance by calculating typical IR performance measures. Another interesting experience might be to examine different types of query formulation and their consequences for retrieval, e.g., in the context of image retrieval: query by sketch, query by example, and tag-based image retrieval.
- *Applying algorithms and formulas manually*: There is a rich set of fundamental IR algorithms that can be applied manually in order to foster understanding. Examples are the PageRank algorithm (Brin and Page 1998) and algorithms determinating the k most similar documents when applying the vector space model (Buckley and Lewit 1985). In addition, IR models are well suited for performing basic calculations by hand. Document representations for a small set of sample documents can be computed and matched against sample queries manually.
- *Reading exercises*: Especially in a master course, students are encouraged to gain some insights into research. Therefore, reading, summarizing, and discussing classical IR papers [e.g., from Sparck Jones and Willett (1997); Moffat et al. (2005)] or selected papers from recent IR conferences are a beneficial experience.

Students with basic programming skills can be asked to implement IR algorithms. Small source skeletons can aid in focusing on critical aspects of the algorithms and avoid tedious programming. Of course, there is also a huge number of IR libraries for different aspects of the curriculum that can be used.[6] Unix tools can also be applied to realize IR systems (Riggs 2002).

Having focused on more fine-grained exercises so far, we will now briefly describe three best practices of IR programming projects:

- *Implementing a basic IR framework from scratch*: Within this project, a small IR framework is implemented using only standard programming libraries without applying a specialized IR library or framework. The project is well suited for a bachelor course in IR. Basic programming skills as well as a course on algorithms and data structures are compulsory. Various subtasks can be identified in order to structure the work packages such as the implementation of a directory crawler, a tokenizer, several filtering steps (case-folding, stop word removal, and stemming), an inverted index, Boolean retrieval, document representations based on TF-IDF, top-k query processing, etc. All programming tasks are extensively explained in short briefings at the beginning of a session. Students can work in teams. If there is additional time, the framework can be extended in many directions, e.g., integrating Web crawling facilities, designing a user interface, or evaluating the system. The educational objective of this project is to deepen the students' understanding of basic IR algorithms.
- *Implementing desktop search using frameworks and libraries*: IR libraries such as Apache Lucene[7] can be used to design a small desktop search engine. Alternatively, one could devise a project concerned with the design of a proto-typical Web search engine (Cacheda et al. 2008). At the beginning, the basics of the IR library that is used are explained to the students. Key concepts such as *analysis*, *documents*, and *fields* are emphasized. In a first step, students index their local file system with the help of a file crawler. Afterward, libraries for extracting the content of different document types are employed. Tools for inspecting the index such as Luke[8] can be employed analyzing the consequences of tokenizing and filtering. After having introduced the basic properties of the query engine (query syntax, document scoring, etc.), students are asked to implement query processing. There are many possibilities to extend this project: designing a user interface, extending the framework with a Web crawler, including linguistic analysis, etc.
- *Design and development of a (small) Web search engine in a Unix environment*: This project covers the aspects of IR from data analysis over indexing to retrieval

---

[6] Middleton and Baeza-Yates (2007) give an overview and compare multiple search engine libraries. A list of links pointing to tools and libraries can also be found in the *Teaching IR* subtree on the web site of FG-IR (http://www.fg-ir.de, last accessed: 2010-10-26).

[7] http://lucene.apache.org/, last accessed: 2010-10-26.

[8] http://code.google.com/p/luke/, last accessed: 2010-10-26.

and evaluation. Students build a tokenizer to analyze some Web pages (can be easily gathered via wgetUnix command). Then, the collection is indexed, and the students prepare a layer that receives queries and returns results and result pages (page construction, snippet generation). The project involves the development of a basic GUI. This project trains the IR and software engineering skills of students, and the motivation is to "beat" a favorite Web search engine for selected queries. Unix tools form a powerful basis for such a project (Riggs 2002).

3.4 Conclusion

When designing a curriculum for IR, the designated content, the appropriate forms of teaching, a useful breakdown into courses, and the relevance for the different target groups have to be considered. In this chapter, we tried to contribute in this respect.

Feedback on our courses which only partly implement the presented ideas at this time shows that in particular the heterogeneity in the previous knowledge and the expectations of the students are a big challenge. Specific courses for the target groups might be a solution – as far as the teaching capacity permits. However, a mixed audience can also be seen as a good preparation for practical tasks, and especially IR-related projects can benefit from the various points of view.

References

Al-Maskari A, Sanderson M, Clough P (2007) The relationship between IR effectiveness measures and user satisfaction. In: Proceedings of the 30th annual international ACM SIGIR conference, Amsterdam, pp 773–774

Baeza-Yates R, Ribeiro-Neto B (1999) Modern information retrieval. Addison-Wesley, England

Bates MJ (1989) The design of browsing and berrypicking techniques for the online search interface. Online Inf Rev 13(5):407–424

Bates MJ (1990) Where should the person stop and the information search interface start? Inf Process Manag 26(5):575–591

Bawden D, Bates J, Steinerov J, Vakkari P, Vilar P (2007) Information retrieval curricula: contexts and perspectives. In: First international BCS workshop on teaching and learning of information retrieval (TLIR 2007), London, UK. http://www.bcs.org/server.php?show = ConWebDoc.8777

Belew RK (2000) Finding out about: a cognitive perspective on search engine technology and the WWW. Cambridge University Press, Cambridge, UK

Belkin NJ (1980) Anomalous states of knowledge as a basis for information retrieval. Can J Inf Sci 5:133–143

Brin S, Page L (1998) The anatomy of a large-scale hypertextual web search engine. Comput Netw ISDN Syst 30(1–7):107–117

Buckley C, Lewit FA (1985) Optimization of inverted vector searches. In: Proceedings of the 8th annual international ACM SIGIR conference, Montréal, Québec, Canada, pp 97–110

Buckley C, Voorhees EM (2005) TREC: experiment and evaluation in information retrieval. Retrieval system evaluation. Digital libraries and electronic publishing series. MIT, Cambridge, MA, pp 53–75

Cacheda F, Fernandez D, Lopez R (2008) Experiences on a practical course of web information retrieval: developing a search engine. In: Second international BCS workshop on teaching and learning of information retrieval (TLIR 2008), London, UK. http://www.bcs.org/server.php? show = conWebDoc.22357

Croft B (1995) What do people want from information retrieval? (the top 10 research issues for companies that use and sell IR systems). D-Lib Mag 1:5

Croft B, Lafferty J (2003) (eds) Language modeling for information retrieval. The information retrieval series, vol 13. Kluwer, Amsterdam

Croft B, Metzler D, Strohman T (2009) Search engines: information retrieval in practice. Pearson Higher Education, Old Tappan, NJ

Ellis D (1989) A behavioural approach to information retrieval system design. J Document 45(3):171–212

Fernández-Luna JM, Huete JF, Macfarlane A, Efthimiadis EN (2009) Teaching and learning in information retrieval. Inf Retr 12(2):201–226

Grossman DA, Frieder O (2004) Information retrieval: algorithms and heuristics. The information retrieval series, vol 15, 2nd edn. Springer, Dordrecht

Hearst MA (2009) Search user interfaces. Cambridge University Press, Cambridge

Ingwersen P (1992) Information retrieval interaction. Taylor Graham, London

Järvelin K, Kekäläinen J (2002) Cumulated gain-based evaluation of IR techniques. ACM Trans Inf Syst Security 20(4):422–446

Jurafsky D, Martin J (2008) Speech and language processing. Prentice Hall, Upper Saddle River, NJ

Kuhlthau CC (1988) Developing a model of the library search process: cognitive and affective aspects. Ref Quart 28(2):232–242

Lieberman H (1995) Letizia: an agent that assists Web browsing. In: International joint conference on artificial intelligence, Montréal, Québec, Canada, pp 924–929

Liu X, Croft BW (2004) Cluster-based retrieval using language models. In: Proceedings of the 27th annual international ACM SIGIR conference, Sheffield, UK, pp 186–193

Mandl T (2008) Recent developments in the evaluation of information retrieval systems: moving towards diversity and practical relevance. Informatica 32:27–38

Mann TM (2002) Visualization of search results from the world wide web. Ph.D. thesis, University of Constance, http://kops.ub.uni-konstanz.de/volltexte/2002/751/pdf/Dissertation_Thomas.M. Mann_2002.V.1.07.pdf

Manning CD, Schütze H (1999) Foundations of statistical natural language processing. MIT, Cambridge, MA

Manning CD, Raghavan P, Schütze H (2008) Introduction to information retrieval. Cambridge University Press, Cambridge, MA

Melucci M, Hawking D (2006) Introduction: a perspective on web information retrieval. Inf Retr 9(2):119–122

Middleton C, Baeza-Yates R (2007) A comparison of open source search engines. Technical Report. http://wrg.upf.edu/WRG/dctos/Middleton-Baeza.pdf

Moffat A, Zobel J, Hawking D (2005) Recommended reading for IR research students. SIGIR Forum 39(2):3–14

Riggs KR (2002) Exploring IR with Unix tools. J Comput Sci Coll 17(4):179–194

Rijsbergen CJv (1979) Information retrieval. Butterworth, London, UK. http://www.dcs.gla.ac.uk/Keith/Preface.html

Robertson S (2004) Understanding inverse document frequency: On theoretical arguments for idf. J Document 60(5):503–520

Robertson S (2008) On the history of evaluation in IR. J Inf Sci 34(4):439–456

Robertson SE, Sparck Jones K (1976) Relevance weighting of search terms. J Am Soc Inf Sci 27(3):129–146

Robertson SE, Walker S, Jones S, Hancock-Beaulieu M, Gatford M (1994) Okapi at TREC-3. In: NIST Special Publication 500–226: Overview of the Third Text Retrieval Conference (TREC-3), pp 109–126

Rölleke T, Tsikrika T, Kazai G (2006) A general matrix framework for modelling information retrieval. Inf Process Manag 42(1):4–30

Salton G, Wong A, Yang CS (1975) A vector space model for automatic indexing. Commun ACM 18(11):613–620

Schaefer A, Jordan M, Klas C-P, Fuhr N (2005) Active support for query formulation in virtual digital libraries: a case study with DAFFODIL. In: 9th European conference on digital libraries, Vienna, Austria, pp 414–425

Shadbolt N, Berners-Lee T, Hall W (2006) The semantic web revisited. IEEE Intell Syst 21(3):96–101

Shneiderman B (1998) Designing the user interface. Addison-Wesley, Boston, MA

Shneiderman B, Maes P (1997) Direct manipulation vs interface agents. ACM Interact 4(6):42–61

Sparck Jones K, Willett P (eds) (1997) Readings in information retrieval. The Morgan Kaufmann series in multimedia information and systems. Morgan Kaufmann, San Francisco

Stein B (2007) Principles of hash-based text retrieval. In: Proceedings of the 30th annual international ACM SIGIR conference, Amsterdam, pp 527–534

Witten I, Moffat A, Bell T (1999) Managing gigabytes: compressing and indexing documents and images. Morgan Kaufmann, San Francisco

Wong SKM, Yao Y (1995) On modeling information retrieval with probabilistic inference. ACM Trans Inf Syst Security 13(1):38–68

Chapter 4
Pedagogical Enhancements for Information Retrieval Courses

Edward Fox, Uma Murthy, Seungwon Yang, Ricardo da S. Torres, Javier Velasco-Martin, and Gary Marchionini

4.1 Introduction

Information retrieval graduate courses have been offered each academic year in the Department of Computer Science at Virginia Tech since 1973. The first author has taught those since 1983, except when assigned to an advanced course on Digital Libraries (DL), which includes some sections on information retrieval (IR). Since the early 1990s, the Information Storage and Retrieval course has been improved through a variety of pedagogical enhancements, many of which are reported below; some may be applicable to learners at other sites.

Our pedagogical enhancements build upon various approaches and theories related to learning. In the broadest sense, our focus has been on learners (Weimer 2002). One of the earliest works discussed, by Slavin, emphasizes the importance of cooperative learning (Slavin 1980). Cooperation inside groups or teams, and on occasion with students at other sites such as at UNICAMP, has been a regular part of all our courses. Networks, including virtual environments, have been part of the environment supporting such collaboration (Hiltz 1997).

Another foundational concept undergirding our pedagogy is constructivist learning (Brown et al. 1989; Duffy and Jonassen 1992) that advocates giving learners control over how they learn and encourages instructors to facilitate discovery rather than directly transfer information. In computer science, this led to Papert's development of Logo and its subsequent spread as a basis for student-controlled learning (Papert 1993). Related to this is scaffolding theory, used to guide the design of learner-centered systems (Quintana et al. 2001). Scaffolding in software provides support tools (e.g., scratchpads, unobtrusive lookups) and thus becomes the mechanisms by which instructors facilitate learning. These theories have led to courses that are team and project based and provide considerable

U. Murthy (✉)
Virginia Tech, Blacksburg, VA 24061, USA
e-mail: umurthy@vt.edu

E. Efthimiadis et al. (eds.), *Teaching and Learning in Information Retrieval*,
The Information Retrieval Series 31, DOI 10.1007/978-3-642-22511-6_4,
© Springer-Verlag Berlin Heidelberg 2011

freedom for the learners to define the specifics of the project within the parameters of the overall course objectives. There are many types of projects in which IR concepts can be illustrated, integrated, and synthesized, such as by building simple Web search engines (Chau et al. 2003). These can help motivate students. Devising a mix of projects and activities can be a key part of creating a set of significant learning experiences (Fink 2003).

When the principles of learning sciences are applied to a learning environment, it tends to increase students' motivation. In "Motivation and Cognitive Engagement in Learning Environment," Blumenfeld et al. (2006) present four determinants that set the stage for motivation and cognitive engagement: value, competence, relatedness, and autonomy. Those determinants could be satisfied when students are engaged in class projects, which deal with real-life problems to which they can relate.

The rest of this chapter is organized as follows. Section 4.2 focuses on the educational goals of our IR courses. Next is a section describing the most effective approaches employed in pursuance of those goals. These rely upon various tools explained in the subsequent section. Section 4.5 gives case studies to explain the teaching and learning further. The final section summarizes, discusses future work, and provides conclusions.

4.2 Educational Goals

Our IR and DL courses, offered to graduate students, some advanced under-graduates, and occasionally to interested faculty, have included general as well as specific goals. In harmony with program level objectives, we seek to ensure that students can communicate effectively, work in groups, contribute to research projects, and advance the state of the art. For example, in the fall 2009 IR course at Virginia Tech, each of the students took about 30 min to present a chapter selected from the textbook (Manning et al. 2008), after adapting (in consultation with the instructor) the online slides provided by the authors. Students with less familiarity with English were paired with those having good facility with the language, so they had additional coaching in addition to the feedback provided by the instructor. These activities also helped prepare students to be able to teach about basic and advanced IR topics.

Course level objectives also include ones particular to IR. Students learning about IR must develop abilities to identify, describe, model, compare/contrast, evaluate, critique, design, build, and synthesize. These skills apply to concepts, theories, models, functions, modules, tools, services, systems, and applications of IR. Consequently, students must gain significant hands-on experience with IR software and tools. They must learn how to apply IR to real-world problems in a variety of contexts and disciplines. Specifically, the course objectives for the IR class (updated as of fall 2009) are as listed below. These can be achieved by the integrated use of a suite of pedagogical approaches. Objectives for the IR course updated as of fall 2009:

1. Commence Masters or Ph.D.-level research in the broad area of information storage and retrieval (IS&R).
2. Read and understand research contributions in this area.
3. Critique, contrast, compare, and evaluate the efficiency, effectiveness, and utility of commercially available and research prototype systems for IS&R.
4. Select, implement, or design and develop algorithms and data structures for IS&R systems, including DL.
5. Effectively use indexing, analysis, search, hypertext and multimedia access systems for common tasks.
6. Communicate effectively using writing and hypertext techniques to demonstrate mastery of course subject matter.
7. Work effectively on teams, including learning content, working exercises, and developing/reporting on applications.

4.3 Approaches

Our pedagogical enhancements are integrated into four main approaches to IR education.

4.3.1 Team-Based Learning

First, we require students to work in teams. Though in earlier years we simply had groups, since early 2008 we have focused on a well proven team-based learning (TBL) approach.[1] Students are assigned to teams early in the term, and work in those same teams throughout the semester. While some of the assignment to teams is based on having a shared interest in a particular project, it is also important that the members of teams have a mix of skills (such as programming, design, writing, presentation, etc.) and diverse backgrounds. Random assignment, coupled with instructor selection of team members so that there is more balance of gender and national/cultural origins, ensures that students will get to know other students. Teams are required to work together on a variety of activities throughout the semester. Typically, students assume a mix of roles, which rotate over the weeks, so the instructor knows more about what each person is doing. Fairness also is partially ensured by grading individual as well as team efforts, and by, at the end of the semester, having teams provide to the instructor confidential assessments (on a 10-point scale) of the quantity and quality of the work of each other team member. This has constituted 20–25% of the project grading, which has usually constituted about 35% of the course grading.

---

[1] http://teambasedlearning.apsc.ubc.ca/.

In the spring 2008 class offering, students worked individually on quizzes, which were graded later, and then immediately worked in teams on the same quizzes, discussing each question before deciding on a team solution. Students quickly learned that team scores were better than all of the individual scores, including those of the brightest students, reinforcing the lesson that working in teams is essential and beneficial. In fall 2009, like in earlier years, teams also worked on team concept maps, as is discussed in Sect. 4.5.2. But most of the time devoted to team efforts was in connection with projects.

4.3.2   Projects

Achieving program and course objectives is facilitated by having students work together on teams to undertake projects. These projects vary in size and scope depending on the particular class offering. In spring 2008, a small number of large projects were identified and divided into phases. Each phase involved a set of subprojects that each could be completed in 2–3 weeks by a different team, such that all subprojects converge into one large project, usually a real-world application. In this way, students work on their projects but also learn about the context of the project and how it connects to a real-world application. They also see how to work in a team on a focused activity that later must be fit together with a different deliverable (e.g., a routine or a set of data/information that had been suitably processed) from a different team. This is a rapid approach to teach basic and advanced IR topics by relating IR concepts to real-world applications. In each project, students were allowed to choose a subproject, which has a clear list of tasks to be done. Students were motivated to complete these subprojects, since the duration of the subproject is short, yet when combined with other subprojects its impact is significant. This modular approach to larger projects also helps students construct their own personalized experience with project management concepts and skills. In the fall 2009 class, one project was assigned to each team on the first day of class, to be carried out over the course of the semester. This assignment was made by the instructor based on top-ranked choices made by each team as well as individual members skills. Four teams were able to choose from five projects. Teams consulted with the instructor and the project client(s), specifying on a wiki their precise plans and the roles assigned to each team member. This became a contract, though in some cases defining specifics was part of the project plan, while in other cases some research and exploration was called for first. Though this approach had been used for many years prior to 2008, as a result of the lessons learning in spring 2008, a clearer split was devised for projects into subprojects, along with a corresponding assignment of parts of a team to particular subprojects. The project examples demonstrate the balance between fully learner-controlled projects that might flounder for weeks and instructor-facilitated projects that give users some control but also good guidance so that their creativity and self-direction can lead to satisfying outcomes.

4.3.3 IR Modules to Teach and Learn

In addition to projects, students also engaged in working with educational resources to ensure their learning of key IR concepts. Since we have long been involved in the building of DL of educational resources related to computing (now, through our leadership role in the Ensemble portal development[2]), using such resources seems particularly appropriate. Experimentation with using chapters in a reading book (Jones and Willett 1997) made clear that it was important to have consistency in notation and style to avoid students becoming confused and missing integrating themes.

In the fall 2008 DL course, building upon our DL curriculum project,[3] we had teams study and lead class discussions of eight previously developed educational modules. Each team also devised, by the end of the semester, a new module, which they presented to the class. Thus, students are not only learners but also active participants in modifying and adding to materials that future students will use.

In fall 2009, this active involvement of students continued, even though we did use a textbook to aid with much of the learning of course content. One team, devising a way to filter out noise in large collections made available by the Internet Archive, found they needed to jump ahead in the textbook to study about SVM; this is much like the flexible and motivating practices that commonly occur in problem-based learning. Another team, which chose educational module development as its term project, had each student prepare a new IR-related educational module, as well as review two other modules created by other team members.

4.3.4 Second Life

Second Life (SL)[4] is one of many shared virtual environments. However, it is large, popular, and has participants connected with many schools, colleges, universities, and corporations. There have been a variety of studies of how SL can help with education (Ausubel et al. 1978; Chau et al. 2003; Fox et al. 2009; Second Life Official Site 2010). UNC-CH and VT, with support from NSF, have developed an SL island called the Digital Preserve, to explore how SL can be of help to those involved in digital curation and preservation. The lead faculty and students involved in this project (all coauthors of this chapter) served as clients for one of the fall 2009 teams in the IR class. Some of the students involved learned that project meetings, as well as activities undertaken (e.g., collecting posters from ECDL 2009 and running an after-conference virtual version of the poster session (ECDL 2009) as well as keynote address), could be carried out "in world." In this way, SL was used as a scaffolding environment for students to explore and create

---

[2] http://www.computingportal.org.

[3] http://curric.dlib.vt.edu.

[4] http://secondlife.com.

Fig. 4.1 Second life in IR courses at Virginia Tech (**a**) Poster building in the "Digital Preserve" Second Life island; (**b**) ECDL 2009 virtual keynote organized by a project team in the IR course in Fall 2009

their own resources while contributing to a large-scale group project with scope beyond any single course. Figure 4.1 shows screenshots of teaching and learning resources developed and used in SL in the fall 2009 IR course at Virginia Tech.

4.4   Tools

There are many tools available that can be used by students so they can understand functions, systems, concepts, and their integration. Some have been developed specifically to aid in learning about IR (Efthimiadis and Freier 2007). Subsections below provide more detail.

4.4.1   Open Source Software

Use of software, such as Lucene, Flickr API, Zend, SVM light, and open source CBIR packages, has become a regular part of our IR courses. While Virginia Tech has developed and used a variety of IR and DL systems to aid in teaching and for project efforts (e.g., SMART, CODER, MARIAN, Envision, CITIDEL, and ETANA-DL), there are many advantages to using packages developed outside. Students often are highly motivated when connecting with a popular system, like Flickr or Facebook. They also realize that delivering a (sub)project that incorporates a popular package or service adds to their skill set, can be listed on their resume, and possibly may be of use in their future endeavors. Working with Lucene and SVM light clearly fit in with this realization.

4.4.2 Concept Maps

Building on constructivist learning theory, concept maps have been used extensively for many of the class sessions. Concept maps are based in Ausubel's subsumption theory (Ausubel 1963; Ausubel et al. 1978), i.e., "the most important single factor influencing learning is what the learner already knows." They were initially proposed by Joseph Novak (1998). In the context of DL, they are particularly important since they can serve to link a variety of educational resources together with learning goals (Sumner et al. 2005).

In our classes, we use IHMC's CMapTools.[5] In fall 2009, each student prepares a concept map for each textbook chapter that is covered. Teams meet to discuss individual maps to prepare a team map that improves on each of the individual maps. Finally, the student who presented the chapter slides earlier to the class takes all of the team maps for that chapter and then builds and presents a class concept map. All team and individual concept maps are submitted to a concept map server. Once the course is complete, the concept maps have public read access. All concept maps that were created in IR classes taught at Virginia Tech by the first author are available at the Virginia Tech (DLRL) CmapServer.[6] Figure 4.2 is an example of a team concept map on "Search Engines."

4.5 Case Studies

To further clarify our pedagogical innovations, we present case studies below. The common components and structure across these course offerings are outlined in Fig. 4.3. A summary of resources used and outcomes from these course offerings is provided online.[7]

---

[5] http://cmap.ihmc.us.

[6] http://boris.dlib.vt.edu/.

[7] http://collab.dlib.vt.edu/runwiki/wiki.pl?TLIRBookChapter.

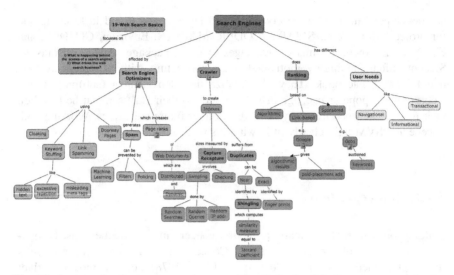

Fig. 4.2 An example of a team concept map on "Search Engines" (authors suppressed due to excessive length)

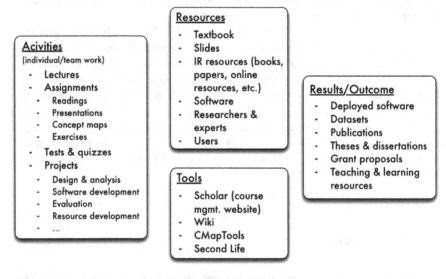

Fig. 4.3 Components and structure of IR courses at Virginia Tech

4.5.1 Information Storage and Retrieval: Spring 2008

In a spring 2008, we used a rapid approach to teach basic and advanced IR topics, such as text retrieval, Web-based IR, CBIR, and fusion search, to Computer Science (CS) graduate students. We designed projects that would help students grasp the aforementioned IR topics. Students, working in teams, were given a practical application to start with. That first application was locally developed: SuperIDR the Superimposed Application for Image Description and Retrieval (Murthy et al. 2009). SuperIDR [earlier, SIERRA (Murthy et al. 2006b)] allows users to associate parts of images with multimedia information such as text annotations. Also, users may retrieve information in one of two ways: (1) perform text-based retrieval on annotations; (2) perform content-based image retrieval (CBIR) on images and parts of images that look like a query image (or part of a query image).

Each team was asked to build an enhancement for this application, involving text retrieval and/or CBIR in 3 weeks' time. The outcome of this activity was that students learned about IR concepts while being able to relate their applicability to a real-world problem. Details of these projects may be found in the course project wiki page.[8] This work eventually led to a demonstration at SIGIR 2008 (Murthy et al. 2008).

4.5.2 Digital Libraries: Fall 2008

As was explained in Sect. 4.3.3, an advanced course on DL was taught in fall 2008. In that class, 13 modules from the DL curriculum project were involved. First, the instructor presented one of the modules, during a single class session. Next, each of four teams presented a module, using two class sessions so there was time for an in-class activity. This was repeated for another set of four modules. Meanwhile, each team developed a new module from scratch. Then they used a single class period for each of these to present that module. Since the class met twice a week for 75-min sessions, and since there were other days for midterm and final project presentations, the above-mentioned activities essentially filled the 14-week semester.

4.5.3 Information Storage and Retrieval: Fall 2009

The fall 2009 offering of Information Storage and Retrieval included most of the approaches and tools used in the aforementioned classes. In addition, students in this class were introduced to the SL virtual environment. This class followed a new textbook (Manning et al. 2008). The class was divided into teams, with four to seven individual members, as mentioned in Sect. 4.3.1. Each team worked together on all activities through the semester. Table 4.1 provides an overview of the activities in the class and their corresponding points (out of a total of 100). As indicated, some activities were undertaken as a team and some individually. Students worked and were graded on concept maps individually and as a team.

---

[8] http://collab.dlib.vt.edu/runwiki/wiki.pl?TabletPcImageRetrievalSuperimposedInformation.

Table 4.1 Grading points distribution for the Information Storage and Retrieval course offered in fall 2009 at Virginia Tech

Points	Activity
35	Team: term project
5	Team: team concept maps
10	Team: exercises
4	Team: Wikipedia entry
20	Individual: Final
14	Individual: Instructor assessment
8	Individual: Chapter lecture
4	Individual: Chapter consensus concept map

Teams could choose from five term projects, where each corresponded to an active grant/project. Project points were divided as mid-term presentation (5), final presentation (10), final report (10), and final deliverables (10). The final project points were adjusted based on peer evaluations of an individual by team members. With regard to exercises (available in the textbook (Manning et al. 2008) and author's Web site[9]), students first worked on them individually, and later as a team. The reason behind this was that team performance would almost always be better than that of the best individual, so students would learn the benefits of teams. One of the class assignments was to extend the coverage in Wikipedia[10] of the field of IR. Students could add new entries (a list of suggested topics was provided) or could make major enhancements to an existing entry. A part of the grading was based on the instructor's assessment of a student's performance in all activities in order to make adjustments for differences within members of a team.

4.6   Results and Impact

Work undertaken in these classes has been published at conferences including SIGIR (Murthy et al. 2008), ECDL (Kim et al. 2005), ICADL (Kim et al. 2006), and JCDL (Murthy et al. 2006a; Yang et al. 2006; Gorton et al. 2006). Some projects have resulted in grant proposals that have been funded, such as CTRnet[11] and Beyond Human Memory: SenseCam Use in Veterinary College and as Assistive Technology.[12] Some have been extended by an individual student, resulting in a master's thesis (Venkatachalam 2008; Raghavan 2005). Many projects have involved real-world clients including various university departments such as the alcohol abuse prevention center,[13] thus providing service learning opportunities that are highly motivational.

---

[9] http://www.ims.uni-stuttgart.de/lehre/teaching/2009-SS/ir.

[10] http://en.wikipedia.org/wiki/MainPage.

[11] http://www.ctrnet.net.

[12] http://www.memex.cs.vt.edu.

[13] http://www.alcohol.vt.edu/.

In the fall 2009 offering of the Information Storage and Retrieval course, we sought feedback from the students on their perception of the course content and structure. Twelve of the 21 students responded to the survey, of which there were one undergraduate, three doctoral, and eight master's degree students – all majoring in CS. Students had varied areas of interest, with most students being interested in Human–Computer Interaction (HCI) (Fig. 4.4A). Students felt they were more

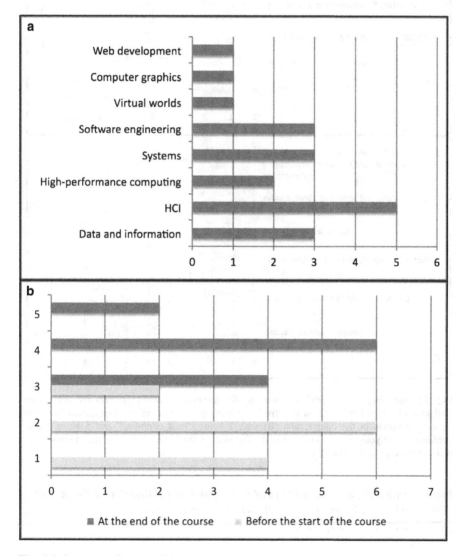

Fig. 4.4 Summary of students' responses to the questions (*x*-axis represents the number of students): (A) what is your area of interest? and (B) with 1 being "Novice" and 5 being "Expert," rate your familiarity and knowledge in information retrieval

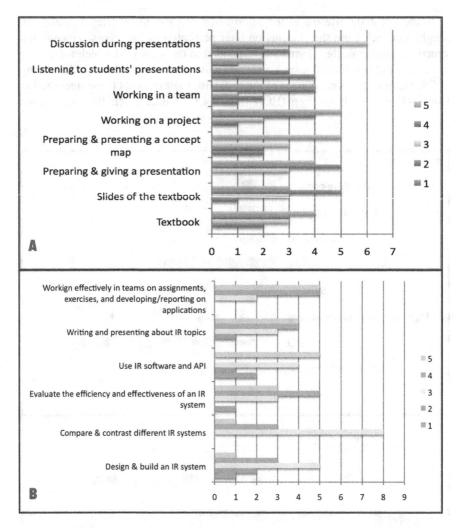

Fig. 4.5 Summary of students' responses to the questions (*x*-axis represents the number of students): (A) with 1 being "least effective" and 5 being "most effective," rate the teaching and learning methods in the course; and (B) with 1 being "least confident" and 5 being "most confident," rate your confidence level in the following tasks based on the skills and knowledge that you have gained in the class

familiar with and knowledgeable in IR at the end of the course than at the start of it (Fig. 4.4B). In addition, students felt that working in teams as well as working on projects was effective approaches to teach and learn IR (Fig. 4.5).

4.7 Discussion and Conclusion

Over the years, the IR class at Virginia Tech has been a fertile ground for experimentation with pedagogical approaches. Since we have had an active program in the digital library field since 1991, we have built and made use of collections of related educational resources. Since we have an active research program in IR and DL, we regularly have project activities that are integrated with class activities or with term project efforts. Students work in teams on those projects, as well as to develop concept maps and other aids to learning. Recently, environments like SL have further enhanced collaboration as well as constructivist learning. We hope that our experiences may be of interest to others involved in IR education. Many of our pedagogical innovations should be applicable to those at other institutions. We offer assistance to those choosing to explore these approaches, and will be happy to collaborate with others involved in similar innovations.

Acknowledgments This material is based upon work supported by the National Science Foundation under Grant Numbers NSF DUE-0840719, IIS-0535057, IIS-0910183, and IIS-0910465. Any opinions, findings, and conclusions or recommendations expressed in this material are those of the author(s) and do not necessarily reflect the views of the National Science Foundation.

References

Ausubel D (1963) The psychology of meaningful verbal learning. Grune & Stratton, New York

Ausubel D, Novak J, Hanesian H (1978) Educational psychology: a cognitive view. Holt, Rinehart & Winston, New York

Blumenfeld P, Kempler TM, Krajcik J (2006) Motivation and cognitive engagement in learning environments. In: The Cambridge handbook of the learning sciences. Cambridge University Press, Cambridge, pp 475–488

Brown JS, Collins A, Duguid P (1989) Situated cognition and the culture of learning. Educ Res 1(1):32–42

Chau M, Huang Z, Chen H (2003) Teaching key topics in computer science and information systems through a web search engine project. J Educ Resour Comput 3(3):2

Duffy T, Jonassen D (1992) Constructivism and the technology of instruction: a conversation. Lawrence Erlbaum Associates, Hillsdale, NJ

ECDL (2009) Online poster session in Second Life. http://www.ionio.gr/conferences/ecdl2009/secondlife.php

Efthimiadis E, Freier N (2007) IR-Toolbox: an experiential learning tool for teaching IR. In: SIGIR '07: Proceedings of the 30th Annual International ACM SIGIR Conference on Research and Development in Information Retrieval, Amsterdam, The Netherlands, p 914

Fink D (2003) Creating significant learning experiences: an integrated approach to designing college courses. Jossey-Bass, San Francisco

Fox EA, Lee SJ, Velacso J, Marchionini G, Yang S, Murthy U (2009) The first international workshop on innovation in digital preservation, held in conjunction with the 9th ACM/IEEE Joint Conference on Digital Libraries, Austin, TX

Gorton D, Shen R, Vemuri NS, Fan W, Fox EA (2006) ETANA-GIS: GIS for archaeological digital libraries. In: JCDL '06: Proceedings of the 6th ACM/IEEE-CS joint conference on Digital libraries, ACM, New York, pp 379–379

Hiltz SR (1997) The virtual classroom: learning without limits via computer networks. Ablex, Norwood, NJ

Jones KS, Willett P (1997) Readings in information retrieval. Morgan Kaufmann, San Francisco

Kim S, Murthy U, Ahuja K, Vasile S, Fox EA (2005) Effectiveness of implicit rating data on characterizing users in complex information systems. In: Research and advanced technology for digital libraries, 9th European Conference, ECDL 2005, Vienna, Austria, 18–23 Sept 2005. Lect Notes Comput Sci 3652:186–194

Kim S, Lele S, Ramalingam S, Fox EA (2006) Visualizing user communities and usage trends of digital libraries based on user tracking information. In: Digital libraries: achievements, challenges and opportunities, 9th International Conference on Asian Digital Libraries, ICADL 2006, Kyoto, Japan, 27–30 Nov 2006. Lect Notes Comput Sci 4312:111–120

Manning CD, Raghavan P, Schutze H (2008) Introduction to information retrieval. Cambridge University Press, New York

Murthy U, Ahuja K, Murthy S, Fox EA (2006a) SIMPEL: a superimposed multimedia presentation editor and player. In: JCDL '06: Proceedings of the 6th ACM/IEEE-CS joint conference on Digital libraries. ACM, New York, p 377

Murthy U, Torres RdS, Fox E (2006b) SIERRA – a superimposed application for enhanced image description and retrieval. In: ECDL 2006: Proceedings of the 10th European Conference, pp 540–543

Murthy U, Torres RdS, Fox EA, Venkatachalam L, Yang S, Gonçalves MA (2008) From concepts to implementation and visualization: tools from a team-based approach to IR. In: SIGIR '08: Proceedings of the 31st annual international ACM SIGIR conference on research and development in information retrieval. ACM, New York, pp 889–889

Murthy U, Fox E, Chen Y, Hallerman E, Torres R, Ramos E, Falcao T (2009) Superimposed image description and retrieval for fish species identification. In: ECDL '09: Proceedings of the 13th European conference on Research and Advanced Technology for Digital Libraries, Corfu, Greece, pp 285–296

Novak J (1998) Learning, creating, and using knowledge: concept maps as facilitative tools in schools and corporations. Lawrence Erlbaum, Mahwah, N.J

Papert SA (1993) Mindstorms: children, computers, and powerful ideas. Basic Books, New York

Quintana C, Soloway E, Norris CA (2001) Learner-centered design: developing software that scaffolds learning. In: ICALT 2001: Proceedings IEEE international conference on advanced learning technology, Madison, WI

Raghavan A (2005) Schema mapper: a visualization tool for incremental semi-automatic mapping-based integration of heterogeneous collections into archaeological digital libraries: the ETANADL case study. Master's thesis, Virginia Tech, Blacksburg

Second Life Official Site (2010) Virtual worlds, avatars, free 3D chat, online meetings – Second Life Official Site. http://secondlife.com/

Slavin R (1980) Cooperative learning. Rev Educ Res 50(2):315–342

Sumner T, Ahmad F, Bhushan S, Gu Q, Molina F, Willard S, Wright M, Davis L, Janee G (2005) Linking learning goals and educational resources through interactive concept map visualizations. Int J Digital Libr 5(1):18–24

Venkatachalam, L. (2008). Scalability of stepping stones and pathways. Master's thesis, Virginia Tech, Blacksburg

Weimer M (2002) Learner-centered teaching: five key changes to practice. Jossey-Bass, San Francisco

Yang S, Congleton B, Luc G, Pérez-Quiñones MA, Fox EA (2006) Demonstrating the use of a SenseCam in two domains. In: JCDL '06: Proceedings of the 6th ACM/IEEE-CS joint conference on Digital libraries, 376. ACM, New York, 376 p

Chapter 5
Pedagogical Design and Evaluation
of Interactive Information Retrieval
Learning Environment

Kai Halttunen

5.1 Introduction

Interactive information retrieval (IIR) has become a commonplace activity in our
networked world. People constantly use various search services in order to find relevant
documents to satisfy their information needs or accessing services, communities, or
people to get answers or recommendations. From a pedagogical viewpoint, IIR
activities have some important properties. These include firstly, task dependence of
information searching. In the real world, searching is bound to various task situations.
Therefore, IIR instruction is seldom successful as a decontextualized activity. Secondly, users of IR systems encounter uncertainty in various phases of searching.
Searching and finding is basically motivated by uncertainty in a situation, i.e., the
need to find information to reduce uncertainty. Uncertainty also relates to selection of
information channels and sources, search keys, and evaluation of search results.
Thirdly, although we can outline the main phases of searching, we seldom can provide
definite rules on how to proceed in IIR tasks. These ill-defined rules for proceeding are
important elements of IIR instruction. Learners should be supported with motivating
cues and hints, without providing too ready-made solutions. IIR instruction should also
equip learners with transferable skills to manage searching in different operational IR
systems and interfaces (Halttunen 2004; Morville and Callender 2010).

Understanding how pedagogical solutions and technology can best support
student learning in diverse learning environments remains a crucial line of educational research and development. Finding a suitable approach to rapid technological
change and the identification of best practices are core ideas of "design
experiments." Collins (1992) describes an educational research experiment carried
out in a complex learning context, which explores how a technological innovation

K. Halttunen (✉)
Department of Information Studies and Interactive Media, University of Tampere, Tampere,
Finland
e-mail: Kai.Halttunen@uta.fi

E. Efthimiadis et al. (eds.), *Teaching and Learning in Information Retrieval*,
The Information Retrieval Series 31, DOI 10.1007/978-3-642-22511-6_5,
© Springer-Verlag Berlin Heidelberg 2011

affects student learning and educational practice (see also Brown 1992; Cobb et al. 2003). The goals of design experiments are to design and implement innovative learning environments and simultaneously understand salient aspects of human cognition and learning involved in those innovations. Design experiments:

- Address learning programs involving important subject matter
- Are usually mediated by innovative technology
- Are embedded in everyday social contexts which are often classrooms, homes, and workplaces where it is hard to control unanticipated events
- Account for multiple dependent variables
- Do not attempt to hold variables constant, but rather identify many variables and the nature and the extent of their effects
- Evaluate various aspects of the design and develop a profile to characterize the design in practice

The present chapter describes continuing development of teaching practice and a research-oriented design experiment where pedagogical solutions like anchored instruction with scaffolding and fading are used. IIR instruction is also mediated with instructional software application QPA (Query Performance Analyzer). Student assessment and feedback is based on their prior conceptions, performance, learning experiences, and learning outcomes. Students' conceptual change and skills development provide base for learning outcomes assessment. The design experiment was conducted in a naturalistic educational environment of a university. The focus of the chapter is to describe design, implementation, and evaluation process in meta-level without concentrating highly on details of design and evaluation. These are described and referenced in original research articles.

5.2 Pedagogical Design of the IIR Learning Environment

Pedagogical design refers to any systematic choice and use of procedures, methods, prescriptions, and devices in order to bring about effective, efficient, and productive learning (see, e.g., Romiszowski 1981). According to Lowyck (2002), most recent models of design incorporate the following components:

- An analysis of a knowledge base of learning and instructional theories
- The frame of reference in which the design is used (i.e., elements like context, learners, and content)
- A set of validated rules or procedures to regulate and realize the design process and product

Most instructional design efforts involve a minimum of four components: namely, a specification of (1) the goals to be met, (2) materials to be used, (3) teaching strategies to be used, and (4) items and procedures for assessment. These components seem to be important for any domain of instruction imaginable. There is also a potential problem with this approach. The more complete the specification of values for each instructional component, the less inclined teachers may be to map onto the unique features of particular students and communities (Cognition and Technology Group at Vanderbilt 1993).

Sfard (1998) points out that all our concepts and beliefs are based on a small number of fundamental ideas, which are carried from one domain to another by the language we use. She states that the current discourse of learning brings about two metaphors, which she names the acquisition metaphor (strengthening of reactions and information processing) and the participation metaphor (knowledge construction). Both of these metaphors are present in recent texts, but the former is more prominent in older writing and the latter in more recent studies. These ideas guide our pedagogical approaches, intentionally or unintentionally.

In many cases, instruction in IIR is based on practical hands-on exercises, which concentrate on search, interface, and document representation features of mostly operational IR systems. Instruction emphasizes active learning: doing and practicing. Learning tasks are often divided into subtasks like practicing author or title search, truncation, use of operators, etc. Exercises are done in a predefined sequence and feedback given with correct solutions. These pedagogical solutions based on strengthening of reactions are in many cases valid to support learning of the basic features of IR systems, but they may not produce transferable skills.

Pedagogical solutions adapted from the information processing metaphor stress the importance of activating long-term memory with the help of learning materials in different formats (text, image, sound). Learners are supported with flowcharts, hierarchies, and concept maps in building their mental models of study topics.

The metaphor of knowledge construction incorporates pedagogical solutions like activation and consideration of prior conceptions, as well as interaction with the environment both individually and socially. Learning is deeply rooted in interaction and participation in communities of practice.

The present learning environment is a place where learners may work together and support each other as they use a variety of tools and information sources in their guided pursuit of learning goals and problem-solving activities (Wilson 1996). In the present design experiment, learning environment has following properties:

- Place consists of classroom and networked environment
- Learners are first-year university students of information studies
- Who work both individually and in small groups
- Support is based on intentional scaffolding provided by teachers, tools, and colearners. Scaffolding and fading refers to various ways to build learning support
- Different kind of tools like operational and instructional IR systems are used
- Lectures, printed materials, and Web pages serve as information sources
- Students are guided in the learning process by teachers providing learning tasks, timelines, feedback, and scaffolding
- Learning goals are based on a curriculum
- Problem-solving activities are present constantly in classroom and Web exercises

Along with the general definition of the elements of the learning environment stated earlier, the design exploits the idea of "phenomenaria," i.e., the area of presenting, observing, examining, and manipulating the phenomena under study (Perkins 1991). Ideas of anchoring instruction to context as well as various pedagogical solutions based on situated learning and cognitive apprenticeship are utilized (Cognition and Technology Group at Vanderbilt 1990). Examples of these include modeling, coaching, and various ways to support learner, i.e., scaffolding and fading. Some of the scaffolding is implemented in the QPA, but teachers and tutors in the classroom do most of the coaching and scaffolding. The learning environment provides learning tasks, goals and activities, feedback, and information sources.

The QPA was originally developed as a rapid query performance analysis tool (Airio et al. 2007; Sormunen et al. 1998, 2002). The goal of the QPA is to provide a realistic environment for demonstrating the performance of queries in different types of search situations.

The basic idea of the QPA arose from the insight that the test collections used in the laboratory-based IR experiments could be used in instruction. A traditional test collection consists of a database, a collection of test topics (search tasks), and relevance assessments indicating which documents are relevant in respect to a given search topic.

The QPA consist of four major components (1) a set of well-specified search tasks for retrieving documents in a database, (2) relevance judgment's explicating which documents of the database match the relevance requirements of each search task, (3) a front-end system supporting and monitoring searching in all appropriate retrieval systems and databases, and (4) a feedback system for measuring and visualizing the performance of any query executed.

5.3   Description of the Learning Environment in the IIR Course

The course "Introduction to Information Retrieval" (6 ECTS credits) at the Department of Information Studies at the University of Tampere, Finland has been intended for first-year undergraduate students from 2000 onwards. They attend the basic course on information retrieval in the first semester of their studies. They are studying either IS as a major or as a minor subject. The course provides an overview of information storage and retrieval as practice and as a research area. Themes like the production and structure of databases, matching algorithms, metadata, subject representation, query languages and formulation, search strategies and tactics, and evaluation are covered in the course. Learning domain is congruent with IR curriculum described in Vilar and Zumer (2009).

The course consists of five instructional elements. First, students' prior conceptions of IR were analyzed in order to form a baseline for evaluation of learning outcomes and as tool for providing ideas for the design of IIR learning environment. Activating these conceptions enhances learning, creates motivation, and makes it easier to concentrate on studying.

Second, lectures are given on basic concepts of information storage and retrieval. Along with the themes covered earlier, lectures present visual and textual advance organizers of topics to be studied and provide interactive feedback and summaries of exercises and learning tasks completed during the course. Mind maps and charts are used as introductory material to form conceptual understanding and serve as advance organizers. They enhance student learning and make it easier to connect new knowledge to prior conceptions and mental models (Ausubel 1960).

Third, weekly Web exercises concentrate on putting the themes covered in lectures into practice. Every participant is working on these exercises making use of Web-based tools and resources. Exercises are reported on the Moodle learning management system. Feedback on these tasks was given during the lectures.

Fourth, tutored exercises in the classroom covered various aspects of information retrieval systems and their effective use. In these sessions, groups of 8–12 students work in pairs. Various kinds of search services are used (OPACs, union catalogs, article reference databases, full text databases, Internet search engines and directories). Performance feedback of the QPA is used in several exercises as well as log-file analysis.

Fifth, a course feedback Web form is filled out at the end of the course. This feedback covered three main areas (1) course design and teaching methods, (2) the learner's self-evaluation and role in the course, and (3) the teacher's role in the course. The course feedback is an integral part of the course and it provides questions to support learners' self-evaluation and reflection. Feedback is also gathered with empathy-based stories, as discussed later in the chapter.

About 85–120 students attend this course, and a lecturer and two to three tutors take care of a part of the tutored sessions' provided instruction. The course outline, material, exhaustive handouts covering the lecture material, a bulletin board and exercises are provided via the University Moodle. Despite of the number of participants, the course can be regarded as highly interactive and task oriented. The learning-by-doing approach is used in several situations. The assessment of learning outcomes is based on weekly Web exercises, tutored exercises, and final examination. The grading one to five is used to indicate how a student has fulfilled the learning objectives.

5.4 Supporting the Learning Process with Anchoring, Scaffolding, and Fading

Anchored instruction is strongly associated with situated learning and constructivist learning environments. A major goal of anchored instruction is to overcome the problem of inert knowledge by teaching problem-solving skills and independent thinking. The Cognition and Technology Group at Vanderbilt (1993) states that an anchored learning environment permits sustained exploration by students and teachers. Furthermore, it enables them to understand the kinds of problems and opportunities that experts encounter and the knowledge that experts use as tools.

Anchored instruction was used to create a macro-context for IIR activities. We used the full-text database of a local newspaper, an image database of a national press agency, and a national bibliographic database on journal and newspaper articles. Based on these tools we created a context of journalistic practice. In other words, IR activities were situated in a simulated work-task situation (Borlund 2000), where search tasks were based on the idea of a journalist searching the text and image databases available in order to find information on certain topics for a forthcoming article. In addition, some topics required the reporter to search national databases on certain topics.

Scaffolding occurs when a student, with the help of an expert, carries out a task that is too difficult for the student to cope with independently. The concept originates from idea of the zone of proximal development introduced by Vygotsky (1978). The metaphor of scaffolding comes from house construction, in which the house is built with the help of the surrounding scaffolding. When the house is complete, the scaffolding can be taken away. In cognitive apprenticeship, the tutor's withdrawal is called fading. Fading consists of the gradual removal of supports until students are completely on their own (Halttunen 2003b). Scaffolding was offered both by tutors and the QPA. Examples of scaffolding in the classroom are presented in Table 5.1.

The teacher can model the search process by providing examples focusing not only on end products (efficient query formulations), but also on the search process. The teacher provides hints, either initially or on an ongoing basis, on query formulation. The provision of examples of possible search keys serves as a scaffold in certain situations. Coaching comments are intended for motivation, providing feedback and advice on performance, and provoking reflection. Different kinds of questions can be set to enhance reflection, for example, pointing out weaknesses and asking about motivation.

The provision of a timeline with fixed timing and goals provides support for goal direction and reflection. The gradual removal of scaffolding, i.e., fading, was based

Table 5.1 Scaffolding implemented in the classroom

Scaffold	Implementation in classroom
Providing examples	Teacher models a search process
Providing hints	Suggesting parts of query formulation
Giving away parts of the solution	Suggesting search terms
Cueing/hinting	Giving cues/hints on operators, syntax
Providing coaching comments	Commenting, for example: "Why did this happen?"
Asking questions	Asking, for example: "How does that effect?" "What problems may that cause?"
Providing a timeline	Presenting a search process timeline

Table 5.2 Software-based scaffolding implemented in the QPA

Scaffold	Implementation in the QPA
Giving away parts of solution	Query performance feedback, relevance information, and search topics
Providing clues	Give a hint on relevant documents
Providing examples	Showing hall of fame containing queries
Providing comparison	Others' queries, p/r curves

on student performance in the exercises. When the students were able to construct queries, scaffolds such as examples and hints were removed. Coaching comments and questions were used throughout the exercises to improve reflection and articulation. Performance feedback provided by the QPA was removed in one of the search tasks, when students selected their own viewpoints on the topic. Table 5.2 describes the instructional scaffolds implemented in the QPA.

The basic idea and functionality of the QPA is that the query performance feedback scaffolds the learner by providing information on query performance. The learner receives feedback on query construction, which enables her/him to evaluate different search strategies and tactics. Learners can concentrate on the analysis of effective query formulation without spending lots of time in analyzing results. The "give a hint" function provides the learner with one nonretrieved relevant document. This document serves as a cue to the selection of appropriate search keys or document structures usable while searching. The possibility of identifying the retrieved relevant documents also serves as a cue in the same respect. The hall of fame provides examples of best queries on the current topic over time. The opportunity to see one's own performance compared to the performance of other users provides an area of comparison and feedback. Search topics can serve as a scaffold, providing examples of search keys and informing searchers about applicable restrictions.

The software-based scaffolds in the QPA are based on the basic idea of "knowing the right documents" for each topic. In a way this approach pays attention to the end product of the process, to effective query formulation with good precision and recall, but not interactive learning process support as such. The face-to-face scaffolding described earlier is needed in this situation (Halttunen 2003a).

5.5 Data Collection for Evaluation and Feedback

In order to evaluate students' prior conceptions and the effect of anchored instruction, scaffolding, fading, and the use of the QPA on learning experiences (student feedback), performance and outcomes, multiple evaluation and feedback data collection and analysis methods were used.

First, prior conceptions represent learners' understanding and experiences of IR know-how at the very beginning of formal instruction. Students' prior conceptions form the basis for learning. Conceptions cover elements of IR skills (e.g., information sources, search engines), phases of the search process (e.g., analysis of information needs, evaluation of results), and background factors (e.g., searcher characteristics, IT skills). Students wrote essays and filled out the questionnaire on conceptions of IR know-how as an in-class assignment in the very beginning of the first lecture. The instruction for essay writing was presented as: "Write an essay-type text, in which you present your own description of information retrieval know-how. You can approach the topic by identifying different kinds of skills, knowledge, elements, etc. which, in your opinion are part of IR know-how." After writing the essay, students filled out the questionnaire, which presents visual analog scales (VAS) of different kinds of conceptions of IR. They presented their views from three different perspectives (1) what the important aspects of IR know-how are; (2) what their present knowledge about these aspects is; and finally, (3) what they expected as the important aspects of IR on the course they were attending. VAS was used because we did not want to categorize the levels of importance in advance, but direct students to form their own categorizations (Halttunen 2003b, 2007; Halttunen and Järvelin 2005).

Second, learning experiences represent students' reactions and feedback to the instruction. These experiences form a basis for the evaluation of instruction as a whole. Students describe their learning experiences concentrating on the elements of learning environments which were felt to be either positive or negative, i.e., factors enhancing or inhibiting learning. (Halttunen and Sormunen 2000). Students described their learning experiences in texts written based on the method of empathy-based stories (MEBS) and in answers to the course feedback question- naire. There were seven major themes of learning experiences, namely: study orientation, domain of study, instructional design, teachers, other students, com- puter skills, and factors of everyday life (Halttunen 2003a, 2007).

MEBS was used for collecting data on students' learning experiences related to the instructional design. This method involves writing short essays according to instructions given by the teacher or researcher. In MEBS, the respondent is given some orientation, which is called the script. This script should be used in conjunc- tion with the respondents' imagination in the writing of the story. The author of the story either continues the situation detailed in the script or describes what must or may have taken place prior to that situation. Variation is crucial to the use of this method, and there are at least two different versions of the same script, which vary with regard to a certain key issue. Such variation distinguishes the MEBS from many other methods of acquiring data (Eskola 1988, 1998). Variation of the scripts was based on good and poor learning experiences. Also a course feedback Web form was filled out at the end of the course. Feedback covers three main areas (1) course design and teaching methods, (2) the learner's self-evaluation and role in the course, and (3) the teacher's role in the course. There were 21 questions out of which 16 were open questions and five were multiple option questions.

Third, performance in IR learning environment covers learners' search sessions, i.e., performance feedback provided by the QPA on four exercises in the course. Student performance was analyzed with the following data: (a) the number of queries, (b) the number of search keys, (c) the average number of search keys per query, (d) qualitative evaluation of use of operators, truncation and field searching, and finally (e) the overall efficiency of best queries based on precision/recall measures provided by the QPA (Halttunen 2003a, 2007).

Log files were gathered in several search exercise sessions. First, search sessions in the QPA were logged within the application. Log files were downloaded from the QPA and converted into spreadsheets. Second, the Dialog system was used in the last search exercise session for the performance assessment of IR skills. These sessions were logged with the aid of the search history of Dialog. Search histories were saved as HTML files and converted into spreadsheets.

Fourth, learning outcomes represent what a student knows and/or what she is able to do as a result of an educational experience. Learning outcomes indicate the change in the knowledge, understanding, skills, capabilities, and values that a student has gained by completing an instructional episode. In the present case, learning outcomes are evaluated on two levels. First, conceptual change is analyzed by comparing students' conceptions of IR know-how at the beginning and at the end of the course. At the end of the course the students were again asked to write an essay-type text on their conceptions of IR know-how in the same manner as at the beginning of the course. Second, the development of IR skills is analyzed by identifying improvement and errors in query formulation in 24 search sessions. The conceptual change consists of the introduction, modification, and neglect of concepts presented in student essays along with enrichment or revision of conceptual structures. The development of IR skills is based on an analysis of query formulation, error types, and effectiveness of queries (Halttunen and Järvelin 2005; Halttunen 2007).

5.6 Analysis of Evaluation and Feedback Data

IIR learning environment is evaluated at three levels: students' learning experiences, performance, and learning outcomes. In order to describe and analyze these different levels, several datasets were gathered as described earlier. The analytical methods for assessment and feedback and corresponding datasets are outlined later.

First, students' subjective learning experiences concerning the learning environment and the QPA are studied using the MEBS (Eskola 1988, 1998) and the course feedback questionnaire. Stories and course feedback were analyzed qualitatively by theme coding, categorization, and with the aid of matrices (Eskola 1998; Miles and Huberman 1994).

Second, student performance in the IIR learning environment was analyzed by assessing their search sessions both in terms of query construction and modification and the overall effectiveness of queries. Query construction and modification was analyzed with the scheme concentrating on (1) the construction of facets and the use of operators, (2) the use of truncation and masking, and (3) the use of field restrictions. The overall effectiveness of best queries of each student within the four exercises was measured by average precision and recall.

Third, learning outcomes were analyzed on two levels, namely, conceptual change and skills development. Conceptual change was assessed with essays and questionnaire. The essays were first analyzed through the phenomenographic approach (Marton 1988, 1994) in order to ascertain students' conceptions of IR and how it may affect the design of learning environment. These conceptions were also used as a baseline for the evaluation of learning outcomes. The analysis of the essays was based on a grounded theory approach, which is common due to the fact that phenomenography is clearly an approach, not a solid method, in the analysis phase (Richardson 1999). The teacher collected all the statements concerning conceptions of IR know-how from each essay and compared the statements between and within essays. In the analysis we were primarily looking for qualitative differences in the way in which students experienced the phenomenon of IR know-how. The evolving pattern of differences and similarities was then captured in a set of categories of description. The categories of description were again applied to the data, which resulted in modification of categories. Prior conceptions of information retrieval were also studied through the questionnaire, which presents VAS of different kinds of conceptions of IR. VAS results are based on the measurement of the point on an axis (0–6 cm). Measurements were categorized into six classes. Student learning benefits from activating prior conceptions. This activation may be used as an advance organizer for learning (Ausubel 1960). Student generated visual representations of IR systems serve well for this purpose (Hendry and Efthimiadis 2008).

Essays written at the beginning and end of the course were analyzed with the aid of concept maps. These maps describe the essence of concepts, and the number of, and connections between, concepts (Kankkunen 1999; Novak and Musonda 1991; Novak 1998). Though concept maps were introduced as vehicles for instruction, studying, and assessment in the situations where they are used by teachers or students, they can also be used as analytical methods by researchers in qualitative inquiry (Miles and Huberman 1994). Concepts referring to IR know-how were extracted and labeled in the essays, likewise the connections between concepts. Top-level concepts are identified within essays as new themes, which did not consist of examples or enriched definitions or descriptions of concepts presented earlier in the essay. Assessment framework for structure of observed learning outcomes (SOLO taxonomy) would also contribute to this approach (Biggs and Collis 1982).

The development of IR skills was analyzed with performance assessment criteria based on search-logs in an assessment situation during the last tutored exercises. This assessment was based on analyzing problems and errors in queries and the effectiveness of queries. A scoring scheme was devised for log-file analysis. It identified all possible errors, which students had made during each session. This raw data was categorized with the aid of previous research on interaction problems in IR and OPAC systems and knowledge types in human–computer interaction (see, for example, Borgman 1996; Shneiderman 1992; Sit 1998). Because of the instructional performance assessment we excluded several factors of previous studies of operational environments, for example, database selection and information need formulation to search task, and concentrated on factors directly present in our learning assignments. The analysis scheme contains the following dimensions: (1) semantic and syntactic knowledge; (2) topical and functional knowledge.

5.7 Reflections on the Design, Evaluation, and Feedback

Writing an essay on prior conceptions of IR at the beginning of the course served as an orientation, and it created an interest in the topic at hand. In this way, writing assignments were used as advance organizers and as a means to bridge and activate prior knowledge and conceptions of the new area of study. Search histories were used to reflect the searching processes and to analyze errors in queries as natural phenomena. The second essay on conceptions of IR know-how was used as reflection and self-evaluation of student learning. Empathy-based stories and the course feedback questionnaire served as tools for course feedback and evaluation as well as instruments for self-reflection. The chosen approach to integrate evaluation and feedback data gathering as an integral part of learning activities seems to work well.

The design and evaluation of IIR learning environment in the present design experiment was highly intuitive but same at the same time innovative for at least two reasons. First, there were few published, available up-to-date models of IR instruction design and evaluation (see, e.g., Fernández-Luna et al. 2009; Lucas and Topi 2005). Second, the design experiment was implemented in a natural setting, with resources and tools available at the time in the course. The strength of the natural setting is the applicability of the pedagogical solutions. The pedagogical design was mainly based on the teacher's understanding of the central problems of IIR instruction, which they have encountered during their own teaching careers. The identification of a need for research and development was motivated by the research on conceptions of learning and learning environments. Anchored instruction was found to be a promising strategy to overcome the problem of decontextualized IIR instruction and ideas from scaffolding provided explicit tools to support learners in their information searching.

The evaluation of learning environment was based on various datasets, containing material on learning experiences, performance, and outcomes. Data gathering was integrated into course activities and also served as an instructional element itself, as described earlier. This approach was highly successful. After collecting and analyzing these datasets, the teacher could reflect the work done by following recommendations or reconsiderations for future: first, allocate more time for essay writing in order to activate prior conceptions. Visual tools and techniques are worth considering. Second, collect some performance data – for example, observations, texts, and interviews – to enrich the log data. Collaborative work by students should be used more and more. Third, develop data collection methods for evaluating learning outcomes. Weekly learning tasks and final examination could be enriched with various ways to make learners work visible to colearners and tutors.

References

Airio E, Sormunen E, Halttunen K, Keskustalo H (2007) Tools and methods for linking information retrieval research and instruction. In: The first international workshop on teaching and learning of information retrieval (TLIR'07), London, 10 Jan 2007

Ausubel DP (1960) The use of advance organizers in the learning and retention of meaningful verbal material. J Educ Psychol 51:267–272

Biggs JB, Collis KF (1982) Evaluating the quality of learning – the SOLO taxonomy. Academic, New York

Borgman CL (1996) Why are online catalogs still hard to use? J Am Soc Inf Sci 47(7):493–503

Borlund P (2000) Experimental components for the evaluation of interactive information retrieval systems. J Document 56(1):71–90

Brown AL (1992) Design experiments: theoretical and methodological challenges in creating complex interventions in classroom settings. J Learn Sci 2(2):141–178

Cobb P, Confrey J, diSessa A, Lehrer R, Schauble L (2003) Design experiments in educational research. Educ Res 32(1):9–13

Cognition and Technology Group at Vanderbilt (1990) Anchored instruction and its relationship to situated cognition. Educ Res 19(3):2–10

Cognition and Technology Group at Vanderbilt (1993) Designing learning environments that support learning: the Jasper series as a case study. In: Duffy TS, Lowyck J, Jonassen DH (eds) Designing environments for constructive learning. Springer, Berlin, pp 9–36

Collins A (1992) Toward a design science of education. In: Scanlon E, O'Shea T (eds) New directions in educational technology. Kustantaja, Paikka, pp 15–22

Eskola A (1988) Non-active role-playing: some experiences. In: Eskola A, Khilström A, Kivinen D, Weckroth K, Ylijoki O (eds) Blind alleys in social psychology: a search for ways out. North-Holland, Amsterdam, pp 239–305

Eskola J (1998) Eläytymismenetelmä sosiaalitutkimuksen tiedonhankintamenetelmänä [The method of empathy-based stories as a method of acquiring data in social research]. TAJU, Tampere

Fernández-Luna JM, Huete JF, MacFarlane A, Efthimiadis EN (2009) Teaching and learning in information retrieval. Inf Retr 12(2):201–226

Halttunen K (2003a) Scaffolding performance in IR instruction: Exploring learning experiences and performance in two learning environments. J Inf Sci 29(5):375–390

Halttunen K (2003b) Students' conceptions of information retrieval: Implications for design of learning environments. Libr Inf Sci Res 25(3):307–332

Halttunen K (2004) Two information retrieval learning environments: their design and evaluation. Ph.D Dissertation. University of Tampere

Halttunen K (2007) Design experiment on two information retrieval learning environments. In: The first international workshop on teaching and learning of information retrieval (TLIR'07), London, 10 Jan 2007

Halttunen K, Järvelin K (2005) Assessing learning outcomes in two information retrieval learning environments. Inf Process Manag 41(4):949–972

Halttunen K, Sormunen E (2000) Learning information retrieval through an educational game: is gaming sufficient for learning. Educ Inf 18(4):289–311

Hendry DG, Efthimiadis EN (2008) Conceptual models for search engines. In: Spink A, Zimmer M (eds) Web searching: interdisciplinary perspectives. Springer, Dordrecht, pp 209–228

Kankkunen M (1999) Opittujen käsitteiden merkityksen ymmärtäminen sekä ajattelun rakenteiden analyysi käsitekarttamenetelmän avulla [Comprehending the concepts and their meanings on learning, and the analysis of structures of thinking with the method of concept mapping], Dissertation. Joensuun yliopisto, Joensuu

Lowyck J (2002) Pedagogical design. In: Adelsberg HH, Collins B, Pawlowski JM (eds) Handbook on information technologies for education and training. Springer, Heidelberg, pp 199–218

Lucas W, Topi H (2005) Learning and training to search. In: Spink A, Cole C (eds) New directions in cognitive information retrieval. Springer, Dordrecht, pp 209–226

Marton F (1988) Phenomenography: exploring different conceptions of reality. In: Fettermann DM (ed) Qualitative approaches to evaluation in education: the silent scientific revolution. Praeger, New York, pp 176–205

Marton F (1994) Phenomenography. In: Husen T, Postlethwaite NT (eds) International encyclopedia of education, vol 8, 2nd edn. Pergamon, Oxford, pp 4424–4429

Miles MB, Huberman AM (1994) Qualitative data analysis: an expanded sourcebook, 2nd edn. Sage, Thousand Oaks

Morville P, Callender J (2010) Search patterns. O'Reilly, Sebastopol, CA

Novak JD (1998) Learning, creating, and using knowledge: concept maps as facilitative tools in schools and corporations. Lawrence Erlbaum, Mahwah, NJ

Novak J, Musonda D (1991) A twelve-year longitudinal study of science concept learning. Am Educ Res J 28(1):117–135

Perkins DN (1991) Technology meets constructivism: do they make a marriage. Educ Technol 31(5):18–23

Richardson JTE (1999) The concepts and methods of phenomenographic research. Rev Educ Res 69(1):53–82

Romiszowski AJ (1981) Designing instructional systems: decision making in course planning and curriculum design. Kogan Page, London

Sfard A (1998) On two metaphors for learning and the dangers of choosing just one. Educ Res 27(2):4–13

Shneiderman B (1992) Designing the user interface: strategies for effective human-computer interaction, 2nd edn. Addison, Reading, MA

Sit RA (1998) Online library catalog search performance by older adult users. Libr Inf Sci Res 20(2):115–131

Sormunen E, Laaksonen J, Keskustalo H, Kekäläinen J, Kemppainen H, Laitinen H, Pirkola A, Järvelin K (1998) IR game: a tool for rapid query analysis in cross-language IR experiments. In: Paper presented at the Joint workshop on cross language issues in artificial intelligence & issues of cross cultural communication, Singapore

Sormunen E, Halttunen K, Keskustalo H (2002) Query performance analyser: a web-based tool for information retrieval research and instruction (Research Notes 1/2002). Department of Information Studies, University of Tampere, Tampere

Vilar P, Zumer M (2009) The Bologna reform at the department of library and information science and book studies, University of Ljubljana. Inf Retr 12(2):102–116

Vygotsky L (1978) Mind in society: the development of higher psychological processes. Harvard University Press, Cambridge, Mass

Wilson BG (ed) (1996) Constructivist learning environments: case studies in instructional design. Educational Technology, Englewood Cliffs

Chapter 6
Shifting Contexts: Relating the User, Search and System in Teaching IR

Frances Johnson

6.1 Introduction

If we are to understand the subject of Information Retrieval (IR) we need to be taught in a curriculum that not only covers the core topics of indexing, search and their systems, but that also provides for an analysis of these in the contexts of users, their queries and searching for information. This chapter explores teaching IR in the contexts of the student's experiences with IR systems and the insights that may be gained from the complementary perspectives of the user and the system. Defining a curriculum for teaching Information Retrieval has been called upon and investigated over the years. Bawden et al. (2007), for example, identified a set of 28 topics from an analysis of IR and its related, yet distinct, subjects of Information seeking (IS) and Human Information Behaviour (HIB). It was considered necessary to broaden the topic to cover and integrate the aspects of IR, IS and HIB in order that a coherent and reasoned curriculum could be constructed from the set of topics, with a perspective or target group in mind. Saracevic and Dalbello (2001), in defining a curriculum for a digital library course, not only posed the question *what* to teach, but also *how* and *why*, and demonstrated the integrative function of the digital library context for learning about the different aspects of IR. The challenge for the curriculum for IR is not so much that the fundamental techniques for IR, what we aim to teach, have changed. This has stood the test of time precisely because these techniques are grounded in the discipline – in the study of the properties of text, documents, collections, language, users, queries and communication. Rather, the challenges faced lie in the organisation of the broad curriculum in which the contexts, particularly our experiences with IR systems, provide the insights for understanding IR as a subject. To this end, the approach presented here is to use an aspect of HIB, specifically user interactions and search processes, as a

F. Johnson (✉)
Manchester Metropolitan University, Manchester, UK
e-mail: F.Johnson@mmu.ac.uk

E. Efthimiadis et al. (eds.), *Teaching and Learning in Information Retrieval*,
The Information Retrieval Series 31, DOI 10.1007/978-3-642-22511-6_6,
© Springer-Verlag Berlin Heidelberg 2011

context in which to analyse and understand the technology and the design of IR systems.

A course in IR is more than a course in engineering a retrieval "solution"; it is a study of the subject area and, as such, the study of the theory, concepts, principles and practise. This chapter focuses not so much on the curriculum content for IR, but on our experience with IR and search engines, to explore a range of shifting contexts which have set up a "need to know" scenario for learning the core principles of IR on Librarianship, Information Management and Web Development courses at the Manchester Metropolitan University.

6.1.1   What Is IR: An Overview for the Curriculum

Sparck-Jones and Willett (1997) define IR in their explanation that it

> Subsumes two related, but different, activities: indexing and searching. Indexing refers to the way documents [. . .] are represented for retrieval purposes. Searching refers to the way the file is examined and the items in it are taken as related to a search query.

This succinctly defines the field in terms of its core yet belies the range of topics typically found in an IR curriculum as required to teach the subject – information organisation, indexing, database, file structures, inverted index, Boolean, probabilistic retrieval, ranking, Web retrieval, relevance, satisfaction, evaluation of information and human information seeking and searching, to indicate a few. Whilst wide ranging, the extent and depth of coverage can be determined and distinguished, in part, by the aims and perspectives of the host course. Croft et al.'s (2010) textbook, aimed primarily at undergraduates in Computer Science, indicates what would be an exemplary programme in which the components of a search engine are developed in detail – including crawling to acquire the information, text processing for creating the inverted index, indexing (based largely on statistical properties of text), query processing, ranking algorithms and their retrieval models, performance metrics, and techniques beyond index search, including classification and clustering. Further extension of the core material indicates areas for postgraduate studies including advanced techniques to capture document content and search techniques for applications such as social and peer-to-peer search.

Information Retrieval as taught on courses in Information or Web Technology is likely to cover similar ground of IR architecture and techniques with emphasis on the Web, for example, as given in Levene's (2006) textbook, *An introduction to search engines and Web navigation techniques*. Likewise a textbook aimed at the student of Library and Information Science will also cover IR techniques but with greater focus on the principles of organising and the representation of information, in the library catalogue and in the broader context of providing information and its services. Others, such as *Web Dragons* (Witten et al. 2007), provide an understanding of how search engines work whilst focusing on the impact of the technology on our lives and our interaction with the world.

6.1.1.1   Educational Goals: The Fundamentals

The IR curriculum may well be tailored to the student, as potential computer scientist, Web technologist, information scientist or librarian, and the technical detail or particular practise suppressed or explained accordingly. Yet in every course there must be a common educational goal to teach the fundamental techniques for IR which, as Belew (2000) points out, are as relevant as they were pioneering. The goal in providing an education in IR, the analysis and appreciation of IR, demands not only the teaching of the practise of IR – the techniques and how the systems work, but also an analysis of "why" they are as they are – the theory, concepts and principles that have underpinned its development. Thus, in learning about IR we seek to understand

- The properties and patterns of language, text and collections that have led to statistical and probabilistic IR or the "best match" model
- The semantic indeterminacy and resultant noise of document representations and searchers' requests which (Blair 2006) refers to as "the IR problem"
- The characteristics and patterns of our information seeking behaviour and our ability to interpret the retrieved information
- How we use IR systems which, as Sparck-Jones and Willett (1997) point out in characterising IR, will become of increasing importance as the field develops

Teaching IR in contexts, such as search, can help organise a coherent curriculum in which the complementary analysis of searches and systems provides essential insights into the principles that underpin the subject. In this broad view of IR, the analysis of the search context and the search system enhances the understanding of both, and resultantly, our ability to apply, use and reason about IR.

6.1.2   Teaching in Contexts

Teaching in context is a fashionable concept with the purpose of providing a motivation for the learner to have explained the ideas and principles of a subject as dictated by the given context (Light et al. 2009). In this chapter the pedagogy of "teaching in contexts", and its relations such as "scaffolding" are not examined in any detail; rather, "contexts" is used simply with the aim to make the subject of IR both interesting, accessible and possibly less abstract to the learner. Consideration of the context can also help determine what needs to be learnt as dictated by the perceived needs of the context, and indeed the resultant "need to know" setup in the mind of the student. Three teaching contexts in IR can be identified – "Search", "Build", and "Design" – where the educational goal remains the same but the shifts in the context are adopted as students' experience of IR systems has broadened. The remainder of this chapter explores what the student may be motivated to learn about the practise of IR, its techniques and technology, so as to be able to participate in the use and design of IR systems. Consideration is also given to the effectiveness of the contexts in helping the understanding of the principles of IR. In effect we begin to unravel, so as to purposefully employ, the reciprocal relationship of the user, their searching behaviour, and the design of the IR system, that is the understanding of IR in principle and in practise. The first of these "contexts" of learning how to search goes back to the early days of IR and what we might consider to be the "traditional" IR system.

6.2   The Search Context

By the 1980s, "computerised information retrieval" was firmly established with the development of the large bibliographic databases, search system hosts and online searching. Searchers were trained, known professionally as search intermediaries, with knowledge of both the procedural and the conceptual skills and techniques for online search. These skills would be taught and honed as part of a course in Library and Information Science on information access covering cataloguing, classification, indexing and online databases and search systems. Students were thus motivated to learn how to search professionally, on behalf of a client with an information need, and to search effectively with knowledge of the central concepts, principles and techniques of information retrieval systems.

Learning to search, utilised as a "context", requires the student to find out how information is stored, indexed and searched in the IR system and how its features facilitate search. Knowledge of the record structures, the parsing rules and the stemming and stop words applied in the creation of the searchable inverted file reveals to the searcher the representation against which their query is matched. Equipped with this knowledge of the logical storage structures and information processing, the student learns the requirement to specify precisely the set of query terms that the sought documents will contain. Understanding that the words in the searcher's expression, and not the concepts, are matched in the full-text Boolean-based system, the student learns to make use of Boolean and word proximity operators with a sense of how they affect retrieval. Proximity operators are used to bring together terms separated in the word index, truncation to expand the word forms, field searching to add precision and Boolean operators to strategically broaden and narrow a search. Thus the student learns to use the search features to gain control and to build detailed and often sophisticated searches, honing the search expression and manipulating the exchange towards a desired outcome.

With practise the student searcher comes to use the system as a tool and gains a certain control over the search outcome as he concentrates on finding the query terms to represent the information sought; in making assessments of the relevance of the retrieved items; and, in using the search terms strategically to obtain feedback from the system to refine the query or to conclude the search. By understanding how the information is processed and stored in the system and by relating the core techniques of the IR system to the practise of search the student learns how to search, and ultimately (hopefully) meets Harter's (1986) textbook aim that "the reader learn[s] *how to think about* online information retrieval" (p. ix).

Effective retrieval requires knowledge of both the domain and the system to formulate a query and to submit for matching to take place on some logical representation of the documents. Learning about the IR system and learning to use the tools of the traditional (Boolean-based) system, it seems, leads to a problem solving approach to the search and thus elucidates the practise of search.

6.2.1   The Shifting Context: From Traditional to Modern Systems

The modern search engine, based on an alternative best match model of retrieval, does not (obviously) present the searcher with command-based search and the opportunity to nurture a strategic approach to search dependent on knowledge of the search system. It has been discussed that classic information retrieval techniques are irrelevant in the environment of the Web (Savoy and Picard 2001). Teaching IR in the context of learning search may be less convincing to today's students – their experience of regular and instantaneous search would seem to have little call for engagement in a well prepared session to conduct a thorough search on a topic. Whilst this may be an effective context to teach students aspiring to search professionally, on behalf of a client, an alternative context is needed to encourage students to find out about the technology that provides their experience of instantaneous search, the modern retrieval system.

6.2.2   Comparing Search in Traditional and Modern Systems

During the 1990s development in search technology – that is to say the emergence out of the labs of the "modern" statistical-based retrieval system – required our students to take more than a cursory look at ranked retrieval systems. Having been taught the traditional retrieval system in the context of search, a comparative study of the functionality of the traditional and modern systems presents a possible basis to learn about the modern IR system. A paper on the historical development of retrieval systems by Hahn (1998) provides just such an opportunity by inviting students to concur with or argue against her conclusion that the lack of search control offered by a search engine is so significant that we should not think of these as successors to the traditional online search system. Entering into the debate, as a set exercise, students are motivated to learn about IR techniques and the models that provide both the control and manipulation afforded by the traditional system and the apparent ease by which we query the search engine which has led Markey (2007) to observe that for most information needs doing a search involves simply that one

connect to the Internet, launch a Web browser, type a query into a search engine's dialogue box, browse ranked retrievals, and link to one or more full-length retrieved documents.

Making the comparison highlights the differences between the Boolean and the "best match" models, and leads to contemplation of the notion of "computational offloading"[1] which is used here to refer to the extent to which the user's effort to search is reduced and "off-loaded" onto the engine's computation to interpret the query and, in effect, make relevance judgements. Thus motivated to learn about how the modern search engine works, the student can explore, with a sense of purpose, the effectiveness of the technologies based on the vector space model and/ or probability and the further clues used in Web retrieval, such as link popularity (as referred to by Battelle (2005) as pre-programmed relevance calculation) as well as a range of other techniques such as relevance feedback, clustering, profiling and trends such as "slice and dice" to bring information to satisfy the user's request and/or to encourage users' interactions with and engagement in search (depending on the stance taken in the debate). Again teaching in context, as we learn more about how the engine processes our queries and returns information, insights are gained into the search activity itself. Have the techniques for pre-programmed relevance or "inferred intent" reduced our search effort for the better, making search easy requiring less time and thought? Does the answer to this depend on the type of the query? Or are there times when we might find searching less of an effort when we utilise the search features and seek to optimise the precision of the search? Or have our intentions simply been artificially narrowed by the similar results we continually retrieve, leading to a disengagement from the search process opting for the easy fix with an expectation of immediate satisfaction? These are some of the questions we might contemplate informed by our acquired knowledge of IR and in particular its application in Web search engines.

6.3   The Build Context

The "search" context, relating IR techniques to the practise of search, provides a structure helping the learner understand and be able to reason about IR. However, for many students, especially in computing, the context may be unconvincing. The "learning to search" context may even be considered too specialised for today's LIS students, who come with experience in searching on the Internet and whose expectations in studying IR increasingly lean towards the developer perspective to learn how to implement search and provide access to a collection. Thus, as the educational goals of the host course shift so does the context for teaching IR. The information retrieval system itself, specifically the search engine, is something that all students will have used and, in itself, provides an interesting, and familiar context to learn about the subject. If asked to name a most frequently used piece of software, a student is likely to refer to the search engine, and the lists of pages in

---

[1] Coined by Navarro-Prieto et al. (1999) to refer to the extent to which a representation reduces the amount of cognitive effort required to understand what is being represented.

response to their searches. The ubiquity of the search engine at once provides a familiar context to learn about these systems and a motivational context to find out more about IR.

Chau et al. (2003) at the University of Arizona make a compelling case for using the familiar Web search engine to interest and motivate students in learning fundamentals of Computer Science (CS). They point out the variety and diversity of core skills CS students need to acquire including databases, data structures, algorithms, Web servers and Web-based interfaces. Furthermore, in a Web-based environment, students will need to be taught application development using and integrating different systems and tools (with script languages and Internet protocols) and project management. Perhaps they allude to a motivational context in their decision to base the project on the building of a domain-specific Web search engine in stating that

> [w]e believe the project is useful for helping students understand some key computer science and information system concepts, acquire sufficient background in Web computing technologies, and obtain experience with various types of real-life challenges in system development projects.

Courses intending to use the "build" context to learn about computing basics as well as specific IR techniques may use existing toolkits that provide the components needed to create a search engine. Tools, such as those listed on the Web site SearchTools.com, can be directed to take a list of Web sites from a user as seed URLs, collect Web pages based on these, index the pages, and set-up a user interface for querying and browsing. Whilst these are interesting for students to look at and to learn about the basic architecture of a search engine with its components of spider, indexer, query processor and search engine, they may not provide sufficient technical detail on the processing involved for understanding data structures and algorithms in a "build" project. For this reason, textbook course tools (e.g., Croft et al. (2010) make use of Galago, open source designed for the teaching of search engines) can provide a transparency of the results from each component to favour later processing in a way that is not possible in the integrated toolkits. Chau et al. (2003) provide students with two simple tools, called the *AI Spider* and the *AI Indexer1*, to collect and store and index Web pages for import into databases whereupon the query engine can be implemented and customised, for example, to improve the ranking of the results or to provide additional functionality such as application of linguistic analysis and clustering to the search results (Chen et al. 2002). Such tools are now widely available to build a searchable index between terms and document. *SMART*, developed by Salton, is an early indexing tool (Salton and McGill 1983) widely used in traditional and Web-based engines and, distributed under open source, both the Lucene[2] and Lemur IR Toolkit[3] are used in a range of commercial applications, primarily due to their scalability, and which

---

[2] http://lucene.apache.org.

[3] http://www.lemurproject.org.

also provide the developer with accessible and flexible tools to build and evaluate search software.

The learning opportunities in the "build" are considerable as students are involved in working with the programmes of search software, including parsing, indexing and computing similarity between query and documents; and the evaluation of the information processing helps develop an understanding of the theory and core concepts in IR, such as term distribution and the discriminating power of a good index term. Belew (2000) takes this further in intimating that the impact of search engines is such that IR techniques and theory may be perceived as central to the discipline of computer science itself (and thus its curriculum), possibly on par with database but providing a distinct technology that is described in probabilistic rather than in absolute terms.

Thus, it would appear that there is a strong rationale in terms of learning opportunities for the build project to motivate the CS student and, with an evaluation element, to ensure that learning goes beyond being about the techniques to an analysis of *why* they are effective. Fairly quickly, a positive learning outcome is achieved as students learn the limitations of the existing tools with regards to the functionality they may want to build in to their "search engine". In an advanced or postgraduate course this could lead to further investigation into the application of semantic or NLP technologies or, for example in advanced techniques for use in emerging digital environments, such as multilingual IR or agent-based discovery. Hearst (2005), for example, writes about her experience to develop a class project in which NLP technologies are applied to provide content analysis to retrieved blogs and comments that a key aspect is learning what is possible but which is outside the scope of a standard semester-based course. Jones (2007), also cognisant of the extent of the required learning, describes a successful problem solving approach to deliver an advanced course in which students research and develop solutions using advanced applications.

6.3.1   The Shifting Context: From Build to Design

IR taught in non-computing departments such as Information Management and Web Technology may also find the "build" context motivational. In these types of courses less emphasis will be given to the acquired and applied skills in programming. However, the engineering approach to build a search system, again, provides a familiar and potentially interesting context on which to enhance the required learning of the concepts and principles of information retrieval. Students on these courses would be expected to be involved in the organisation and representation of information as well as the implementation of search technologies for the retrieval of information. The availability of software and commercial systems provides the opportunity to be involved in the "design" of search systems informed by an acquired understanding of IR.

Ruthven et al. (2008) describe a project developed at the University of Strathclyde which requires students to engineer a design for the storage and retrieval of a given collection of information objects. This course used the Lucene toolkit, thus focusing less on the computing skills required in the implementation and more on the design, as they explain:

> The use of Lucene meant that the group did not have to invest time in implementing low-level retrieval and indexing code but could concentrate on appropriate design decisions for their documents, e.g. whether to use stemming, to use index fields or whole texts.

The driving force, as explained was the constructivist principles of learning, which goes beyond the motivational notion of "contexts", in suggesting that active engagement with material provides the means to construct knowledge.

The context has thus shifted from development to the importance of design in providing search and retrieval. Students involved in the design will be making decisions regarding the provision of Boolean, free text searching, fielded or faceted search, vocabulary browse, clustering and ranked retrieval with or without relevance feedback all based on knowledge of the index and search methods of the system. Thus the student is motivated to have explained these techniques and the associated back end information processing involved. The potential learning opportunities, however, goes further as the design is also informed from the reasoning about the users' search behaviour and assumptions made regarding the user's interactions with the system. The final section thus concentrates on "design" as a teaching context and again considers the learning opportunities in finding out about the technology in the context of the search activity the system is designed to support.

6.4 The Design Context

Students may be involved in a "design project" via a series of exercises or in a complete user centred project with finished product. In either scenario the context sets up the "need to learn" about search and information behaviour as varied as it is complex. There are times when we want to be able to specify our query, to gain control of the search and go for an exact match on the stored information. Boolean may be off-putting to the untrained user, but there are alternative models that can be used to design for the specific search. Faceted search, for example, has gained popularity for its functionality, especially on e-commerce Web sites. On the other hand there are times when we do not come to the engine with our honed search formulation, but with the immediate feedback of retrieved results we can quickly learn how best to ask for the information. It has been noted, usually with a degree of concern, that users typically enter only two or three keywords to represent their query. However at the same time it has been noted that the people have learnt how to search and are more likely to enter a promising keywords or phrase, such as "body mass index" rather than ask "Am I fat?" (in this instance, to retrieve documents to find out if you are overweight). And, there are other times when our research has not a finite answer and we seek a more tempered approach to searching, along the lines of the berry picking model (Bates 1989) wherein thought is involved in associating prior knowledge and in interpreting the information retrieved. Whilst factors will end the query, with this sort of inquiry it is difficult to judge the outcome of the search – the line between "satisfiction" and satisfaction may be impossible to decipher. It is, however an approach to search which involves the elements of exploration and learning which make it quite distinguishable from the immediateness of the "popular" query, stopping where we have found some-thing – anything – and from the well-formed targeted query when we have a good idea of what we are looking for and seek to optimise the precision of the retrieved results.

A class exercise can be used to encourage students to think about these three main search activities beyond the immediately apparent surface procedural activity of querying a search engine. In observing the search behaviour of oneself and of others insights are gained into the activity of search and the processes deciphered by relating thoughts and actions, if at all, to established search models, such as Bates's (1989) berry-picking or Kuhlthau's (1988) stages of [re]search. Such practical exercises have always had a place in the IR course, for example to demonstrate inter-inconsistency in indexing documents, and which aim to reveal the issues and challenges for IR (rather than as a piece of valid and tested research). Observing search behaviour is, of course, non-trivial and we have found that the following (non-validated, but functional) categories have worked well to help students iden-tify differences in their seeking behaviour and associated system requirements: the "*anything-will-do dialogue*", the "*precision dialogue*", and the "*concept dialogue*" as are outlined in the above discussion.

The aim of learning about user search behaviour is to reveal the challenges for the design of the search interface. Searching is not a homogeneous activity. Korfhage (1991) argued that designing for the simple search can inhibit the searcher and suggests what is needed is a range of search tools from which users could pick the most suitable for their current query. The user may have a preference for simple search and immediate results (and for computational off-loading), but the observed brief query and subsequent scanning of the retrieved results may signify the searcher engaged in a more complex cognitive or conceptual process, making mental connections to concept build and learn about the search topic. Effectively the "design" context, in encouraging the student to think about search behaviour and the resultant challenges for the IR system guides the student towards learning about IR principles and practises in the realm of HCIR (Human Computer Informa-tion Retrieval). HCIR, as coined by Marchionini (2006), is to design IR systems in a way that reflects the needs and behaviour of its users during the interactive communicative process of IR. If the goal of HCIR is to bring the user back into the system by interacting with the information sought and taking responsibility and control for successfully retrieving information, we need to design not only for known item searching but also for exploration and the high level learning and investigative processes in which searchers engage to understand the concepts about which they seek information. The *concept dialogue* in the class exercise thus sets the greatest challenge in the design task, and optimises the potential for learning about IR, in aiming for what might be considered to be "low computational off-loading" and high user engagement with the information and the search features at the interface. The ensuing shift in the context is best realised with reference to our first "context" which by relating the principles and practises of IR systems to the activity of search, encouraged the searcher to *think* about search. The design context focuses on what can be done at the interface to facilitate the searcher in searching and in interacting with the information, concentrating the mind on the query and again encouraging the searcher to think about search.

6.4.1 Search Design

Designing for search thus provides a context in which to motivate the student to learn about IR techniques and technologies to decide on the best search model for the proposed system. For example, important design decisions need to be taken to show to the user how or why their results were found in supporting an exploratory search. Further inspiration into how the study of the search interface is informed by the theory and practise of IR (and HCI) can be drawn from recent textbooks focusing on the search interface, such as Hearst (2009). And, whilst it is possible that a highly motivating course could be built around the intersection of IR and Interface Design, we need to keep reminded of the intention of "teaching in context". For this reason, it is suggested here that the analysis of information visualisations used in the design of the search interface can provide the desired effect of a motivational context to meet the goal of learning IR. Visualisation is about exploration and understanding (presenting the information in a way that facilitates its interpretation and its use). Clustering technologies, for example, can be used to group results or generate categories or facets to guide search. Thematic visualisations of the clusters aim to present an overview of a subject domain or the document set. Early examples of search results of visualisation are discussed in Korfhage (1991) and Hearst (1999) which cluster, based on the statistical similarity of documents, and then map the resulting groups into a galaxy type visualisation [e.g., Korfhage's 2D (VIBE) or 3D (GUIDO)]. These visualisations may be useful to a searcher new to a topic as it provides a snapshot of the significant areas in the subject. It may also be of use to more established researchers as an aid to spotting gaps in their knowledge and where new connections might be established. Throughout the 1990s and into the 2000s a wide range of experimental visualisation systems have been developed, such as InfoCrystal and TileBars (Hearst 1999), Kartoo (online) and Grokker (online), which present potentially useful search aides in the visualisations of concepts and their relationships within and across documents. Conceptual visualisation is a major development in the promotion of search as a holistic process, as compared to the atomised bytes of the linear text-based results. It offers a way of exploring and comprehending the complexity and connectedness of information, rather than the relatively straightforward task of retrieval. It aims to assist in the learning in search, to allow access to subject areas the searcher did not know existed and did not know to ask questions about; and, to expand the searcher's broader understanding of the domain of interest. Perhaps this is akin to what (Marchionini and Shneiderman 1988) allude to in their writing on hypertext retrieval systems, claiming that when an information system presents results it engages in a process of structuring knowledge and resultantly, *"the systems themselves affect how users think when using them"*. The evaluation of these visualisations may demonstrate a desire from users to stay with the status quo presenting significant barriers to the development of the visual concept-based search interface. However, and the important point made with regards to teaching IR is that their analysis serves the goal of bringing together the student's knowledge of search behaviour, retrieval techniques and their relations in understanding and reasoning about modern principles and practises of IR.

6.5   Assessment and Conclusions

The topics that may be covered in a course in IR are many, and their effective delivery requires the curriculum content to be organised in some way to help the student come to an understanding of IR. In essence the educational goal is to develop the students' ability to reason about IR – that is, to have knowledge not only of the core techniques and technologies for search and retrieval but also to have gained insight into concepts and principles that have led to the generation of these systems. The analysis of the complementary aspects of IR, the user perspective of searching for information and the system perspective of search and retrieval suggests that the latter when taught in the familiar context of the former can help motivate to have explained the practises and principles of IR.

With the developments that have taken place, these contexts have shifted in accordance with the students' experience and expectations. The context of "learning to search (expertly)" guides the learning about the core techniques of the "traditional" retrieval system and, in the process, gives insight into the processes of search as a skilful and intellectual activity. It also provides a sense of the problem of "semantic indeterminacy" to which Blair (2006) refers and insight into the problem with the notion of information retrieval as some sort of matching process suggested in the bibliographic description and vocabulary control. The modern retrieval system based on a similarity between the query and document in turn invites comparisons and to contemplate their role in fostering the searcher engagement in some form of "computational off-loading". This debate (based on Hahn's 1998 comment on the evolution of the search engine) has proved useful to encourage student's exploration of search and to have elucidated the workings of the search engine. Furthermore students have declared that the investigation has made them more confident in their ability to search, possibly as a result of transferring some of the conceptual and strategic processes of traditional search into the modern search environments. It would be interesting to evaluate this, possibly as an assessment of the value of teaching search per se, but in the meantime it is assumed that the student has benefited from learning about search, or about retrieval technology, or from insight from learning a bit about both. Students in Computer Science, on the other hand, may find there is more motivation to be had in learning "how to build" a search engine and the learning opportunities are considerable as students work on the use, evaluation and possible modifications of the components of search engine software. Working with IR programmes helps to develop a key sense of the statistical and linguistic properties of text which underpins so much of IR. A final shift in the contexts is to "design" which draws on knowledge of both search behaviour and on retrieval techniques and technologies. Learning about search behaviour, especially open-ended exploratory search, in which the searcher interacts with information in a holistic and iterative way provides the student of IR with a basis on which to appraise the search interface and information visualisations in facilitating our interpretation and understanding of information. Focusing on what we have referred to as the "*concept dialogue*" learnt through an appreciation of search using IR systems, provides the student of IR working in the design context, with a basis on which to learn about the search features provided by the underlying retrieval model and to appraise the design of the search interface in reducing the user effort in interpreting and understanding the information and ultimately facilitating search.

In recommending the teaching context, whether it be search, build or design, the goal, however, is not so much as to teach how to provide "search solutions", but rather to motivate the student to have explained the concepts and the techniques of IR. Relating the principles of IR to the activity of search delivers a coherent curriculum and, brings these aspects together towards explaining how IR works and why. For some time the user aspects of IS and HIB and the system perspectives of retrieval technology have gone about their business in harmony but never quite connecting. But research and development in IR evolves, as do our teaching contexts, possibly towards shared perspectives and, at the least, towards a complementary understanding of the aspects of IR.

References

Bates MJ (1989) The design of browsing and berrypicking techniques for on-line search interface. Online Rev 13(5):407–424

Battelle J (2005) The search: how Google and its rivals rewrote the rules of business and transformed our culture. Portfolio, London

Bawden D, Bates J, Steinerov J, Vakkari P, Vilar P (2007) Information retrieval curricula; contexts and perspectives. In: MacFarlane A, Fernadez-Luna JM, Ounis I, Huete JF (eds) Proceedings of the first international workshop on teaching and learning of information retrieval. British Computer Society, London, pp 55–60

Belew RK (2000) Finding out about: a cognitive perspective on search engine technology and the WWW. Cambridge University Press, Cambridge

Blair D (2006) Wittgenstien, language and information 'Back to the rough ground'! Springer, Dordrecht

Chau M, Huang Z, Chen H (2003) Teaching key topics in computer science and information systems through a web search engine project. ACM J Educ Resour Comput 3(3):1–14

Chen H, Chau M, Zeng D (2002) CI Spider: a tool for competitive intelligence on the Web. Decis Support Syst 34(1):1–17

Croft WB, Metzler D, Strohman T (2010) Search engines: information retrieval in practice. Pearsons, New Jersey

Grokker. http://www.grokker.com. Accessed 20 Dec 2009

Hahn TB (1998) Text retrieval online: historical perspectives on Web search engines. Bull Am Soc Inf Sci 24(4):7–10

Harter SP (1986) Online information retrieval: concepts, principles and techniques. Academic, Orlando, FL

Hearst M (1999) User interfaces and visualization. In: Baeza-Yates R, Ribeiro-Neto B (eds) Modern information retrieval. Addison-Wesley, Harlow, pp 257–323

Hearst M (2005) Teaching applied natural language processing: triumphs and tribulations. In: The second association of computational linguistics workshop on effective tools and methodologies for teaching natural language processing and computational Linguistics, Michigan, USA, pp 1–8

Hearst MA (2009) Search user interfaces. Cambridge University Press, Cambridge

Jones G (2007) Using research questions to encourage creativity and assess understanding in teaching of information retrieval. In: MacFarlane A, Fernadez-Luna JM, Ounis I, Huete JF (eds) Proceedings of the first international workshop on teaching and learning of information retrieval. British Computer Society, London

Kartoo. http://www.kartoo.com. Accessed 20 Dec 2009

Korfhage RR (1991) To see, or not to see – is that the query? In: Proceedings of the 14th Annual international ACM SIGIR conference on research and development in information retrieval, Chicago, pp 134–141

Kuhlthau CC (1988) Developing a model of the library search process: cognitive and affective aspects. Ref Quart 28(2):232–242

Levene, M. (2006). *An introduction to search engines and web navigation*. London: Addison Wesley

Light G, Calkins S, Cox R (2009) Learning and teaching in higher education: the reflective professional, 2nd edn. Sage, London

Marchionini G (2006) Exploratory search: from finding to understanding. Commun ACM 49(4):41–46

Marchionini G, Shneiderman B (1988) Finding facts vs. browsing knowledge in hypertext systems. Computer 21(3):70–79

Markey K (2007) Twenty-five years of end-user searching, Part 2: Future research directions. J Am Soc Inf Sci Technol 58(8):1123–1130

Navarro-Prieto R, Scaife M, Rogers Y (1999) Cognitive strategies in web searching. In: Proceedings of the 5th conference on human factors & the web. Gaithersburg, Maryland. http://zing.ncsl.nist.gov/hfweb/proceedings/navarro-prieto/index.html. Accessed 1 Mar 2010

Ruthven I, Elsweiler D, Nicol E (2008) Designing for users: an holistic approach to teaching information retrieval. In: Proceedings of the second international workshop on teaching and learning of information retrieval (TLIR 2008). British Computer Society, London. eWiC proceedings online. Accessed 01 Mar 2010

Salton G, McGill MJ (1983) Introduction to modern information retrieval. McGraw-Hill Education, New York

Saracevic T, Dalbello M (2001) A survey of digital library education: libraries in the digital age. Proc Am Soc Inf Sci Technol 38:209–223

Savoy J, Picard J (2001) Retrieval effectiveness on the Web. Inf Process Manag 37(4):543–569

Sparck-Jones K, Willett P (eds) (1997) Readings in information retrieval. Morgan Kaufmann, San Francisco

Witten IA, Gori M, Numerico T (2007) Web Dragons. Morgan Kaufmann, San Francisco

Chapter 7
A Technical Approach to Information Retrieval Pedagogy

Rafael López-García and Fidel Cacheda

7.1 Introduction

Computing Science (CS) is a young discipline whose curricula have to be constantly renewed and tend to be divided into different specializations (IEEE-CS 2001). Information Retrieval (IR) is one of them and syllabi in IR are usually disparate too. Duration can oscillate from a few sessions to months and students with no previous knowledge of the subject or even of programming can fulfill the admission criteria. Actually, as IR is a multidisciplinary science, approaches can be really heterogeneous, from holistic (Ruthven et al. 2008) and philosophical (Thornley 2008) to detailed and technical (Cacheda et al. 2008).

Fortunately, experts in technical IR identify two components of IR systems: the indexer and the search engine. A third one, the crawler, is usually added in Web environments. There are lots of common and interesting concepts and techniques related to those components (Robertson and Sparck-Jones 1997; Manning et al. 2008; Croft et al. 2009) (e.g., MIME (Freed and Borenstein 1996) types, robots exclusion standard (Koster 1994), stop words, stemming (Porter 1980), weighting models (Zobel and Moffat 1998), etc.). Teachers have to decide how many and which concepts are going to be part of their syllabi.

Whatever the characteristics of the subject, there is a significant need for methodologies and teaching materials in order to improve students' understanding. Most of the classic systems, like Apache Lucene and Terrier (TERabyte RetrIEveR), are too complex to be understood or changed by inexperienced students. There are some simpler and pluggable initiatives, like IR-Base (Calado et al. 2007), but the number of systems fulfilling these features is not high.

R. López-García (✉)
Facultad de Informática, Department of Information and Communication Technologies,
University of A Coruña, Campus de Elviña, A Coruña s/n. 15071, Spain
e-mail: rafael.lopez@udc.es

E. Efthimiadis et al. (eds.), *Teaching and Learning in Information Retrieval*,
The Information Retrieval Series 31, DOI 10.1007/978-3-642-22511-6_7,
© Springer-Verlag Berlin Heidelberg 2011

The first goal of this chapter is to present some methods which help technical teachers to solve some of their problems and to facilitate several tasks like, for example, presenting the main problems of IR to their students, guiding them to the solution of these problems, establishing their coursework, and evaluating their theoretical and technical comprehension.

Another aim of this chapter is to present the IR-Components system as a candidate to help teachers to solve the proposed problems and to fulfill the afore-mentioned needs. The system is specially oriented to this purpose, since it is simple and its design pays special attention to modularity.

7.2   Related Work

Among the multiple disciplines involved in IR, Library and Information Science (LIS) has become one of the most important since 1951, when Mooers introduced the term in that context (Mooers 1951). Nevertheless, IR makes use of computer-related technology, and that was the reason for IEEE and ACM to include it in the CS curricula (IEEE-CS 2001). Some authors like Zhu and Tang (2006) presented their own proposals for degree and postdegree levels too.

Fernández-Luna et al., who have recently published a literature review of pedagogical methods for teaching and learning IR (Fernández-Luna et al. 2009), have identified three main educational goals about IR in the CS curricula and literature. The first one, understanding fundamental aspects of IR, has already been developed by some authors like Henrich and Morgenroth (2007), Efthimiadis and Hendry (2005), and Hendry and Efthimiadis (2008). Other authors go into higher detail and teach advanced techniques, like Herrera-Viedma et al. (2007) in fuzzy systems and Goharian et al. (2004) in data mining, but those concepts are out of the scope of this chapter.

The second, training in search strategies, is more typical of the LIS curricula. In this kind of syllabi, teachers usually show students how to choose among different search engines and how to exploit their features, but they never force them to program their own solutions and hardly ever teach technical details [although there are exceptions like Johnson (2008)].

Besides, Airio et al. presented a tool for measuring the features of IR systems (Airio et al. 2007) in order to improve students' search skills.

Finally, the last aim Fernández-Luna et al. found – to acquire skills to develop new IR methods using software modules – has also been researched by several authors. Efthimiadis and Freier (2007) proposed an approach in which students do not have to program. Jinguji et al. (2006) designed a customizable answering system, but it is not exactly a document retriever and its complexity makes it oriented to advanced courses. De Campos et al. (2007) presented an object-oriented framework for the research and teaching of IR, but this system is oriented to Probabilistic Graphical Models (PGM) and structured document formats like XML. Chau et al. (2003) submitted another initiative, but their proposal for the coursework is to give two complete applications to their students, AI Spider and AI

Indexer, and make them develop the search engine starting from scratch to get a medium/large-scale project. IR-Components, on the contrary, forces students to understand each of the applications by means of completing a skeleton, programming only the most illustrative parts and focusing on the essential concepts and techniques of IR chosen by the teacher.

The main alternatives to IR-Components seem to be IR Framework (Wade and Braekevelt 1994), and IR-Base, presented in 2007 by Calado et al. (2007). Unfortunately, in the case of IR-Base, the authors do not provide high level of details about its design nor provide any information on how to use the system in teaching and research. In fact, they have announced that the system is still under development. Another difference among IR-Base, IR Framework, and IR-Components is that while the first ones only provide a framework and a pool of components which the programmer has to plug in order to create the applications, the last one provides the components in a format that makes easier the creation and execution of IR applications.

Independently of these educational goals, classroom materials (text books, slides, problems, etc.) are another of the great needs of IR teaching. Jones (2009) regretted that lack in his inquiry-based learning approach. He also noticed that feedback from students is another useful tool for improving the goals of the subject. The approaches of Henrich and Morgenroth (2007) and Sacchanand and Jaroenpuntaruk (2006) could be appropriate for some courses too. However, the methodology presented in this paper tries to offer materials in the way of Croft et al. (2009), but linking theoretical and technical concepts in a bit different and stronger way.

7.3   The Technical-Oriented IR Methodology

The multidisciplinary nature of IR almost invariably causes LIS researchers to focus on abstract or high-level matters, delegating the technical or low-level ones to computer scientists and engineers (e.g., distributable systems, index compression techniques, etc.). Hence, CS students have to be able to analyze the abstract requirements and transform them into programming code. The traditional way to make them familiarized with this procedure is to include some laboratory classes where students often have to program their own applications starting from an informal specification. Nevertheless, this approach gives rise to a couple of problems. On the one hand, a stronger association between theoretical concepts and programming code is needed in order to make this transition easier. On the other hand, students' time and effort should not be wasted in programming a complex and nonillustrative code in laboratory classes.

Another problem of the courses with a high level of technical detail is the search or development of sample applications. Although there are a lot of available and mature IR systems on the Internet, their code is often too complex to be explained to students. It would be better for teachers to have at their disposal a simpler custom system that illustrates the concepts at the appropriate detail level. At this point, teachers have to choose between a set of sample applications and a framework.

While the first alternative allows users to test immediately how the code works, the second one helps programmers to create or modify applications or components.

The problem of achieving a stronger linkage between theoretical concepts and the final programming code can be solved by means of the inclusion of the appropriate design diagrams and pieces of code in the course notes or slides. Even when the pedagogic materials become harder to maintain, this technique helps to create a better association between both parts of the subject. Furthermore, if the diagrams and the pieces of code are placed immediately after each theoretical concept or procedure, students will obtain a first aid guideline to solve each problem.

The aforementioned election between sample applications or a framework is especially interesting when the course notes or slides contain sample code. On the one hand, if students had at their disposal the complete application from where the code was taken, they could easily verify how it works. On the other hand, a framework could guide them in the correct development of their coursework. Fortunately, it is possible to take advantage of all those features at the same time by means of the combination of both ideas, through a simple framework and a little set of implementations from whose fusion the sample applications will result. That will allow the teacher to choose either to provide the students only with the framework or to give them the full sample applications.

With regard to the coursework, an alternative to the problem of developing an application or a component from scratch could be to provide the students with a set of interfaces and a skeleton, making them develop the rest of the code. The skeleton would cover all the nonillustrative parts of the application or component they have to develop, whereas the guidelines offered by the set of interfaces would force students to follow a standard in the completion of the rest of the code. Orienting the framework to this structure of skeletons and interfaces will make the coursework more interesting for students.

Moreover, coursework evaluation could be easier for teachers too because following this approach students only have to implement a reduced and concrete number of classes specified by their corresponding interfaces, so their evaluation could also be reduced to a simple checklist about the number, versatility, and efficiency of the implementations programmed by each student. The effectiveness of those modules would also become easy to check, since teachers would only have to plug them in their skeleton instead of their default implementations. Efficiency can also be checked by adding measuring techniques in the appropriate points of the skeleton.

In short, the approach presented in this chapter consists of two main parts. The first one is helping to link theoretical concepts and software products, generally by means of the inclusion of diagrams and sample code in the course notes or slides and the second one is improving coursework selection, avoiding nonillustrative tasks in student's coursework. In order to follow this methodology, the teacher has to choose the right materials. A good selection can help with both points and make the evaluation easier.

The IR-Components framework is presented in this chapter as the pedagogic tool that will fulfill the requirements of the explained approach, so teachers will not have to create it from scratch. In addition, some of its features, like its modularity, will make it valid for other tasks, like the quick developing and testing of new IR techniques. Nevertheless, its educational purpose does not make it appropriate as a commercial system or as high-performing researching environment, capable of operating with large collections of documents and queries like .GOV2.

7.4   IR-Components

The IR-Components project[1] has been designed as an object-oriented framework for developing IR applications. The entire software product has been developed using only the J2SE API of the Java programming language, XML files, the Apache log4j framework for log file generation (Apache log4j), and the JUnit framework for unit test generation (JUnit), so a programmer can read or modify all the code only knowing these four technologies. It is important to remark that the IR-Components project has been designed according to several design patterns, most of them introduced in order to create a robust and scalable architecture with pluggable components.

The IR-Components framework provides developers with a set of components which will have to be interconnected to build IR applications. This interconnection is a relatively easy task, since it only consists of one component invoking at least one of the APIs provided by another component. Internally, each of the components contains a pair of modules. On the one hand, programmers have the "API module," which offers them a set of interfaces and it can also offer the skeleton of an algorithm. Some of the aforesaid interfaces are APIs for externally invoking the functionalities of the component, while the rest are facades for completing the internal tasks delegated by the skeleton. On the other hand, they have the "implementation module," which consists of several classes that implement all the interfaces provided by the API module. The IR-Components project includes a default implementation module for each API module, but programmers could develop their own third-party implementations. The change of implementation would be very easy, since they would only have to choose their own classes in a configuration file. Figure 7.1 shows the structure of a component and how they are interconnected.

The naming convention used in this project is the following: applications are named according to the MiniXXX notation (e.g., a searcher application should be called MiniSearcher). Components, which are part of applications, follow the XXXComp format (e.g., a component containing the search engine of a searcher application should be called SearchEngineComp). Finally, for the modules that constitute a component, API modules follow the XXXAPI notation, whereas

---

[1] Current URL: http://www.tic.udc.es/~rlopezga/ir-components/index.html. User: "reviewer". Password: "tlir2010"

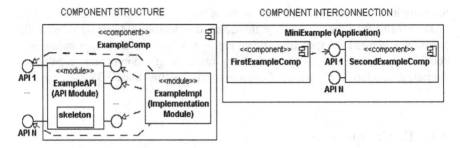

Fig. 7.1 Component structure and interconnection

implementation modules are named according to the XXXImpl format (e.g., a component called SearchEngineComp should be formed by the SearchEngineAPI and the SearchEngineImpl modules).

IR-Components could be used in at least three ways:

- To combine the provided components using their API and default implementation modules in order to quickly create an IR application.
- To generate a new implementation module for at least one component in order to change its behavior. Then, the programmer should combine the new component with others in order to create a different application.
- To use the source code of a certain component to explain how it works.

While the first use of IR-Components does not have much relevance for the CS staff, the second one is especially interesting for teachers who want to provide their students with a starting point for the coursework. In this case, it is recommended that a library be generated (e.g., a jar file) with each of the API modules of the components, and then provide students with those libraries and their respective documentation in order to force them to create their own components through the development of the respective implementation modules. It is important to highlight that, as students do not possess the sources of default implementation modules, reverse engineering is not possible for them. The second use of IR-Components could also be interesting to programmers who want to quickly develop and test their new techniques, expecting the new component to be more efficient or versatile than the one generated using the default implementation. Finally, the third use could help teachers to explain with a higher level of detail how a certain component works.

The project components are particularly oriented to build three applications: MiniCrawler, MiniIndexer, and MiniSearcher.

MiniCrawler is an implementation of the traditional Web spider that uses a single thread to perform a breadth-first traversal of the target Web site and downloads the pages that match the specified file types, creating a data structure that stores the main attributes of the file. It also has support for the robots exclusion standard. The main educational objectives that have been identified for MiniCrawler are the following:

- To illustrate the breadth-first traversal in the crawling algorithm.
- To know how to access a URL and how to save its content (simple text file, compressed file, or even by means of a database).
- To establish an access policy for URLs, taking into account several factors like their content type, whether they belong to the crawled Web site or not, whether they are excluded for robots or not, and so on.
- To parse different kinds of files (plain text, HTML, XML, etc.) in order to get new URLs to be accessed.

In order to achieve those aims, MiniCrawler only needs one component called CrawlerComp. The API module of this component is mainly formed by a skeleton (class Crawler) and some interfaces to which the skeleton delegates the illustrative parts of the algorithm, expecting to be coded in the respective implementation module. The diagram presented in Fig. 7.2 shows this organization.

The first educational objective is covered by all the classes in general, but the skeleton provided by the class Crawler is the most important contributor. The second objective is fulfilled by the RemoteAccess interface. The third one is reached by means of the RobotsParser, TypeFilter, and URLNormalizer interfaces, which provide methods to check the robot exclusion standard, the content type of the URLs and its belonging to the crawled Web site, respectively. Finally, the fourth objective is covered by the PageURLsParser interface and the PageURLsParserManager class, which is a pool of PageURLsParser objects.

Each of those interfaces can be implemented following several strategies. For example, a programmer can create an implementation of the TypeFilter interface either based on the file extension (efficient but not valid in every case) or the MIME

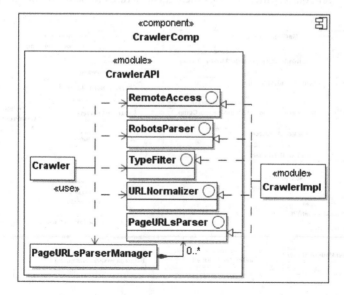

Fig. 7.2 Architecture of MiniCrawler and its components

type offered by an HTTP request (more correct but inefficient). In the default implementation module, the developers chose a class based on the file extension.

The purpose of MiniIndexer is to create a document index and a term index for a document collection. The application has at its disposal different ways to store the indexes in memory and on disk (plain text, Java serialized objects, etc.) and it also supports as many MIME types as plug-and-play parsers are installed in the system (plain text, HTML and XML documents by default). What is more, MiniIndexer also supports some other term processing advanced configurations, like the stop words mechanism, the list of characters that have to be treated as separators (e.g., hyphen, plus sign, etc.) and the list of special characters that may be transformed into others (e.g., those which contain tilde, dieresis, etc.). The primary teaching goals that have been identified for MiniIndexer are:

- To illustrate an indexing algorithm.
- To extract the tokens of various documents with different structures.
- To be conscious of the problems brought by some special characters that should be normalized and some others that should act as separators.
- To determine which tokens are significant enough to be included in the term index, generally by means of the stop words technique.
- To experiment with several data structures, file formats, and loading and storage techniques for the index.

The architecture and components of MiniIndexer are shown in Fig. 7.3.

The component of MiniIndexer that contains the skeleton of the indexing algorithm is IndexerComp. In order to improve extensibility, it detaches from the index format and operations, delegating this responsibility to a component called IndexManagerComp, which decides the data structures to be used, the file format,

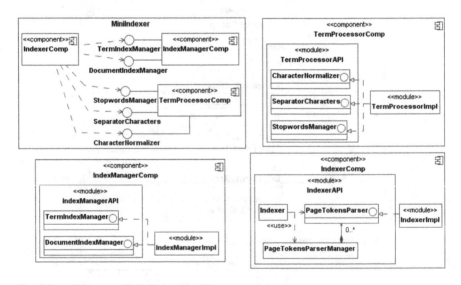

Fig. 7.3 Architecture of MiniIndexer and its components

and the loading and storage strategies (cache, etc.). The term "processing techniques" is also encapsulated in a component called TermProcessorComp.

The API module of IndexerComp is principally formed by the aforementioned skeleton (class Indexer) and some more classes and interfaces. The skeleton delegates the illustrative parts of the algorithm to those classes and interfaces and also to the other components that constitute the MiniIndexer application, covering the first educational aim. The PageTokensParser interface and the PageTokensPar-serManager class, which acts as a pool of PageTokensParser objects, are in charge of reaching the second teaching goal of the application.

The second component, TermProcessorComp, is only constituted by a set of APIs for term processing and their respective implementations. It lacks a template for an algorithm. The CharacterNormalizer and SeparatorCharacters interfaces and their implementations are responsible for covering the third educational goal, whereas the StopwordsManager interface is in charge of the fourth teaching aim.

Finally, the third component, IndexManagerComp, only provides a mechanism of APIs and implementations for term and document index managing (creation, update, lookup, load, and storage). The DocumentIndexManager and TermIndexManager interfaces and their respective implementations fulfill the fifth pedagogic objective of MiniIndexer.

The versatility of MiniSearcher lies in its capability of being configured to act as a standalone search engine or as a broker of a distributed environment in combination with multiple query server instances. In any case, the application accepts multiple user interfaces (interactive console, batch process, and window interface), multiple weighting models, and the same term processing techniques as MiniIndexer (stop words, separator character configuration, etc.). On the other hand, when MiniSearcher is acting as a distributed environment, it supports broker hierarchy, asynchronous result reception, several transport protocols (e.g., TCP and UDP with and without multicast), multiple types of data encoding to send the results through the network, and multiple algorithms to get the best results at the broker. The pedagogic objectives of MiniSearcher are the following:

- To illustrate the overall process of query solving in centralized and distributed environments.
- To evaluate the usability of the different types of user interfaces.
- To study in depth the advantages and problems brought by normalized characters, separator characters, and stop words.
- To detail the functioning and features of the different weighting models.
- To implement a result sorting algorithm and to evaluate its performance.
- To implement the communications between brokers and query servers and to learn the consequences of using different transport protocols.
- To investigate the advantages and disadvantages of the different encodings for sending the data through the network.
- To know the problem of result selection in distributed environments.

The components of MiniSearcher have to be interconnected in different ways depending on the scenario in which the application is running (standalone,

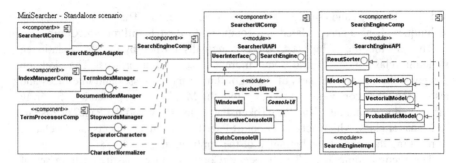

Fig. 7.4 Architecture of MiniSearcher in a standalone scenario

distributed with a broker and some query servers, or distributed with a complete hierarchy of brokers and query servers). The simple change of a parameter in a configuration file is sufficient to change from one to another. Every scenario uses some more components than the previous one, so the standalone scenario where the user interface directly connects the search engine is the simplest one. Figure 7.4 shows that architecture.

As some needs of MiniSearcher are the same as in other applications above, the programmer can reuse some components from them. For example, as a search engine needs to lookup the indices in order to solve the queries, the IndexManagerComp used in MiniIndexer is now reused in MiniSearcher. Other components like TermProcessorComp can also be reused, but as the term processing can be done in several places of the searcher, the programmer must decide where it is going to be placed. This is how the third pedagogic aim is covered.

The first new component is the user interface (SearcherUIComp), which covers the second teaching goal of the application and provides an API for the possible user interfaces and some classes that could be used in its implementations. Most of those classes are graphical components, with the exception of SearchEngineAdapter, that communicates the user interface with the search engine. In order to prove that the API can be used by console user interfaces and graphical user interfaces, the default implementation of the module consists of an interactive console, a console that executes a batch process and a window environment.

The search engine is also independent from the rest of the application, so it is confined in a component called SearchEngineComp. As it is shown in Fig. 7.4, the component has a set of interfaces for the different weighting models supported by the engine (Model, BooleanModel, VectorialModel, and ProbabilisticModel). This way, the fourth teaching goal is covered. There is another interface for result sorting (ResultSorter). Its implementations are responsible for covering the fifth teaching goal.

The second and third scenarios consist of a distributed architecture. Figure 7.5 shows a simple schema of both scenarios. In the second one, there is only a root broker (RB) and a variable number of query servers (QS). In the third one, there is a hierarchy composed of a RB, some intermediate brokers (IB), and the QS which are the leaf nodes of the tree. Figure 7.6 shows the architecture of the third scenario, since the second one is a particular case of the third without any IB.

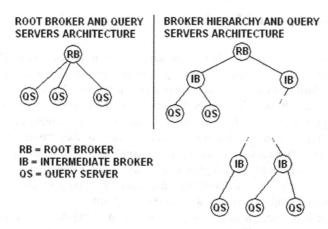

Fig. 7.5 Distributed scenarios for MiniSearcher

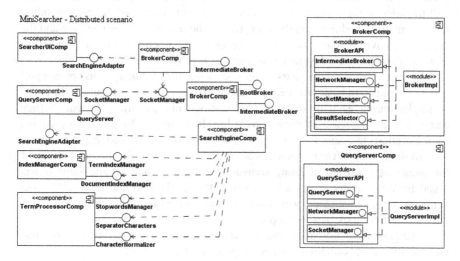

Fig. 7.6 Distributed scenarios for MiniSearcher

In order to develop both scenarios, two new components are needed: BrokerComp and QueryServerComp.

BrokerComp provides another implementation of the SearchEngineAdapter facade from the SearcherUIComp when it acts as the RB; and it uses its own IntermediateBroker interface when it works as an intermediate broker. In both cases, the SocketManager, NetworkManager, and ResultSelector interfaces are in charge of developing the sixth, seventh, and eighth teaching goals, respectively.

QueryServerComp offers an API (QueryServer interface) for component invocation, and it also offers the SocketManager and NetworkManager interfaces, which are responsible for reaching the sixth and seventh teaching goals, respectively, from the QS's side.

7.5 Assessment and Feedback

The first time that Professor Fidel Cacheda taught a subject about IR at the University of A Coruña (Spain), it was in a master degree in the academic year 2007–2008. Professor Cacheda and some other contributors related their experience in Cacheda et al. (2008). Their methods were focused on the decomposition of the different typical problems of IR and on the strategies to implement the low-level solutions. They also enumerated some inconveniences of their "Internet Information Retrieval" subject and its practical coursework. As a solution to the problems, Cacheda proposed some "live-programming" classes and the possibility to offer the students a basic implementation of the subsystems that compose the coursework (crawler, indexer, and searcher) as a basic starting point.

For the next course, Cacheda changed the format of the practical coursework, using the first version of IR-Components as the aforementioned starting point. In particular, the students were provided with a set of binary libraries containing the API modules of the framework and they were told to create all the corresponding implementation modules with the exception of the searcher's user interface and the distributed environment. They also were given the documentation associated to those modules, so their first task was learning how to use the libraries.

In order to compare both years' results, students took an anonymous opinion poll about the course. In basic outline, they had to give their opinion about the difficulty of implementing each of the proposed components and the contribution they entailed to the increase of their knowledge. In addition, the poll also included some questions to assess the contribution of using some other pedagogic resources (design diagrams, software documentation, the coursework forum, etc.). Some of the questions consisted of rating something between 1 and 10 and some others asked for an extended explanation. In both the 2007–2008 and 2008–2009 academic years, seven students were called to answer the questions, but in both cases only six of them took part in the poll.

In the general section about the coursework, students had to rate the workload and the difficulty. Numerical results are given in Table 7.1.

In the additional comments, one of the students asked for some more techniques to be applied (e.g., a ranking algorithm like HITS or Page-Rank). Another student suggested starting the coursework with some parts already implemented, alleging that they were too tedious to be implemented by the students and their contribution to his/her knowledge was insufficient. Nevertheless, a third one suggested exactly the opposite, in other words, that all the coursework was interesting and it should be mandatory to implement the three applications from scratch. A fourth student

Table 7.1 Coursework general results

	Score 2007–2008	Score 2008–2009	Ratio of variances	Significance
Workload	7.5	7.57	1.5906	>97%
Difficulty	6.7	6.43	1.7427	>99%

compared the workload of making the applications in Python and in Java, and he suggested that it is easier to implement them in the first programming language.

Even though the global rates did not change significantly for the second year, everybody agreed that having the IR-Components APIs as a starting point is clearly an advantage. The main reason given by the students was that they avoided a lot of tedious work. Unnecessary complexity was removed and the students could concentrate on the most important parts of the engine. Most of them also agreed that the main inconvenience of this kind of coursework is that some parts of the software act as a black box, making it more difficult to understand in the beginning, but they also clarified that the design diagrams and the documentation are sufficient to overcome this initial problem. In addition, every student of the second course declared that the workload is sufficient, but five out of six affirmed that a PageRank module could be a good extra exercise for the next course since it is historically important in IR and it is the only part of the theoretical contents that had not been reflected on the practical coursework.

Regarding the different resources offered to the students, in both academic years everybody agreed that the forum is convenient for sharing some information about the development of the applications. However, they also agreed that personal attention is also necessary in some cases, especially for the students of second year whose interaction with an unknown API makes them more prone to technical problems. The acceptance of some other resources was remarkable too. Some of these materials, such as hints to help students to solve some programming problems, were available in both years, while the others, programming documentation and design diagrams, were only available to the second year of students. Numeric results are given in Table 7.2.

In spite of the fact that there were only seven students in each promotion, four thorough statistical tests were made in order to analyze the average and the variance of the difficulty of implementing each feature and the contribution that they entailed to the knowledge of the students. Unfortunately, the lack of a sufficient number of samples determines that no conclusion can be reached when the average of the different factors is studied.

More interesting conclusions can be reached when the variance is studied. Table 7.1 shows the ratio of variances for the difficulty and the contribution of the coursework in both groups. As in both cases the variance is significantly smaller for the second year and the analysis of the p-value also shows a high degree of certainty for this hypothesis, the first conclusion extracted from the statistical study is that the application of the new methodology reduces the number of students who think that the coursework is too difficult or easy, or that it contributes a lot or

Table 7.2 Statistics about teaching resources

Resource	2007–2008	2008–2009
Forum	7.67	8.57
Hints	8.6	9.57
Programming documentation	N/A	9.33
Design diagrams	N/A	9.33

nothing at all to their knowledge. Even when decreasing the third of the four groups too is a bad partial result, the combination of the previously presented methodology and materials constitute an improvement in the subject.

On the teachers' side, the opinion is quite different. In small- and medium-scale projects like this, working with new APIs and continuing other people's work is more difficult than starting a project right from scratch, so coursework in the second academic year was harder. However, the difficulty did not change significantly in the poll. Also, the number of questions asked by the students was significantly bigger during the second year, so the teachers think that the students were more interested in the second year's coursework and this helped them to overcome difficulty.

7.6   Conclusions and Future Work

This chapter has presented a technical approach to teaching IR which is of interest mainly for teachers working on CS curricula. As the global idea lies on helping students to make the transition from theoretical concepts and specifications to final software products, this methodology is based on a strong linkage between theoretical contents and programming code, not reducing its utilization to laboratory classes and practical coursework, but including it in the classroom materials (notes, slides, etc.). In addition, this methodology also focuses on other problems like the coursework evaluation and the difficult choice of sample applications, since there is a lack of appropriate materials.

This chapter has also submitted IR-Components, a multimodule object-oriented software product which combines the ideas of an IR framework and the common IR sample applications. The project has been studied in depth in order to show how several pedagogic objectives of IR subjects could be fulfilled by means of its use. Moreover, this project could be useful not only for teachers, but also for programmers who are in need of a simple starting point to test their new techniques and algorithms.

This chapter has also evaluated the difference between using and not using the aforementioned methodology and materials. To that end, the students of 2 years of a postgraduate Internet Information Retrieval class took an anonymous opinion poll. The results given by the students suggest three interesting conclusions. First of all, the availability of a wide range of resources (discussion forum, programming documentation, design diagrams, source code) and their integration with theoretical concepts is really useful to improve students' interest and understanding. These resources are really necessary for the development of their coursework. Secondly, the availability of an IR framework as a starting point for students' coursework helps them to avoid tedious and nonillustrative parts of the coursework and it also guides them to the correct design of IR applications. Finally, the approach described in this chapter significantly reduces the variability of their opinions about the difficulty and the contribution of the coursework. Hence, the number of students who think that the coursework is too difficult or easy or that it makes too big or to small contribution to their knowledge is reduced.

On the teacher's side, the usage of IR-Components makes easier to evaluate students' work, since they have only to check which of the proposed functionalities were implemented and how they were programmed.

However, it is clear that the full fruition of this methodology will be reached only after several years of application, so it will be necessary to continue improving and adapting it, generally by means of the feedback submitted by teachers, students, and researchers. The immediate future work of the general approach is, mainly, to improve the way of linking theoretical concepts and the final programming code. This will mean more experiments in this respect and a more thorough monitoring in student's learning process.

Regarding to IR-Components project, two different paths will be followed in the future. The first one will consist of adding new features to the framework with two aims in mind: to include some IR concepts which can be interesting for students and to make IR-Components become not only an educational framework, but also a research tool. As a first step, the next versions will include the IR concepts that the students suggested in the opinion poll (e.g., PageRank), some other interesting ones (e.g., query expansion, stemming, more weighting models, etc.), and some wrappers for a few research engines, like MG4J (Managing Gigabytes for Java) and Terrier (TERabyte RetrIEveR).

The other path to follow is to research a way to extend IR-Components in order to help teachers and students of other branches (e.g., LIS). The application resulting from this extension would consist of a canvas where the user could create a search engine without editing a single line of programming code, but simply dropping and interconnecting some visual representations of several parts of IR-Components. This would allow students of nontechnical branches of IR to be introduced in the technical concepts at a level of abstraction appropriate for their particular studies.

Acknowledgments This work was partially supported by the Spanish Government under project TIN 2009–14203, the European Social Fund and the Dirección Xeral de Ordenación e Calidade do Sistema Universitario de Galicia of the Consellería de Educación e Ordenación Universitaria – Xunta de Galicia (Spain).
We would also like to thank Professor Fernando Bellas for his educational guidance on the architecture of IR-Components.

References

Airio E, Sormunen E, Halttunen K, Keskustalo H (2007) Integrating standard test collections in interactive IR instruction. In: Proceedings of the first international workshop on teaching and learning of information retrieval (TLIR 2007). http://www.bcs.org/server.php?show=ConWebDoc.8783
Apache log4j. http://logging.apache.org/log4j
Apache Lucene. http://lucene.apache.org
Cacheda F, Fernández D, López R (2008) Experiences on a practical course of web information retrieval: developing a search engine. In: Proceedings of the second international workshop on

teaching and learning of information retrieval (TLIR 2008). http://www.bcs.org/server.php?show=ConWebDoc.22357

Calado P, Cardoso-Cachopo A, Oliveira A (2007) IR-BASE: an integrated framework for the research and teaching of information retrieval technologies. In: Proceedings of the first international workshop on teaching and learning of information retrieval

Chau M, Huang Z, Chen H (2003) Teaching key topics in computer science and information systems through a web search engine project. ACM J Educ Resour Comput 3(3):article 2

Croft B, Metzer D, Strohman T (2009) Search engines: information retrieval in practice. Addison-Wesley, Harlow

De Campos LM, Fernández-Luna JM, Huete JF, Romero AE (2007) A flexible object-oriented system for teaching and learning structured IR. In: Proceedings of the first international workshop on teaching and learning of information retrieval (TLIR 2007). http://www.bcs.org/server.php?show=ConWebDoc.8769

Efthimiadis EN, Freier NG (2007) IR-toolbox: an experiential learning tool for teaching IR. In: Proceedings of the SIGIR conference, p 914

Efthimiadis EN, Hendry DG (2005) Search engines and how students think they work. In: Proceedings of the SIGIR conference, pp 595–596. http://portal.acm.org/citation.cfm?id=1076034.1076145

Fernández-Luna JM, Huete JF, MacFarlane A, Efthimiadis EN (2009) Teaching and learning in information retrieval. Inf Retr 12:201–226. doi:10.1007/s10791-009-9089-9

Freed N, Borenstein N (1996) Multipurpose internet mail extensions (MIME) part one: Format of internet message bodies. RFC 2045, 31 p. http://www.ietf.org/rfc/rfc2045.txt

Goharian N, Grossman D, Raju N (2004). Extending the undergraduate computer science curriculum to include data mining. In: Proceedings of the international conference on information technology: Coding and computing (ITCC'04), pp 251–254

GOV2 collection. http://ir.dcs.gla.ac.uk/test_collections/gov2-summary.htm

Hendry DG, Efthimiadis EN (2008) Conceptual models for search engines. In: Spink A, Zimmer M (eds) Web searching: Interdisciplinary perspectives. Springer, Heidelberg, pp 277–307

Henrich A, Morgenroth K (2007) Information retrieval as e-learning course in German – lessons learned after 5 years of experience. In: Proceedings of the first international workshop on teaching and learning of information retrieval (TLIR 2007). http://www.bcs.org/server.php?show=ConWebDoc.8765

Herrera-Viedma E, Alonso S, Cabrerizo FJ, Lopez-Herrera AG, Porcel C (2007) A software tool to teach the performance of fuzzy IR systems based on weighted queries. In: Proceedings of the first international workshop on teaching and learning of information retrieval (TLIR 2007). http://www.bcs.org/server.php?show=ConWebDoc.8767

IEEE-CS & ACM (2001, 2005) The joint task force on computer curricula IEEE-CS & ACM (2001, 2005) Computing curricula 2001 and Computing curricula 2005. Computer science. http://www.acm.org/education/curricula-recommendations

Jinguji D, Lewis W, Efthimiadis EN, Minor J, Bertram A et al (2006) The University of Washington's U WCLMA QA system. In: The 15th Text Retrieval Conference (TREC 2006) proceedings

Johnson F (2008) On the relation of search and engines. In: Proceedings of the second international workshop on teaching and learning of information retrieval (TLIR 2008). http://www.bcs.org/server.php?show=ConWebDoc.22355

Jones GJF (2009) An inquiry-based learning approach to teaching information retrieval. Inf Retr 12(2):148–161

JUnit. http://www.junit.org/

Koster MA (1994) Standard for robot exclusion. http://www.robotstxt.org/orig.html

Managing Gigabytes for Java (MG4J). http://mg4j.dsi.unimi.it/

Manning CD, Raghavan D, Schütze H (2008) Introduction to information retrieval. Cambridge University Press, Cambridge, MA

Mooers CN (1951) Making information retrieval pay. Zator, Boston

Porter MF (1980) An algorithm for suffix stripping. Program 14(3):130–137. http://tartarus.org/~martin/PorterStemmer/def.txt

Robertson SE, Sparck-Jones K (1997) Simple, proven approaches to text retrieval. Cambridge Technical Report, Cambridge. http://www.cl.cam.ac.uk/techreports/UCAM-CL-TR-356.pdf

Ruthven I, Elsweiler D, Nicol E (2008) Designing for users: a holistic approach to teaching information retrieval. In: Proceedings of the second international workshop on teaching and learning of information retrieval (TLIR 2008). http://www.bcs.org/server.php?show=ConWebDoc.22356

Sacchanand C, Jaroenpuntaruk V (2006) Development of a web-based self-training package for information retrieval using the distance education approach. Electron Libr 24(4):501–516

TERabyte RetrIEveR. http://ir.dcs.gla.ac.uk/terrier

Thornley C (2008) Teaching information retrieval (IR) as a philosophical problem. In: Proceedings of the second international workshop on teaching and learning of information retrieval (TLIR 2008). http://www.bcs.org/server.php?show=ConWebDoc.22354

Wade S, Braekevelt P (1994) IR framework: an object-oriented framework for developing information retrieval systems. Program Autom Libr Inf Syst 29(1):15–29

Zhu L, Tang C (2006) A module-based integration of information retrieval into undergraduate curricula. J Comput Sci Colleges 22(2):288–294

Zobel J, Moffat A (1998) Exploring the similarity space. In: SIGIR Forum

Chapter 8
Using Multiple Choice Questions to Assist Learning for Information Retrieval

Andrew MacFarlane

8.1 Introduction

In MacFarlane (2007), a number of different challenges in supporting postgraduate library and information science students were outlined. The challenge has come about for two main reasons: there is evidence of a decline in mathematical skills for students entering tertiary education in the UK (Croft 2002), and some key skills such as calculus are no longer taught at GCSE level (Appleby and Cox 2002) in the UK; many of the students who entered postgraduate LIS courses have a first degree in Arts and Humanities, and have very little exposure to relevant mathematical concepts for search. A number of different solutions have been put forward to resolve this problem, including the use of online Multiple Choice Questions (MCQs) to support the students in their learning. In this chapter, we address this issue by examining the parts of information retrieval (search and evaluation) to which MCQs can most usefully be applied – namely discrete mathematics and numeracy. In Sect. 8.2, we describe related work. An outline of using MCQs for assessment is provided in Sect. 8.3, after which the areas of search which can be supported (and which relate to the mathematics part of the syllabus) are outlined in Sect. 8.4 together with a proposed strategy for designing question sets. Given this background, the strategy for implementing MCQs in search is illustrated in Sect. 8.5 using example questions to highlight the issues. A summary and conclusion is provided at the end.

A. MacFarlane (✉)
Department of Information Science, City University London, Northampton Square, London EC1V 0HB, UK
e-mail: andym@city.ac.uk

E. Efthimiadis et al. (eds.), *Teaching and Learning in Information Retrieval*,
The Information Retrieval Series 31, DOI 10.1007/978-3-642-22511-6_8,
© Springer-Verlag Berlin Heidelberg 2011

8.2   Related Work

The various pedagogic challenges in teaching and learning search with information science students were first outlined in MacFarlane (2007), which focused on three main areas of mathematics which require support in some way to assist in the understanding of search – numeracy, discrete mathematics, and probability/statistics. In this light, the issue of diagnostic tests, delivery of material and summative assessment was addressed. This led to further work on using a tutorial style of delivery to support students in MacFarlane (2009), which demonstrated that a proactive style of teaching has a positive effect on the teaching of mathematics for search. A large-scale review of teaching and learning in IR (Fernández-Luna et al. 2009) indicated that there has been some work on using online tests in assessment, e.g., Sacchanand and Jaroenpuntark (2006), which was focused on using a Web-based training package in distance learning. However, this research focused on search in general and used other forms of online interactivity such as multimedia to achieve its aims. There is a clear need therefore to investigate the use of MCQs to support student learning in search, in particular for understanding mathematics.

8.3   Using MCQs for Assessment

MCQs are one of a number of different types of objective assessments, which can either be used for formative and summative assessment (Higgins and Tatham 2008). Each question is made up of a stem (the text of the question) with a number of options as the answer to the question; the key – the correct answer, and a number of distracters which are incorrect answers (McKenna and Bull 1999). Care needs to be taken when designing questions (Higgins and Tatham 2003) to ensure that no clues are given away as to the answer, contain obviously incorrect answers, etc. A number of problems with regard to using MCQs for assessment have been identified (Higgins and Tatham 2003). We tackle each of these in turn using the context of mathematics in search.

A key issue with the use of MCQs for assessment is the accusation that there use means "dumbing down", e.g., testing facts drawn from lecture materials or only testing part of the syllabus for the module. This is a concern in the domain as certain concepts in search (such as undertaking relevance assessments) are subjective and cannot be examined by objective assessment methods. This restricts their use in the field to a subset of objectively testable concepts such as Boolean logic and precision/recall calculations. Note that questions set must test higher level concepts (such as interpretation of results) and not simple calculations. Targeting MCQs at the correct area of search alleviates the "dumbing down" problem.

The potentially "easy" nature of poorly designed or targeted MCQs leads to two other problems, namely unrealistically high scores and the "lucky monkey" problem where students can guess their way to success. Search being a very practical subject should be assessed summatively using reports where the student provides evidence of knowledge though examining search and evaluation with online search systems for a given information need. MCQs can be used in a supporting role in formative assessment, for that part of search which can be objectively tested. Adopting this strategy avoids both score-related issues, however care must be taken to ensure that the purpose of both formative assessment (with MCQs on Boolean Logic) and summative assessment (a written report on search and evaluation) is made clear to ensure that students who do well in the former have realistic expectations about their performance in the latter (Higgins and Tatham 2003).

Two further problems are identified by Higgins and Tatham (2003) that of the inability to test oral/written skills by MCQs and encouraging surface learning by deploying them. We do not advocate using MCQs to test oral/written skills, which must be assessed by other methods (see above). The issues of surface learning can be tackled by setting questions which allow the student to show analytical skills, e.g., provide a stem with an information need which requires analysis, tackling the various areas of mathematics with each proceeding set of questions. We make use of this idea below.

Given the above, it is our contention that MCQs are best used when there are clear objective right and wrong answers to a problem. As stated in MacFarlane (2007) and reinforced above, much of learning IR cannot be supported by this form of assessment as important elements contain subjective aspects, e.g., information needs, relevance assessment. However the underlying mathematics used to support search (such as Boolean logic, numeracy) do allow objective questions to be posed, and it is therefore possible to use them in a supporting role. It is our contention that using MCQs for summative assessment (MacFarlane 2007) is not appropriate (see above), and we therefore focus on formative assessment. Using MCQs to support teaching and learning mathematics for search is useful in the formative context – they can either be used for diagnostic tests in order to ascertain the prior experience of the cohort, or just in a supporting role for those who feel the need for extra tuition.

8.4 Areas of Learning in IR Supportable by MCQs and a Proposed Strategy to Implement Question Sets

We now turn to the specific areas of search in IR, which are mathematically focused and to which MCQs can be applied to objectively assist teaching and learning. We identify six different areas of the search process which require knowledge of mathematics to some degree:

- Boolean logic: operational IR systems only use three-core Boolean operators: AND (set intersection), OR (set union), and AND NOT (set difference). These are used to connect terms together to create quite complex queries, expanding and narrowing search as necessary.

- Extended Boolean logic: operational IR systems also provide extensions to Boolean logic, such as proximity operators and truncation or wildcards. Proximity operators come in a number of different forms (adjacency, within text block, e.g., sentence, paragraph, within a range of words or near) and are used to narrow down the search further – they are a special case of AND (set intersection). Truncation operators are used to specify variations of a useful word, e.g., break* would retrieval break, breaks, breakers, breaking, etc., and are used to expand the search – they are a special case of OR (set union). Truncation operators are generally postfix, but infix or prefix operators can be supported.
- Ranking and ordering documents: statistics such as term frequency, inverse document frequency, and document length are used to build ranking models for ordering documents. The cohort only needs a high-level understanding of these concepts, and their effect on search.
- System syntax: operational search systems have their own query syntax and form, which varies from system to system particularly for extended Boolean operators, e.g., proximity operators (within, near) or truncation operators (*,?). Examples of variations can be found in Dialog (2010) and Factiva (2001).
- Boolean search strategies: there are a number of command line systems which allow quite complex search strategies, e.g., successive fractions and building blocks. These require an understanding of set theory and merging sets through both Boolean and extended Boolean operators (see above).
- Evaluation measures: the core precision and recall measures (Cleverdon 1967) must be understood, plus important variations such as mean average precision (TREC n.d.). This assumes binary relevance. Graded relevance assessment measures such as the Discounted Cumulative Gain (DGC) measure can also be tackled (Kekäläinen and Järvelin 2002).

MacFarlane (2007) applied the "Mathematical Assessment Task Hierarchy" (MATH) taxonomy defined by Smith et al. (1996) to the building blocks for mathematics required for information retrieval (see Table 8.1).

In this table dependencies flow from left to right, e.g., Group B knowledge is dependent on Group A, Group C is dependent on Group B. The logical flow of questions, therefore, is to address Group A issues followed by Group B, then Group C. We apply this framework to the six elements of information retrieval which require mathematical knowledge identified above to derive a strategy for building a set of MCQs to support student learning of mathematics in IR. See the following strategy for building MCQ sets for learning mathematics in Search:

Table 8.1 Building blocks for mathematics required for information retrieval (Macfarlane 2007)

Group A	Group B	Group C
Numeracy	Forming Boolean queries	Search strategies (different uses of
Set theory	analyzed from a user's	Boolean and Adjacency operators
Transformation rules,	information need	and terms)
e.g., commutativity,		Evaluation of results
associativity		
Statistics and probability		

- Group A: Boolean and Extended Boolean Logic. Ranking and Ordering of documents. Precision and Recall measures.
- Group B: Systems search syntax (implemented Boolean and Extended Boolean logic). Applying precision and recall measures.
- Group C: Boolean search strategies (using systems search syntax). Evaluation of precision and recall measures.

The strategy requires that questions be built on knowledge gained at the previous level of the taxonomy outlined in Table 8.1 and elaborated in the list above, therefore we proceed through the taxonomy from group A to group C issues in the set of questions. The key contribution of this chapter is the derivation of the strategy from educational theory and applying it in the requisite areas of mathematical knowledge needed for understanding key parts of search.

8.5 Implementing the Strategy to Support IR Learning by Deriving MCQs

We outline the strategy identified in Sect. 8.4 by using an example question set to show how it can be implemented in practice – the focus is very much on illustrating the strategy rather than providing a question set. This should be born in mind by the reader as they go through each of the questions. The example questions provided are based on the author's personal experience of teaching an IR module to LIS students. We provide different views of the mathematical material to be delivered including some which are more mathematical focused, and some which are put in the context of searching using examples of highlighted text. Each example given takes the following form:

- Stem: this is the text of the question for the student to answer.
- Options: different answers to the question, of two types:

  – Key: the correct answer to the question.
  – Distracters: incorrect answers which are plausible and are typical wrong answers for the given question.

The advice given in McKenna and Bull (1999) is used to generate the example questions, readers should refer to this paper on writing pedagogically useful MCQs. The structure is based directly on the taxonomy derived in MacFarlane (2007) and the strategy derived from it in Sect. 8.4. In Sects. 8.5.1–8.5.3, we address query-based issues. Section 8.5.1 is focused on Group A issues in search such as Boolean logic and extended Boolean logic. The information in Sect. 8.5.2 is then developed further in the context of Group B issues, by addressing the issue of system search syntax. Group C issues are then tackled in Sect. 8.5.3 by developing search strategies using the search syntax used in Sect. 8.5.2. Section 8.5.4 is focused entirely on evaluation issues, and proceeds from group A to C using standard evaluation measures in IR. Due to space issues, we do not address the issue of ranking and ordering of documents.

8.5.1 Boolean and Extended Boolean Operator Querying (Group A Questions)

The first area to address is Boolean logic, firstly via set theory and then using examples in context. All the simple examples given here focus on AND, but variations would be provided for the OR, AND NOT operators. An understanding of Boolean operators would be tackled first (see Fig. 8.1).

Variations would be provided for OR and NOT operators. The stem can utilize Venn diagrams to help the student find the answer (see above). Questions on Boolean transformation rules could also be addressed here, e.g., associativity, commutativity, etc. This question set would be followed by MCQs focused on highlighted text, see Fig. 8.2.

Care needs to be taken when mixing AND and OR queries, otherwise two right answers can be provided, complicating the option design, e.g., information OR retrieval would also be a correct answer for the example given in Fig. 8.2. Proximity operators, a special case of AND can also be tackled (perhaps directly after the questions on the AND operator to help the student distinguish between the two types of query). Proximity operators are addressed in Fig. 8.3.

Variations for other types of proximity operator could also be provided, e.g., same block of text, with a specified distance etc. Truncation operators, as a special

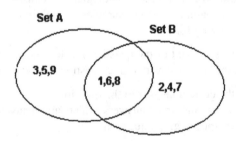

- Stem: What is the result set for {1,3,5,6,8,9} AND {1,2,4,6,7,8}?
- Key: {1,6,8} – correct! Elements must be in both sets
- Distracters:

    o{1,2,3,4,5,6,7,8,9} - No: this is a Boolean OR (set union), A OR B. Recall that the real world use of AND is different from a formal setting such as this.

    o{3,5,9} – No: this is a Boolean NOT (set difference), A NOT B.

    o{2,4,7} – No: this is a Boolean NOT (set difference), B NOT A.

Fig. 8.1 Example set theoretic question (AND) – Group A

- Highlighted Text: "**Information retrieval** is the art of the possible. Most people—no matter what society they live in—are involved in some kind of information seeking. For example the **Bushmen** of the Kalahari need information on waterholes in the desert. Although they live in a non-technical society, their thirst brings about an information need, in this case to find a waterhole."
- Stem: Which of the following queries would retrieve this document?
- Key: *information AND retrieval* – Correct: this document contains both terms in the query.
- Distracters:
  - *information AND extraction* – No: the text does not contain the right hand term 'extraction'.
  - *sahara AND bushmen* – No: the text does not contain the left hand term 'sahara'.
  - *technological AND seekers* – No: the text does not contain either query terms.

Fig. 8.2 Example highlighted text question (AND) – Group A

- Highlighted Text: "**Information retrieval** is the art of the possible. Most people—no matter what society they live in—are involved in some kind of **information seeking**. For example the **Bushmen** of the **Kalahari** need information on waterholes in the desert. Although they live in a non-technical society, their thirst brings about an information need, in this case to find a waterhole."
- Stem: Assuming a proximity operator named ADJ, which retrieves documents with two terms directly next to each other in the specified order - which of the following queries would retrieve this document?
- Key: *information ADJ retrieval* – Correct: this document contains both terms in the query and they are next to each other in the specified order.
- Distracters:
  - *seeking ADJ information* – No: the text does contain both terms and they are directly next to each other, but not in the specified order of required by the query.
  - *Bushmen ADJ Kalahari* – No: the two terms are in the correct order, but the words 'of' and 'the' are between them.
  - *information ADJ seekers* – No: the text does not contain term 'seekers'.

Fig. 8.3 Example highlighted text question (ADJ) – Group A

case of OR are addressed in Fig. 8.4. All operators presented so far can then be used in a series of questions with much more complex Boolean expressions in them, an example is given in Fig. 8.5.

Common errors and misunderstanding on Boolean expressions must be addressed. The reader experienced in Boolean logic may regard the question design to be at somewhat a low level, but the remedial focus of questions at the Group A stage is prerequisite for this cohort before they attempt question sets at the Group B level. Questions on Boolean transformation rules can also be provided using Boolean expressions to augment the set theoretic questions.

- Highlighted Text: "Information retrieval is the **art** of the possible. Most people—no matter what society they live in—are involved in some kind of information **seeking**. For example the **Bushmen** of the Kalahari need information on waterholes in the desert. Although they live in a non-technical society, their thirst brings about an information need, in this case to find a waterhole"
- Stem: Assuming a postfix only wildcard operator *, which truncated a query term and selects a variety of documents with the [stem]*, which of the following queries would retrieve this document?
- Key: *seek** - Correct: the text contains seeking which contains the stem "seek," with "-ing" picked up by the wildcard operator
- Distracters:
  - *Seek*ng* – No: this is an infix operation, so although the term "seeking" is in the document, a postfix only operator would not retrieve this text.
  - *men*– No: this is a prefix operation, so although the term 'bushmen' is in the document, a postfix only operator would not retrieve this text.
  - *arts** – No: the term "art" is in the text, but the character "s" after "art" would mean that the text would not match with this postfix only example.

Fig. 8.4 Example highlighted text question (Wildcard) – Group A

- Highlighted Text: "**Information retrieval** is the art of the possible. Most people—no matter what society they live in—are involved in some kind of **information seeking**. For example the **Bushmen** of the **Kalahari** need information on waterholes in the desert. Although they live in a non- technical society, their thirst brings about an information need, in this case to find a waterhole."
- Stem: Which of the following Boolean expressions would retrieve the above text?
- Key: *(information ADJ retriev*) AND (information ADJ seek*)* - Correct: all proximity operators in combination with wildcards and the connecting AND operator will retrieve this text.
- Distracters:
  - *(Bush* ADJ Kalahari) AND (information ADJ seek*)* – No: all the search terms are valid, but "of the" is between the terms "Bushmen" and "Kalahari," so the left hand adjacency operators would not match the text. Both right hand and left had expressions either side of the AND operator must be satisfied for the text to be retrieved.
  - *(information ADJ retriev*) AND (information ADJ science)* – No: the text does not contain the term "science" therefore the right hand adjacency operator would not match the text. Both right hand and left had expressions either side of the AND operator must be satisfied for the text to be retrieved.
  - *(information ADJ retrieval) AND (information ADJ seeker*)* – No: the right hand expression contains a wildcard operator "seeker*" which would not match the text. Both right hand and left had expressions either side of the AND operator must be satisfied for the text to be retrieved.

Fig. 8.5 Example highlighted text question (Boolean expression) – Group A

8.5.2   Query Syntax (Group B Questions)

In our examples, we assume Dialog syntax (Dialog 2010). For those unfamiliar with Dialog, we provide brief details of the language syntax in Table 8.2. We present examples of correct and incorrect syntax and/or use, and then take the examples from Sect. 8.5.1, asking the same kind of questions using the appropriate Dialog form. Figure 8.6 shows an example of correct and incorrect syntax – this lends itself to the choice of true/false from a set of given statements.

Table 8.2   Dialog Syntax used in example questions

Select search terms
   SELECT
   abbreviated **S**, and search term, e.g., S material
   truncation is indicated by the **?** symbol, e.g.,
      "S material?" [to include material, materials, . . .]
   Proximity is indicated by brackets with N,W to indicate "near" or
   "within," e.g.,
      "library (w) science" [both words are directly adjacent]
Combine sets
   COMBINE, abbreviated **C** and set numbers with Boolean operators,
   e.g.,
      C 1 and 2 [Boolean AND of sets 1 and 2]

- Stem: Assuming the Dialog search syntax, how many of the following search statements are correct?
   1. SEARCH information
   2. S retrieval
   3. C information AND retrieval
   4. SELECT extraction
- Key: *Two*: Correct - statements 2 and 4 are valid Dialog search statements, statement 1 is wrong as dialog does not support the command "search," statement 3 is wrong as you can only apply <u>combine</u> to sets already generated by <u>select</u> statements.
- Distracters:
   - *One* – No: Incorrect - statements 2 and 4 are valid Dialog search statements, statement 1 is wrong as dialog does not support the command "search," statement 3 is wrong as you can only apply <u>combine</u> to sets already generated by <u>select</u> statements.
   - *Three* – No: Incorrect - statements 2 and 4 are valid Dialog search statements, statement 1 is wrong as dialog does not support the command "search," statement 3 is wrong as you can only apply <u>combine</u> to sets already generated by <u>select</u> statements
   - *Four* – No: Incorrect - statements 2 and 4 are valid Dialog search statements, statement 1 is wrong as dialog does not support the command "search," statement 3 is wrong as you can only apply <u>combine</u> to sets already generated by <u>select</u> statements

Fig. 8.6   Example Dialog syntax question: Group B

- Highlighted Text: "**Information retrieval** is the art of the possible. Most people—no matter what society they live in—are involved in some kind of **information seeking**. For example the **Bushmen** of the **Kalahari** need information on waterholes in the desert. Although they live in a non-technical society, their thirst brings about an information need, in this case to find a waterhole."
- Stem: Which of the following Boolean expressions would retrieve the above text?
- Key: *SELECT   (information(w)retriev?)   AND   (information(w)seek?)* - Correct: all proximity operators in combination with wildcards and the connecting AND operator will retrieve this text.
- Distracters:
    o *SELECT (Bush?(w)Kalahari) AND (information(w)seek?)* – No: all the search terms are valid, but "of the" is between the terms "Bushmen" and "Kalahari," so the left hand adjacency operators would not match the text. Both right hand and left had expressions either side of the AND operator must be satisfied for the text to be retrieved.
    o *SELECT (information(w)retriev?) AND (information (w)science)* No: the text does not contain the term "science" therefore the right hand adjacency operator would not match the text. Both right hand

    and left had expressions either side of the AND operator must be satisfied for the text to be retrieved.
    o *SELECT (information(w)retrieval) AND (information (w)seeker?)* No: the right hand expression contains a wildcard operator "seekers?" which would not match the text. Both right hand and left had expressions either side of the AND operator must be satisfied for the text to be retrieved.

Fig. 8.7   Example Dialog Boolean question: Group B

Further questions on sessions in Dialog could also be asked to address the confusion students have in building a search statement with the service. Variations could include testing any confusion between systems when using different online systems, e.g., the truncation operator ? as against *. Building on this we then test the students with valid Dialog forms, but testing Boolean logic again in this context – see Fig. 8.7 (modified version of Fig. 8.5).

A variation would be to augment these Boolean expression question sets with examples of correct and incorrect Dialog syntax. The next stage is to build on questions presented on Boolean expressions and Dialog syntax in terms of search strategies.

8.5.3   Search Strategies (Group C Questions)

At this stage we can start looking at higher level search concepts (group C), such as search strategies. We concentrate on the types of strategies available on command line interfaces such as Dialog, i.e., quick search, building blocks, and successive fractions. We assume some confusion between strategies particularly building

- Stem: Given the search terms "human," "computer," and "interaction," which of the following is a valid form of the "building blocks" search strategy?
- Key: Correct—sets are built up one by one, and the final result set generated at the end of the strategy.
  Set1 = human
  Set2 = computer
  Set3 = interaction
  Set4 = 1 AND 2 AND 3
- Distracters:
  o *Set1 = human AND computer AND interaction*
     – No: this is an example of a quicksearch – in building blocks sets are built up one by one, and the final result set generated at the end of the strategy.
  o *Set1 = human*
     Set2 = computer AND Set1

     Set3 = interaction AND Set2
     – No: this is an example of successive fractions, which builds up intermediate sets incrementally – in building blocks sets are built up one by one, and the final result set generated at the end of the strategy.
  o *Set1 = human*
     Set2 = computer
     Set3 = interaction
     Set4 = 1 OR 2 OR 3
     – No: while the first three stages are correct for a Building Blocks strategy, AND is always applied to sets, as each intermediate set represents a facet, therefore the application of OR at the last stage is invalid in this kind of search strategy.

Fig. 8.8 Example search strategy question: Group C

blocks and successive fractions, which require knowledge of intermediate sets and building a final search from these sets. An example question set for search strategies is provided in Fig. 8.8.

The issue of confusing applying AND and OR between and within facets can also be tested further. Other strategies, such as "Citation Pearl Growing," could also be investigated. Building on this, we can then present questions on search strategies using valid Dialog search syntax (see Fig. 8.9).

In Fig. 8.9, the building blocks strategy is used, but variations of different strategies also tackling important misconceptions within the given search strategies.

8.5.4   Measures in IR Evaluation (Groups A to C Questions)

We now turn to evaluation measures, proceeding from group A/B questions on calculations for precision/recall and interpreting and evaluating those figures and group C question on high-level evaluation using query examples from earlier query sets. Figure 8.10 shows an example for mean average precision, addressing typical misconceptions of students on the measure.

A further addition to the question set would be to ensure that the student understood that either negative (−) precision or results greater than 1.0 are invalid.

- Highlighted Text: "**Information retrieval** is the art of the possible. Most people—no matter what society they live in—are involved in some kind of **information seeking**. For example the **Bushmen** of the **Kalahari** need information on waterholes in the desert. Although they live in a non-technical society, their thirst brings about an information need, in this case to find a waterhole."
- Stem: Which of the following Boolean expressions would retrieve the above text?
- Key: *Set1 = SELECT (information(w)retriev?)*
  Set2 = SELECT (information(w)seek?)
  COMBINE 1 AND 2
  - Correct: all proximity operators in combination with wildcards and the connecting AND operator will retrieve this text.
- Distracters:
  o *Set1 = SELECT (Bush?(w)Kalahari)*
     Set2 = SELECT (information(w)seek?)
     COMBINE 1 AND 2
     - No: all the search terms are valid, but 'of the' is between the terms "Bushmen" and "Kalahari," so the left hand adjacency operators on the first select statement would not match the text. Both right hand and left hand expressions either side of the AND operator must be satisfied for the text to be retrieved using the combine statement.
  o *Set1 = SELECT (information(w)retriev?)*
     Set2 = SELECT (information (w)science)
     COMBINE 1 AND 2
     - No: the text does not contain the term 'science' therefore the right hand adjacency operator on the second select statement would not match the text. Both right hand and left hand expressions either side of the AND operator must be satisfied for the text to be retrieved using the combine statement.
  o *Set1 = SELECT (information(w)retrieval)*
     Set2 = SELECT (information (w)seeker?)
     COMBINE 1 and 2
     - No: the right hand expression on the second select statement contains a wildcard operator 'seeker?' which would not match the text. Both right hand and left hand expressions either side of the AND operator must be satisfied for the text to be retrieved using the combine statement.

Fig. 8.9 Example Dialog Boolean search strategy question

Variations of this question could address the issue of Recall, and perhaps other measures such as BPREF or DCG. We may then complete the full circle by looking a search strategies using Dialog syntax and examine the effect on precision and recall by narrowing and expanding searches. Figure 8.11 gives an example on the effect of narrowing down searching and its effect on precision.

Variations of this would include recall examples, different forms of search strategy, and different combinations of both Boolean and extended Boolean operators.

8.6   Summary and Conclusion

We propose a strategy for building a set of MCQs in order to support Library and information science students – inexperienced with the mathematics required for search – and assist their learning. This strategy is the key contribution of this

- Stem: If relevant documents occur at positions 1, 3 and 7 of the results list, assuming that 10 documents are relevant, what is the correct value for average precision on this search.
- Key: *0.21* – Correct: Average precision is calculated by adding the calculations of every relevant document instance at N retrieved, and dividing by the total number of relevant documents known, therefore the result for this search would be (1.0+0.667+0.428)/10 = 0.21.
- Distracters:
  - *21%* – No: All precision figures are report 'between 0-1. Average precision is calculated by adding the calculations of every relevant document instance at N retrieved, and dividing by the total number of relevant documents known, therefore the result for this search would be (1.0+0.667+0.428)/10 = 0.21.
  - *2.09* – No: The final stage of dividing but the number of relevant documents has not been applied. Average precision is calculated by adding the calculations of every relevant document instance at N retrieved, and dividing by the total number of relevant documents known, therefore the result for this search would be (1.0+0.667+0.428)/10 = 0.21.
  - *0.20* – No: this is a rounding error. Average precision is calculated by adding the calculations of every relevant document instance at N retrieved, and dividing by the total number of relevant documents known, therefore the result for this search would be (1.0+0.667+0.428)/10 = 0.21.

Fig. 8.10 Example question on precision calculations: Group A/B

- Stem: Which of the following Dialog search strategies would narrow down a search, thereby increasing precision at the expense of recall.
- Key: *Set1 = SELECT (information(w)retriev?)*
  Set2 = SELECT (information(w)seek?)
  COMBINE 1 AND 2
        - Correct: of all the queries presented, this would yield the narrowest set of results (a small set of documents), and would increase precision.
- Distracters:
  - *Set1 = SELECT (information AND retriev?)*
    Set2 = SELECT (information(w)seek?)
    COMBINE 1 AND 2
    - No: the AND operator used to generate Set1 is more expansive than the adjacency operator (w), and would therefore increase recall at the expense of precision. It is therefore a more expansive search.
  - *Set1 = SELECT (information OR retriev?)*
    Set2 = SELECT (information(w)seek?)
    COMBINE 1 AND 2
    - No: the OR operator used to generate Set1 is more expansive than the adjacency operator (w), and would therefore increase recall at the expense of precision. It is therefore a more expansive search
  - *Set1 = SELECT (informat?(w)retriev?)*
    Set2 = SELECT (informat?(w)seek?)
    COMBINE 1 and 2
    - No: the truncation operator on the term "informat?" used to generate both Set1 and Set2 is more expansive than "information," and would therefore increase recall at the expense of precision. It is therefore a more expansive search.

Fig. 8.11 Example question using queries to show effect on precision: Group C

Table 8.3 Strategy for building MCQ sets for learning mathematics in Search ...(Revisited)

• Issues in group A of the taxonomy would be addressed first, e.g., an understanding of Boolean operators.
• This would then allow the testing of knowledge at group B, e.g., the formulation of Boolean expressions and translating them to a relevant online system search syntax.
• Group C knowledge would then build on the knowledge gained by testing knowledge of search strategies.

Table 8.4 Proposed Strategy for iterative refinement of MCQs

1. From Prior knowledge, write a set of 20/30 questions for each level of the taxonomy.
2. Build these questions into an online learning environment (Moodle).
3. Collate results of MCQs for all students and calculate averages, standard deviations etc.
4. Collate coursework results and measure impact on results from the previous years cohort (differences in averages, SD, etc).
5. Collate student feedback and analysis qualitative and quantitative data on impact of MCQs.
6. Take evidence from 3, 4 and 5 and revise the question sets developed in stage 1.
7. Return to step 2.

chapter. The strategy we propose builds up knowledge from simple calculations and operations in evaluation and search, to higher level knowledge in three steps (Table 8.3).

Our strategy would eventually tackle the issue of the effect of searching on evaluation, providing a holistic picture of the application of mathematics to information retrieval problems.

The examples given in the chapter are just that, and are by no means complete. The next stage is to implement this strategy and build a full set of questions for the test. We envisage a set of around 20/30 questions each for three question sets, at group A, B, and C levels of the taxonomy we put forward above. Iterative refinement to the question sets will be essential, in order to build up knowledge about the cohort and the problems they have in understanding the mathematics required for search. Any problems we outline here are by no means exhaustive. The strategy we propose to use is detailed in Table 8.4.

Further work in the area could include addressing the issues of understanding how ranking works or even moving into the area of computer science which entails the examination of other types of mathematics including term ranking, probability and statistics matrix algebra and mathematical vectors. Each element of the strategy (A, B, and C) could be identified for any types of mathematical knowledge needed for search. Thus the ideas in this chapter are not only useful for those who work in Library and Information Science department or Information Schools, but could be of potential benefit for those teachers who focus is more on implementing information retrieval software and who need a much deeper understanding of retrieval models. Thus teachers in Computer Science departments or schools can also use the strategy to build MCQs to assist their student learning. It should be noted that there is potential to use MCQs in summative as well as formative assessment in this field.

References

Appleby J, Cox W (2002) The transition to higher education. In: Kahn P, Kyle J (eds) Effective learning and teaching in mathematics and its applications. Kogan Page, London, pp 3–19

Cleverdon CW (1967) The Cranfield test on index language devices, ASLIB Proceedings, 19. In: Spark Jones K, Willet P (eds) Readings in information retrieval. Morgan Kaufmann, San Francisco, pp 47–59

Croft T (2002) Mathematics: the teaching, learning and support of non-specialists. In: Kahn P, Kyle J (eds) Effective learning and teaching in mathematics and its applications. Kogan Page, London, pp 144–157

Dialog (2010) Dialog pocket guide. http://support.dialog.com/searchaids/dialog/pocketguide/. Accessed 19 Oct 2010

Factiva (2001) Inside out – the complete reference for Factiva.com. http://factiva.com/learning/F-646InsideOutguide.pdf. Accessed 19 Oct 2010

Fernández-Luna JM, Huete JF, MacFarlane A, Efthimiadis EN (2009) Teaching and learning information retrieval. Inf Retr 12:201–226

Higgins E, Tatham L (2003) Exploring the potential of multiple-choice questions in assessment, learning and teaching in action 2:1, winter. http://www.celt.mmu.ac.uk/ltia/issue4/higginstatham.shtml. Accessed 19 Oct 2010

Higgins E, Tatham L (2008) Assessing by multiple choice question (MCQ) test. The Higher Education Academy. http://www.ukcle.ac.uk/resources/assessment-and-feedback/mcqs/. Accessed 19 Oct 2010

Kekäläinen J, Järvelin K (2002) Using graded relevance assessments in IR evaluation. J Am Soc Inf Sci Technol 53(13):1120–1129

MacFarlane A (2007) Pedagogic challenges in information retrieval – teaching mathematics to postgraduate information science students. In: Huete J, Fernández-Luna JM, MacFarlane A, Ounis I (eds) First International Workshop on Teaching and Learning of Information Retrieval (TLIR 2007). http://www.bcs.org/server.php?show=nav.8704. Accessed 19 Oct 2010

MacFarlane A (2009) Teaching mathematics for search using a tutorial style of delivery. Inf Retr 12:162–178

McKenna C, Bull J (1999) Designing effective objective test questions: an introductory workshop. CAA Centre, Loughborough University, 17 June. http://www.caacentre.ac.uk/dldocs/otghdout.pdf. Accessed 19 Oct 2010

Sacchanand, C, Jaroenpuntaruk, V. (2006) "Development of a web-based self-training package for information retrieval using the distance education approach", Electronic Library, The, Vol. 24 Iss: 4, pp 501–516

Smith G, Wood L, Crawford K, Coupland M, Ball G, Stephenson B (1996) Constructing mathematical examinations to assess a range of knowledge and skills. Int J Math Educ Sci Technol 30:47–63

TREC (n.d.) Text Retrieval Conference. http://trec.nist.gov/. Accessed 19 Oct 2010

Chapter 9
Information Retrieval Systems Evaluation: Learning and Teaching Process

Juan-Antonio Martínez-Comeche and Fidel Cacheda

9.1 Introduction

The study of Information Retrieval (IR) is relatively recent, having begun in the mid-twentieth century, but as Mooers (1951) has shown, from the beginning IR has been included among the educational goals of LIS studies. As IR has evolved the number of disciplines that address the study of IR within their curricula has grown, due not only to technological developments, but also to the incorporation of a large part of the world population as users of retrieval systems, thanks to the popularization of the Internet and search engines. However, two major disciplines have addressed the teaching of IR since its origins: Computer Science (CS) and Library and Information Science (LIS).

We can summarize the teaching orientation of each of these disciplines by stating that CS students focus on a technical approach to IR (development of programs that enable automated retrieval of information), while LIS students focus on the search task as intermediaries and experts in information units, as noted (Ingwersen 1992).

Nevertheless, knowledge of the principal technical terms would be desirable for LIS students so they could take full advantage of the retrieval systems in search tasks. Similarly, a better understanding of user needs and how users perform a search process would be desirable for CS students so they could incorporate or take into account the point of view of the user in future retrieval programs.

The principal aim of this paper is to describe how the addition of new learning tools: the WebCT forum, a wiki, and concept maps, have dramatically changed the outcomes for students with a very limited background in mathematics and CS in classes on IR systems evaluation that are taught from a technical perspective. We discuss the difficulties teachers encounter in trying to transmit technical knowledge

J.-A. Martínez-Comeche (✉)
Department of Library and Information Science, University Complutense Madrid, Madrid, Spain
e-mail: juaamart@pdi.ucm.es

E. Efthimiadis et al. (eds.), *Teaching and Learning in Information Retrieval*,
The Information Retrieval Series 31, DOI 10.1007/978-3-642-22511-6_9,
© Springer-Verlag Berlin Heidelberg 2011

to such students, and how the addition of these tools appears to help overcome these difficulties.

The remainder of this chapter is organized as follows: Section 9.2 explains the most common approaches used in the teaching of IR systems evaluation. Section 9.3 presents the specific context of the courses on IR which are taught as part of LIS studies at the University Complutense Madrid, and how one of them addresses IR systems evaluation from a systems perspective among other topics. Section 9.4 describes the educational goals and cognitive objectives of that part of the course for LIS students on IR systems evaluation that is taught from a systems perspective. Section 9.5 summarizes the main topics covered in IR systems evaluation from a systems perspective. Section 9.6 explains the general methodology we use (examples, exercises, and practice) in teaching IR systems evaluation from a systems perspective, and those new learning tools we use to facilitate the learning process. In this section we discuss the main features of the forum, the wiki and the concept map that can solve specific difficulties encountered by students with poor background in mathematics, and how we use each of them to overcome these difficulties. Section 9.7 presents an evaluation of the proposed methodology by a comparison between two groups of students: the first group was given a traditional course of instruction, while the second group was taught using both traditional and nontraditional instructional techniques. Finally, Sect. 9.8 presents some conclusions and future works.

9.2 IR Courses and System Evaluation

Courses on IR use different approaches to the teaching of evaluation. In this section we will try to summarize the most common methodologies and the approach followed in this paper.

The IR courses that take a technical approach usually dedicate a small percentage of the course (less than 10%) to the evaluation problem, always including the analysis of measures of effectiveness, and in some cases the analysis of efficiency. The Illinois Institute of Technology (IIT) teaches such a course (Illinois Institute of Technology 2010). The most common objective is the development of a prototype of an information retrieval system. Thus, at IIT, students must "Design and implement a search engine prototype using the storage methods, retrieval models and utilities" (Illinois Institute of Technology 2010). There are not many specific objectives about evaluation from the end-user perspective. For an example of that, the School of Information of The University of Texas at Austin includes among their objectives one about "Analyzing Web search logs interaction" (The University of Texas at Austin 2010), which implies a more user-centered perspective. The methodology used is based predominantly in exercises and projects, in-class discussions, and the use of various tools such as Lucene, as in the case of the Portland State University (2010).

The IR courses for LIS students in Europe are characterized by two basic common features (Fernández-Luna et al. 2009): first, the study of IR is approached from the point of view of the use of information retrieval systems as part of an information-seeking process to resolve an information need, as noted by Bates et al. (2005); and second, the evaluation of information retrieval systems is made from the user perspective, relegating evaluation from a systems perspective to less importance, as is shown in QAA (Quality Assurance Agency for Higher Education 2000) where the skills required of LIS students are enumerated: "2.6 The ability to identify, analyze and evaluate the information needs of different groups and make informed decisions to satisfy them. Students should be aware of methods of obtaining feedback from users."

Therefore, there are basically two opposite perspectives on the evaluation of information retrieval systems, one centered on the system (for the CS students) and the other centered on the user (for the LIS students).

These divergent approaches prevent the development of rewarding collaborations between researchers from both disciplines who are trying to develop better information retrieval systems. It is true that the development of retrieval systems requires the expertise of CS professionals, but it is also true that it is the end user, because of his or her information needs, who is the ultimate reason for the existence of retrieval systems; in the same way, it is the end user, or the documentalist on behalf of him or her, who ultimately must use and evaluate the system's performance (Martínez-Comeche 1995). It follows from this that it would be highly advantageous if programmers could participate jointly with documentalists, as specialists in user information behavior, in the design of information retrieval systems. This approach necessarily involves a greater interconnection between the educational goals of the IR curricula in both main disciplines.

This union between technical and user aspects already exists in some courses for CS students and also for LIS students, but always with a focus on the technical approach.

Among the courses on IR for CS students with a more interdisciplinary approach, we can mention CS926 at the University of Strathclyde, one of whose objectives is to "demonstrate an advanced understanding of the theory and technology used to construct modern Information Retrieval systems," but at the same time to "demonstrate the ability to show how findings from information seeking theory and practice can inform the design of information retrieval systems" (University of Strathclyde 2010). We can also mention here the case of the University of Glasgow. One of the objectives of their course on IR is the "understanding of and ability to implement a standard information retrieval (IR) system," but also the "ability to discuss how an IR system should be evaluated in terms of the system's performance and the user's satisfaction with the system" (University of Glasgow 2010). A mathematical background is required of students who want to attend these courses, and the methodology is based mainly on exercises and projects, although e-learning tools such as Moodle are used.

There are also some courses on IR for LIS students with an interdisciplinary approach that focus on CS issues. This is the case at the University of Amsterdam

(Riesthuis 2002) and the University Complutense Madrid. This provokes more difficulties from an educational standpoint, because of students' lack of mathematical and technological background that would facilitate an interdisciplinary approach.

Teaching LIS students about evaluation from a systems perspective has several advantages. First, it enables the LIS students to learn how a retrieval system really works, and how the variation of the elements considered in the design affects the results obtained. Second, it gives students the essential concepts used in evaluation from the point of view of the system, thus enhancing their understanding of the phenomenon of evaluation in information retrieval, beyond feedback from the end users. Finally, the LIS students learn the most common measures used in system-centered evaluation, exposing them to other evaluation methods, complementary to the methods employed in the Social Sciences.

This paper describes the course entitled "Búsqueda y recuperación de información" (number 800945) at Universidad Complutense Madrid, an IR course for LIS students that teaches evaluation from a systems perspective rather than an end-user perspective, even though it entails more difficulties from pedagogically, both in teaching and learning.

9.3   Context

LIS was instituted as a course of study at the university in the early 1990s, and is considered a part of the Social Sciences, with a strong component of Humanities (in the case of the Faculty of Documentation Sciences), at the University Complutense Madrid. Therefore, our students have very little background in Mathematics and Computer Science, and only two subjects (Information Retrieval and Statistics) handle concepts related to Mathematics.

At the University Complutense we divide the teaching of IR into two courses. The one included in this study, "Búsqueda y recuperación de información" (number 800945), analyzes several IR issues, including basic information storage, classic retrieval models, and evaluation from a systems perspective, while the other course, "Sistemas de recuperación e Internet," addresses mainly the characteristics of the information retrieval systems when we face with very large collections of documents in Internet, the ordering of the documents based in link analysis, and the evaluation of the results of searches from the end-user point of view.

The main topics covered in course number 800945, "Búsqueda y recuperación de información," can be summarized as follows:

1. Information concept by Shannon
2. Text processing and storage

   2.1. Tokenizing
   2.2. Stops Words
   2.3. Stemming

3. Boolean model
4. Vector Space model
5. Probabilistic model
6. Information Retrieval Systems evaluation

In this paper we focus only in the last point, the evaluation from a systems perspective. The whole course lasts 60 h in total, including theory (50%) and practice (50%), and from all this time, we only dedicate 8 h to IR systems evaluation, just over 10% of the time.

The fact that we spend less time on evaluation than on other topics like the classic retrieval models, and the fact that we spend precisely the last 8 h of the course to this topic, may adversely affect the students' attitude towards the learning of evaluation issues, as we will see later.

9.4   Educational Goals and Cognitive Objectives

The educational goals about evaluation of course "Búsqueda y recuperación de información" (number 800945) can be summarized as follows:

- Understand the purpose of evaluating IR systems from a system perspective.
- Be knowledgeable of the core concepts employed in IR systems evaluation from a system perspective.
- Understand and use the most important measures in IR from a systems approach.

These educational goals can be achieved through the following cognitive objectives:

- Given examples of texts written from a systems perspective, students will be able to distinguish what concept or concepts are involved in the texts and discuss in writing about their features or characteristics mentioned in the texts.
- Given a description of an aspect of evaluation that must be achieved, students will be able to identify what concept from the system approach is required, and enumerate the reasons why it is that concept and not another one.
- Given the numeric results of a comparison between two systems through one well-known measure and a test collection, the student will be able to compare the figures and conclude which system shows better performance.
- Given a system, a query, the relevant documents in the collection, and the response order of the documents produced by that query, the student will be able to calculate one of the measures employed in IR systems evaluation.

Students from the Computer Science domain are used to dealing with concepts through formal definitions (mathematically, for example), while LIS students assimilate the same concepts better through indirect, rather than direct, means. That is, they are better able to grasp a concept by understanding its purpose or through the feature that tries to represent or measure. This is the reason why the first and second objectives focus on students' ability to discern characteristics or concepts, rather than demonstrate their knowledge through questions about definitions. Similarly, an LIS student will have to understand perfectly the results obtained when two systems are compared, instead of having to know how to write a program to carry out the comparison. This is why the third objective focuses on comprehension of results, instead of developing a comparison, although the student will learn how to use a tool (e.g. Terrier) to compare the systems' performance.

9.5 Content

We can summarize the main topics about effectiveness evaluation covered in the course "Búsqueda y recuperación de información" (number 800945) as follows:

1. Core concepts

    1.1. Effectiveness
    1.2. Relevance
    1.3. Recall
    1.4. Precision

2. Measures of effectiveness based on recall-precision graph

    2.1. Measures based on points of the graph
    2.2. Measures based on interpolation and averaging

As is known, the most frequently used measures of effectiveness currently employ interpolation and calculation of average values from the dots of the recall-precision graph. A complete understanding of these effectiveness measures requires that one be able to explain perfectly the concept of interpolated precision (maximum precision value of the graph for some value of recall or greater) and the concept of average precision (arithmetic mean of the precision values of those points on the curve where a relevant document is retrieved, increasing recall). It is especially relevant at this point to include various examples and in-class exercises, to ensure the complete assimilation of these concepts by the student, emphasizing that these measures try to summarize a portion or the entire recall-precision graph.

9.6 The Problem and the Solution: New Learning Tools

The main problem we face is how to transmit technical knowledge with enough depth to students not accustomed to the principles, mode of reasoning, and mathematical notation required, to make dialog between CS and LIS specialists possible. That students often react negatively to learning these topics adds to the problem.

The solution we have found affects both the course content and the methodology employed. In terms of content, we try to transmit mathematical knowledge with just the necessary breadth and depth, never abandoning the key concepts, but without forcing the student to work with concepts too complex and not useful in the future. This usually requires additional effort by the teacher when the concept is particularly complex or difficult for our students.

Regarding the methodology used, first we always try to avoid the purely mathematical point of view which is largely lacking in the background of our LIS students. Instead, we emphasize the understanding of the phenomenon being observed, and what ideas are involved in a certain concept or evaluation measure. Secondly, we think that the transmission of knowledge is much faster when a new concept is explained using only the student's prior knowledge, and making sure that the student has fully grasped the first concept before moving on to other concepts based on the newly acquired knowledge.

Besides these basic methods, we have found that the cognitive objectives that we pursue can be better achieved by the use of a forum, a wiki and a conceptual map. These new tools allow students to think and reflect on these concepts, enabling learners to take care of their own learning process, as noted by Redecker (2009). The main objective, common to all the tools described below, is that the student raises questions relating to evaluation, in such a way that the answers to those questions include the concepts, the measures or the procedures that are being addressed at the time. In this way, students not accustomed to mathematical reasoning are able to contextualize the various measures or techniques, helping greatly in their assimilation. In turn, each of the tools (forum, concept map, and wiki) presents peculiarities that influence which tool to use depending on the specific educational objective to be achieved in each case.

When we focus on evaluation in general, trying to explain its main purpose or the differences between the system and the user perspective, we prefer to use the forum, available in WebCT or Moodle, platforms used at our university. After introducing the first concepts and basic objectives of evaluation, we urge all our students to use the forum tool to share any questions or problems they have with their classmates and teachers, being sure that they will better understand this content if it is socially constructed through conversations and interactions with others, as Brown and Adler (2008) noted. This also enables the instructors to detect which elements have not been well assimilated from the beginning, or what topics have drawn the attention of the students and require more attention in class. The students' posts in the forum allow us to promptly detect any initial misunderstandings about this aspect of IR, allowing us to appropriately focus on its purpose, its limitations, and procedures. This educational method is particularly relevant when students are not accustomed to quantitative analysis, as is the case in the Faculty of Documentation Sciences of the University Complutense Madrid.

> For example, we introduced the following question in the forum: "The information retrieval in Internet introduces peculiar characteristics, including the unknown number of documents in the collection relevant to a given query. This involves a problem if we want to evaluate the search engines performance. Could you give us any ideas?"

Several posts to this question did not mention the recall concept and a problem related to it, but the convenience of asking the users their opinion about the relevance of each result shown by the search engine.

After these answers, which show an end-user perspective in the students' mind, we reinforced in class time that evaluation from a systems perspective initially uses recall, implying that all the relevant documents to a question must be known.

We think that using concept maps is a good way to ensure that students learn the core concepts employed in IR systems evaluation from a system perspective. The main advantage of the concept map over other tools is that the student is forced to relate the concepts presented in class, making explicit the particular type of relationship between them. This exercise forces students to reflect on the scope and objectives of each concept, and differentiate each one from the others. Furthermore, the concept map allows the students to display the whole evaluation process, enabling them to place each concept in its context near to other concepts related to it, but different and complementary at the same time.

Here is the concept map the students developed in class with the core concepts employed in IR systems evaluation from a systems perspective. As we can see in the figure, the students have been able to identify the key concepts of evaluation and have defined the type of relationship that exists between them (Fig. 9.1).

Mastering the most important measures in IR from a system approach requires the use of a tool that forces the students to summarize in a few lines both the definition and the procedure to be followed for the calculation of each of these measures. A user-friendly tool that facilitates this dual exercise of reflection and synthesis is the wiki (there are a lot of free wiki programs available in Internet: MediaWiki, TikiWiki, or DokuWiki, for example), where we designate one article for each measure. First, the students feel that their work will be visible via the Internet, which motivates their interest. And second, the ability to edit the material produced by their peers in previous courses forces them to reflect on the articles written about other measures, trying to improve them. Therefore, it seems a priori an appropriate tool to use for the third and fourth of the cognitive objectives outlined previously. This method, like the concept map, involves working in groups.

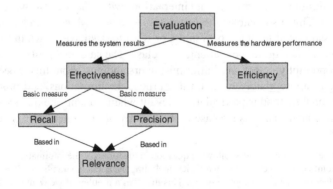

Fig. 9.1 Concept map showing the principal concepts of evaluation

For example, here is the definition of MAP the students decided it was the best one to put in the wiki article after the discussion in class: "MAP is a number that measures the effectiveness of an information retrieval system in relation to a set of queries." As we can see, there is a great effort of synthesis in this definition: it is a measure of effectiveness that summarizes in a single figure the system performance considering a set of queries, not only one. After that, the students described in the article the process needed to calculate this number.

These three tools are not used in courses for the CS students, but we think they are useful in courses for the LIS students. The forum's main function is to provide timely detection of gaps in the learning process, which can be achieved if the teacher introduces threads on those concepts that are more difficult to understand or more complicated mathematically. The inclusion of short essays on a wiki and the development of one conceptual map allows the students, by working in groups, to make a joint effort of assimilation, to summarize and express in writing the various measures of evaluation, and to discover the relationships that exist between the key concepts, all of which reinforce learning.

The employment of these new tools does not preclude the simultaneous use of other learning techniques, more traditional than forums, wikis, and conceptual maps. It is always necessary to include a sufficient variety of examples, exercises, and practice in the classroom, to ensure complete assimilation of these concepts by the students. This effort must be done by the teacher. Following the theory, students must complete their training doing evaluation in practice. Students should be familiar with some TREC test collections (e.g. WT2G), and a platform specifically designed for research and evaluation, such as Terrier. The practice should make the student understand how changing any element in the system design (such as the inclusion or exclusion of stemming, for example) leads to different system behavior, and consequently, a modification of the measures of the effectiveness previously discussed.

9.7 Assessments and Feedback

To test if the learning process has been successful, we employ two complementary methods to check the level of assimilation achieved by students: the first is a self-assessment, by means of a test developed in WebCT or Moodle with questions about all the principal aspects of the subject, that the student can complete several times along the course, whenever he or she wants. After giving the final score obtained by the student, he or she can check why one certain question was answered wrongly, because this test includes the correct answers to all the questions. In this way a student can know at any time which is approximately his or her level of knowledge about the subject. The second method is an exam in class, at the end of the course, which includes several questions about the cognitive objectives described earlier. The score obtained in this exam reflects the knowledge acquired finally by the student.

We must assess to what extent this teaching and learning experience is useful in comparison with a more traditional approach. To measure the improvement in learning, we provided the same material to two groups, but the methods employed with each group were different:

- One group, named A, received the material, with examples and exercises in the classroom, but without the use of the forum, wiki, or concept map in the teaching process. With this group, then, we used more traditional learning and teaching techniques. This group consisted of 41 students, the larger of the two groups.
- The other group, named B, received the same material, the same examples and exercises were made in class, but the students were given a forum where they were encouraged to give their point of view on issues concerning evaluation, especially its core concepts, its purpose, and different possible perspectives on IR systems evaluation. Later, in groups, the students had to develop a concept map with the core concepts discussed in the course (part 1 of the content of the course; see above) and had to write one article for the wiki with an explanation of one of the measures analyzed during the course. The use of these tools represented a more practical approach to teaching and learning techniques. It only took us four more hours of class, although a little more time for the students who answered the different questions posted in the forum. This group consisted of 13 students, one-third of the former, due to the more personalized attention that it is necessary with this teaching and learning methodology.

Comparison of the final exam results of the two groups gave us an objective method to evaluate the improvement provided by the new methodology. We included four questions about evaluation in the test exam, one for each of the cognitive objectives of the course:

- The first question summarized one of the objections to laboratory-based evaluation in IR discussed by Ingwersen and Järvelin (2005), and students had to distinguish the main concept involved and from what perspective it is characteristic.
- The second question was about what measure we could use to evaluate the performance of an IR system without employing the concept of recall.
- The third question presented the numeric results of the comparison between two systems through the tables related to their 11-point interpolated average precision, and students had to determine which system had better performance.
- The fourth question gave a system, a query, the relevant documents in the collection, and the response order of documents to that query. The students had to calculate the R-precision.

In Table 9.1 we show the results obtained from the exam. As noted previously, traditional techniques were employed with Group A, while the forum, concept map, and wiki tools were employed with Group B: The differences between the groups are statistically significant for all questions, as demonstrated by the first, second, and fourth questions with $p < 0.0001$ and the third question with $p = 0.004$ (using Chi-square tests with a significance level of 0.05).

Table 9.1 Results of the comparison between two groups taught with different methodologies

Question	Group	Right answer (%)	Bad answer (%)	No answer (%)
First	A	7.32	9.76	82.92
	B	38.46	0,00	61.54
Second	A	7.32	14.63	78.05
	B	53.85	7.69	38.46
Third	A	14.63	17.07	68.30
	B	30.77	7.69	61.54
Fourth	A	29.27	14.63	56.10
	B	69.23	0,00	30.77

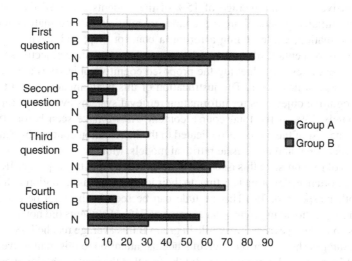

Fig. 9.2 Results for two groups taught with different methodologies

We can illustrate the results of the comparison between a more traditional teaching methodology (group A) and the employment of new tools like forums, concept maps, and wikis (group B) in the following figure, where:

- R represents "Right Answer"
- B represents "Bad Answer"
- N represents "No Answer"

As we can see in the figure, in all the questions the results achieved by the 13 students of group B (who were taught with the use of new tools) are better than the results achieved by the 41 students of group A (who were taught under a more traditional methodology). The percentage of correct answers is always higher in group B, and simultaneously the percentage of students who answered incorrectly is always lower in group B than in group A. Finally, the percentage of students in group A that do not answer the questions included in the test is always higher (Fig. 9.2).

9.8   Conclusions

With these data we can conclude that, undoubtedly, in the case of students with a poor background in mathematics, the added use of new tools such as forums, concept maps, and wikis facilitates the process of learning about evaluation in information retrieval systems. The percentage of students that mastered the cognitive objectives of the course using these new tools is much higher than the percentage of students that mastered the cognitive objectives of the course when only traditional methods were employed: examples, exercises, and practices. This difference can be summarized as follows: when traditional teaching methods were used exclusively only an average of 15% of the students achieved the cognitive objectives initially proposed in the course in relation to information retrieval systems evaluation, while adding a forum, a concept map, and a wiki increased the average of percentage of students who passed these cognitive objectives to 48%.

The success rates for achieving the proposed cognitive objectives are still low, despite the use of new tools. The justification of this phenomenon lies in the fact that the cognitive objectives for information retrieval systems evaluation represent approximately 10% of the total course content. As we have seen before (vid. 3. Context), the rest of the course is dedicated to the information concept by Shannon, the text processing, and the classic retrieval models. Moreover, we devote only the last classes of the course to this issue. Students thus often put this aspect of IR to last place in importance, devoting less time to their learning and assimilation in this area than to other aspects of IR. This attitude can be seen in the high percentage of unanswered questions: in group A an average of 71% of students did not answer the questions concerning evaluation, while in group B this average reached 48%. These high percentages show a serious lack of students' attention to this matter over other aspects of IR discussed in the course. But the fact that the new methodological tools have succeeded in increasing the percentage of students who answer these questions from 29% to 52% is an improvement that should be highly valued.

Finally, although we have had some informal discussions with some students on how to assess the use of these new tools, it would be necessary to get more reliable data. That is why we plan to give a questionnaire to the students in the future. In this way, we will gather students' opinions on the methodologies used, and which aspects of the different methods employed we should add to, modify, or remove. We would thus have subjective input about the best way to learn about this subject to accompany our objective test results, data that would help us to improve the results shown here.

References

Bates J, Bawden D, Cordeiro I, Steinerova J, Vakkari P, Vilar P (2005) Information seeking and information retrieval. In: Kajberg L, Lorring L (eds) European curriculum reflections on library and information science. Royal School of Librarianship and Information Science, Copenhagen

Brown JS, Adler RP (2008) Minds on fire: Open education, the long tail, and learning 2.0. Educause Rev 43(1):16–32

Fernández-Luna JM, Huete JF, MacFarlane A, Efthimiadis EN (2009) Teaching and learning in information retrieval. Inf Retr 12:201–226

Illinois Institute of Technology (2010) Course CS429: Introduction to information retrieval. http://www.ir.iit.edu/~nazli/cs429/index.html

Ingwersen P (1992) Information retrieval interaction. Taylor Graham, London

Ingwersen P, Järvelin K (2005) The turn: integration of information seeking and retrieval in context. Springer, Dordrecht

Martínez-Comeche JA (1995) Teoría de la información documental y de las instituciones documentales. Madrid

Mooers CN (1951) Making information retrieval pay. Zator, Boston

Portland State University (2010) Department of Computer Science. Course CS510: Information retrieval on the internet. http://web.cecs.pdx.edu/~maier/cs510iri

Quality Assurance Agency for Higher Education (QAA) (2000) Librarianship and information management subject benchmark. http://www.qaa.ac.uk/academicinfrastructure/benchmark/honours/librarianship.asp

Redecker C (2009) Review of learning 2.0 Practices: Study on the impact of web 2.0 innovations on education and training in Europe. European Commission, Joint Research Center. http://ftp.jrc.es/EURdoc/JRC49108.pdf

Riesthuis GJA (2002) Teaching of information storage and retrieval at the Department for Information Science of the University of Amsterdam. http://www.ifla.org/IV/ifla68/papers/024-144e.pdf

The University of Texas at Austin (2010) School of information. Course: Web Information retrieval/evaluation/design. http://courses.ischool.utexas.edu/donturn/2009/spring/INF_385D/assignments.html

University of Glasgow (2010) Department of Computing Science. Course: Information retrieval. http://www.dcs.gla.ac.uk/courses/masters/msc/courses.html

University of Strathclyde (2010) Course CS926: Information retrieval. http://www.strath.ac.uk/cis/localteaching/localpg/cs926

Chapter 10
Teaching Web Information Retrieval to Computer Science Students: Concrete Approach and Its Analysis

Stefano Mizzaro

10.1 Introduction From IR to Web IR

Information Retrieval (IR) has been taught for decades in various curricula: computer science, computer engineering, information science, and library science. Until about 10 years ago, although the research in the IR field was steadily progressing, the scenario was quite settled in terms of topics taught. Topics chosen in IR courses depended on the emphasis: more soft-science[1]-oriented curricula (e.g., library and information science) used to concentrate on the user side, studying cognitive aspects. More hard-science-oriented curricula (e.g., computer science and engineering) concentrated on IR formal models, algorithms, data structures, and implementation techniques. In the last 10 years, the situation has changed, due to the Web and the need for Web Search. Indeed, the Web has changed many computer- and information-related disciplines; however, in the IR case the changes have been rather dramatic, and what might be considered a new discipline, namely Web IR (WIR), was born. In WIR the emphasis shifts on Web issues: search engines, crawling, models of the Web graph, link analysis, Web technologies, languages and protocols, search with mobile devices, etc.

More in detail, one can say that WIR is different from classical IR for two kinds of reasons: concepts and technologies. On the conceptual side, there are several Web-specific issues which do not show up in classical IR circles, are not mere technicalities at all, and often rely upon well-established fields: modeling of the Web graph (including graph theory, random graphs, scale-free, and small world networks); links between PageRank/HITS and other notions of centrality in Social

---

[1] I rely on the soft/hard science dichotomy. Although it has obvious limitations and it is quite rough, it is also well known (http://en.wikipedia.org/wiki/Hard_and_soft_science) and it will do here.

S. Mizzaro (✉)
Department of Mathematics and Computer Science, University of Udine, Udine, Italy
e-mail: mizzaro@uniud.it

E. Efthimiadis et al. (eds.), *Teaching and Learning in Information Retrieval*,
The Information Retrieval Series 31, DOI 10.1007/978-3-642-22511-6_10,
© Springer-Verlag Berlin Heidelberg 2011

Network Analysis; crawling; low quality content and quality issues; heterogeneous users (not just librarians); etc. On the technological side, the lecturer that wants to follow the rapid evolution of search engines in the real world is overwhelmed with several technicalities. These might be disregarded as ephemeral and transitory, but I believe that this would be a double mistake. First, because the technical issues are often very effective in raising students' motivation; and second because often technical issues are very important and do make a difference. For instance, Google would not exist without the carefully designed architecture of the so-called Google cluster (Barroso et al. 2003).

This paper reports on my experience as lecturer of a course on Web Information Retrieval at Udine University in the last 5 years.[2] In Sect. 10.2, I describe the course (students population, syllabus, books, reading material, students' activities and projects, and assessment). In Sect. 10.3, I present some feedbacks from the students, gathered by means of a questionnaire filled in by students at the end of each year. In Sect. 10.4, I discuss a crucial alternative in topics order when designing a WIR course. The last section summarizes the paper and draws some conclusions.

10.2 WIR at Udine University

The following subsections describe the Web Information Retrieval course I have been teaching at Udine University in the last years.

10.2.1 Students Cohort

I have been teaching a Web Information Retrieval course for two Master's degrees, in Computer Science and in Information Technology, at the Faculty of Science of the Udine University for the last five academic years (2004/2005, 2005/2006, 2006/ 2007, 2007/2008, and 2008/2009). The duration of the course was one term (48 class hours), and about 15–20 students each year attended the lectures, i.e., about 75–100 students in total. The total number of students that have already passed their exam is 58: 17 + 17 + 10 + 7 + 7 (17 in 2004/2005, 17 in 2005/2006, 10 in 2006/ 2007, 7 in 2007/2008, and 7 in 2008/2009); thus about 15–40 more in total have attended the lectures but have not passed the exam yet.[3] The majority of the students were graduate, but about 2–4 each year were undergraduate.

---

[2] I am still teaching the same course this academic year, with almost no changes and about 20 students, but I am not presenting any data from this year.

[3] In Italy students can try the exam when they want after course end, even in the subsequent years.

10.2.2 Educational Goals

Briefly stated, the aim of the course is to present the basics of IR and WIR. More in detail, being aimed at technical students, the slant of the course is rather technical and scientific, falling in the hard-science approaches mentioned in Sect. 10.1. There are some other aims, though. Since I have been doing research in IR since mid-1990s, and since the course is rather advanced (it is for a Master's degree), I provide the students with a basic understanding of the research frontier as well, by describing some open research problems, in both IR and WIR fields.

Moreover, being the developments in the WIR field quite recent, I try to present a historical perspective on WIR research in the last 10–15 years. This is useful not only per se (the history of a field helps to understand it better) but also to approach the research frontier in a smooth way, as discussed below.

10.2.3 Syllabus

The Web Information Retrieval course is divided into two parts; the syllabus is (there have been only minimal changes along the 3 years):

- Part I: IR

  - Introduction to IR: what IR is, models, systems, evaluation, problems and difficulties.
  - IR models: Boolean, vector space, probabilistic, BM25, language models, latent semantic indexing, neural nets.
  - Inverted index: structure, construction, use.
  - Query languages and reformulation techniques.
  - Human Computer Interaction and IR: examples of user interfaces for IR.
  - Clustering: main algorithms, usage in IR.
  - Evaluation: relevance, test-collections, user studies, metrics.

- Part II: Web IR

  - Statistics on Web and Web users.
  - Models of the Web Graph: random graphs, scale free and small world networks, power laws, bow-tie, Web host graph.
  - Link analysis for ranking: PageRank, HITS, etc.
  - Spam, duplications, mirrors.
  - Search engine architecture.
  - Crawling.

I chose these topics starting by an analysis of the existing IR books, and on the basis of my knowledge of the field.

10.2.4   Textbooks and Reading Material

There are several (W)IR-related textbooks. In classical IR courses, in the pre-Web period, several reference texts were available; indeed, rather old texts like van Rijsbergen (1979), Salton and McGill (1984), Salton (1989), Blair (1990), Frakes and Baeza-Yates (1992), and Ingwersen (1992) were sometimes preferred to newer ones like Korfhage (1997), Marchionini (1997), Baeza-Yates and Ribeiro-Neto (1999), Witten et al. (1999), Belew (2000), Grossman and Frieder (2004), van Rijsbergen (2004), and Ingwersen and Järvelin (2005). More soft-science-oriented curricula usually adopted reference texts among Belew (2000), Blair (1990), Ingwersen (1992), Ingwersen and Järvelin (2005), and Marchionini (1997). More hard-science-oriented curricula usually adopted texts among Baeza-Yates and Ribeiro-Neto (1999), Belew (2000), Frakes and Baeza-Yates (1992), Grossman and Frieder (2004), Korfhage (1997), Salton (1989), Salton and McGill (1984), van Rijsbergen (1979, 2004), and Witten et al. (1999). A more recent text is Manning et al. (2008). Very few IR books deal with WIR-specific issues, and often in a very limited way.

To my knowledge, there are only three textbooks specifically devoted to WIR issues: Chakrabarti (2003), Levene (2006), and Liu (2007).[4] All of them start directly with WIR issues, and IR topics are presented when needed. The first one is more mathematical and conceptual-oriented; the second one deals with technological issues to a greater extent; the third one is more devoted to data mining and machine learning issues. All of them touch upon classic IR issues (the vector space model, the tf.idf weighting scheme, etc.), although these are not discussed and presented per se, but as means to Web search engines implementation. Another WIR book has been published last year (Croft et al. 2009), it starts directly with WIR issues, and also deals in detail with classic IR. This is probably the first book of this kind, and it might change, in the next years, the way we teach IR.

In my WIR course I relied for Part I mainly on Baeza-Yates and Ribeiro-Neto (1999), Manning et al. (2008), and Croft et al. (2009), and for Part II on a set of research papers, like, for instance, Albert and Barabasi (1999), Albert et al. (1999), Barroso et al. (2003), Bharat et al. (2001), Brin and Page (1998), Broder et al. (2000), Cho and Garcia-Molina (2000), Fetterly et al. (2004), Gulli and Signorini (2005), Kleinberg (1999), Lawrence and Giles (1998, 1999), and Page et al. (1998). These "classic" WIR papers are freely available on the Web, and are good substitutes for WIR books (see below).

---

[4] Indeed the first and the third ones are more Web data mining than WIR books; however, the two disciplines overlap quite a lot and the boundaries between them are not so clear.

10.2.5   Term Projects

Besides normal lessons, the course also features some students' presentations as simple term projects, on voluntarily basis. These presentations require about 1 week of study and preparation, last 1 h (or less) and are either on specific conceptual issues (e.g., read one or more research papers and summarize it/them) or on technological issues (e.g., analyze and summarize a specific system or technology). So far, students' presentations have been on the following topics: BM25; language models; stemming algorithms; Average Distance Measure (ADM), a specific IR effectiveness measure; link analysis for ranking algorithms; efficient PageRank computation; Google desktop; Spotlight; Google architecture (massive parallelization, hardware management, power consumption and refrigeration, etc.); IR in peer-to-peer networks; video retrieval concepts and systems (Google Video, YouTube, Yahoo!); Self Organizing Maps; open source and IR; Vivisimo; CREDO, a clustering engine; Search Engine Optimizers (SEO); and Web 2.0.

I have found students' presentations extremely positive. When focused on conceptual topics, they were useful to the speaker and understandable to the audience; when concerning technological issues, they were sometimes even more detailed than what I could have done; the audience looked very interested; and during the exams, questions on the main concepts were correctly answered. Some of the early years topics have been added to the course syllabus in the following years (e.g., BM25, Google architecture).

Students can also complement their course with a more substantial term project, requiring about 3 weeks of work and allowing them to acquire five more credits for their degree. Past term projects have been on the following topics (some of them were group work by two students): analysis of the Citeseer citation graph; implementation of a simple crawler; an AJaX-based term suggestion function (similar to "Google suggest") for PubMed; an AJaX-based implementation of a clustering search engine for mobile devices; a survey on meta search engines; a survey on Geographic IR; an analysis of alerting of mail messages; and quality mechanisms in Wikipedia.

10.2.6   Assessment and Feedback

The final students assessment is divided into two parts: an optional extra activity in the form of a simple term project as just described in Sect. 10.2.5, and a mandatory oral examination. The oral examination lasts about 45 min (from 30 min to 1 h) and ranges over all the topics of the course. If the student chooses the more substantial term project, the optional extra activity is not necessary.

Student feedback is gathered through an official channel, i.e., a standard user satisfaction questionnaire, provided by the university and filled in by the students in an anonymous form during one of the last lectures. The results are quite good overall, above the average and with normal fluctuations over the years. But I also gathered additional and more targeted feedback over the years, by means of a targeted questionnaire, as discussed in the following Sect. 10.3.

10.2.7 PhD Course

I also taught an intensive WIR course for PhD students in December 2009. The PhD course is based on the previously described Master's course, and although there are some differences, it is very similar. The syllabus was similar to that presented in Sect. 10.2.3, the course lasted 20 class hours over 3 weeks, and the final exam is project-based: the students have to do some experimental and/or research activity and present it in a talk. I had about 5–10 students: 10 students attended the lectures, and 5 intend to take the exam (only one has so far).

The same targeted questionnaire was provided to the students, but I have not taken into account their answers in the analysis outlined earlier for several reasons. Only two PhD students have answered so far (20% answer rate), by no means a reliable sample; their answers are very different, with a high variance, thus with different opinions; the numeric figures presents in the following would remain almost unchanged anyway, so adding them would not change anything in what follows.

10.3 Students' Feedback

Some feedbacks have been gathered from the students of the last 5 years by means of an anonymous questionnaire, designed by myself and administered either on paper during the final lecture or sent by email at the end of the course. The questionnaire is shown (translated from Italian to English) in the Appendix and consists of 22 items, divided into two parts. The first part (six items) aims at collecting students' background knowledge before they attended the lectures; the second part gathers students' opinion about the topics included (or not included) in the course, the difficulty of specific topics, the students' presentations, etc. Most of the answers are on a five-point Likert scale; some of them are in free text; and there are two semantic differentials collecting students' impressions on the IR and WIR parts of the course.

The main findings are:

- 45 students returned the questionnaire (45% of the 100 potential participants), 9 of them from the 2004/2005 academic year, 14 of them from 2005/2006, 13 from 2006/2007, 3 from 2007/2008, and 6 from the 2008/2009 year.
- Three questionnaire items (1, 4, 5) were aimed at roughly assessing students' knowledge of WIR before course start. Before course start, students knew what a

Table 10.1 Answers on IR and on WIR

	Interesting	Easy	Important	Pleasant	Simple	Useful
IR	4.8	3.6	5.3	5.0	2.6	6.1
WIR	5.6	3.5	5.4	6.1	2.5	6.5

search engine is (average of 4.0 on the 1–5 five-point scale, i.e., about one unit above the medium scale value, which is 3).[5] The concepts of crawler (2.8) and inverted index (1.9) were less known. The number of search engines used, on average (item 2) is rather low (1.8); Google was used by all the 45 respondents; Altavista, Microsoft, and Yahoo! were much less used (by 10, 7, and 10 respondents, respectively).

- Three questionnaire items (6, 7, 8) were aimed at understanding if classical IR is somehow less enjoyable than WIR, which turned out not to be the case: WIR is just slightly more interesting than IR (3.4); WIR issues are not perceived as more difficult than IR (2.8); and students' desire of more emphasis on WIR topics is very small (3.5).
- Further evidence is given by the results of the two semantic differentials (items 18, 19), that ask if the IR (WIR) part of the course is interesting/boring, difficult/easy, important/unimportant, unpleasant/pleasant, simple/complex, useless/useful. The average results (on a seven-point scale and "normalized" on the positively polarized items – higher values mean higher interest, ease, etc.) are summarized in Table 10.1: IR is as easy, important, and simple as WIR, and WIR is judged more interesting, more pleasant, and slightly more useful than IR.
- Students' presentations (item 17) are considered rather interesting, useful, and understandable (3.8). Other questionnaire items confirm that the syllabus is generally perceived quite positively: as already mentioned, more Web issues (item 6) are requested only to a limited amount (3.5); deepening of specific topics (item 11) is only slightly suggested (3.1), and the most mentioned topics in item 12 are multimedia, mobile, and implementation details; and less emphasis on some issues (item 13) and further topics (item 15) are requested to an amount lower than the medium scale value (2.7 and 2.8, respectively) – the most requested further topic being peer-to-peer IR.
- There are no appreciable differences over the three academic years: means and trends are very similar.

Overall, students' feedback on the course is positive. This is also confirmed by informal discussion that I had with some of them, by the answers to item 20 (on average, students would prefer to increase the number of class hours of the course, from 48 to an average 60), and by the number of students that decided to attend the course, which is higher than the average.

---

[5] I did not perform any deep statistical analysis of these data. I just note that using the median, instead of the mean would lead to similar considerations, and that I do not analyze variance (or interquartile range) values, nor statistical significance.

10.4   IR First or WIR First?

From the discussion in Sect. 10.2, it is clear that the teacher of a course including both classical IR and WIR issues has to choose among several alternatives, like syllabus and topics taught, textbooks and/or reading material, term projects, etc. However, one of the crucial issues is the choice between two alternatives (1) to teach the classical pre-WIR issues first and present the Web-specific issues later, as an add-on; or (2) to teach directly the WIR discipline per se, dealing with classic IR issues when needed. The first approach has the advantages of building on prerequisite knowledge, of presenting the historical development of the discipline, and, probably, of appearing more natural to most teachers, who have followed the historical development of the field. The second approach has the advantage of concentrating on a more modern view of the field and, probably, of leading to a higher motivation in the students, since the more appealing Web issues are dealt with right at course start. This section discusses the two alternatives more in detail, taking into account different aspects.

10.4.1   Textbooks Support

Of course, the availability of a good textbook following either of the two approaches might lead to prefer one of the two. From the available textbooks, listed in Sect. 10.2.4, it is clear that classical IR topics are much more covered than more recent WIR topics. This is not surprising, since classic IR has a longer history and it is very difficult, if not impossible, to have a book which is fully up to date about the last technological issues.

Since there are several classical IR books, the IR first approach would benefit from pure WIR books presenting the Web issues as an evolution of classic IR, and taking classic IR techniques and methods as prerequisite. Perhaps surprisingly, almost no such books are available: either WIR issues are dealt with (often marginally) at the end of IR books (e.g., in Manning et al. 2008), or WIR issues are introduced right from the beginning of a WIR book (e.g., in Croft et al. 2009). This might seem a serious hindrance to the IR first approach.

However, there is a solution to this problem: all "classic" WIR papers, like those mentioned in Sect. 10.2.4, are freely available on the Web, and, as I already mentioned at the end of Sect. 10.2.4, they are excellent substitutes for WIR books. Indeed, since WIR is in its beginning, these papers are usually free from too technical and difficult details and methods, and they can be easily read and followed by students. Reading research papers has also the positive effect of making students aware of the scientific method, of how researchers work, and of the main conferences and journals of the field. Finally, the most recent technological developments will not be found in books: rather, it is necessary to access resources on the Web like, major search engines pages, or specialized Web sites (e.g., search enginewatch.com or searchengineshowdown.com). Thus, the IR first approach does not suffer from the scarcity of WIR books that take IR as a prerequisite.

Turning to the WIR first approach, we see that it is supported by four books: Chakrabarti (2003), Levene (2006), Liu (2007), and Croft et al. (2009). Of course, four books are not many, but in my opinion they are quite good books, although in different respects. Moreover, the situation will change for sure in the near future, with many more WIR books being published.

Summarizing this short analysis, both approaches are compatible with currently published books.

10.4.2   Related Disciplines

Another way to study the alternative between IR first and WIR first is to analyze what is done in other fields. I see two approaches here. On the one side, well established disciplines (calculus, algebra, physics, chemistry, etc.) are more detached from the historical development. On the other side, more recent disciplines (typical examples can be found in computer science subtopics, like programming languages, operating systems, database theory, etc.) seem to be somehow reminiscent of the historical development of the field. For instance, when teaching programming language courses it is not uncommon to follow the historical evolution of the languages: Assembly, Fortran and Cobol, Algol and other structured programming languages, Object-oriented, etc.

Another similar and well discussed issue concerns introduction to computer programming courses. Among several alternatives (IEEE and ACM 2001, pp. 29–30), two are of interest here: whether to adopt an imperative-first approach and teach structured and procedural programming first, moving later to object-oriented issues perhaps going through the Abstract Data Type concept, or whether to choose an object-first approach, and teach programming directly in object-oriented terms. Both these approaches are feasible and supported by several textbooks, and none of them is criticized in IEEE and ACM 2001. During the last 10 years or so I have been adopting the imperative-first approach in first year introduction to programming courses for Engineering, Computer Science, and Information Technology students, and I am satisfied with this approach.

To summarize, although analogies and metaphors have always to be taken with caution, and this analysis is obviously rather limited, it can be said that both approaches have found their own place in other disciplines.

10.4.3   Students' and Lectures' Feedback

Two items in the questionnaire presented in Sect. 10.3 concern the Web first or IR first question, and support the "IR first stance." The answers to item 9 show that students do perceive the usefulness of classic IR to understand WIR (4.3). Also, the perception is rather strong: the 4.3 value is the higher value among all answers, and it is as high as IR usefulness to understand historical development (item 10), which is probably an unquestionable statement.

A preliminary version of this paper, focused on the Web first or IR first alternative, has been presented at TLIR'07, the First International Workshop on Teaching and Learning of Information Retrieval (Mizzaro 2007). During the presentation, and before expressing my preference to avoid any bias, I asked the about 20 attendees, several of them IR lecturers as well, which approach would they prefer. The great majority (all the audience but one) preferred the IR first approach.

10.5 Conclusions

In this paper, I have reported about my experience in teaching Web Information Retrieval at graduate level. In Sect. 10.2 I presented my course, briefly describing the syllabus, providing a (hopefully useful) list of the available textbooks and reading material, and mentioning some term projects for students. I have also maintained the effectiveness of having class presentations by students on specific technical and/or conceptual issues. In Sect. 10.3 I provided some evidence, gathered by means of a questionnaire, that students are satisfied with the course.

In Sect. 10.4, I have discussed whether a WIR course should deliver WIR issues right at course start (WIR first approach) or after a classical–historical description of classic IR issues (IR first approach). I have not found yet any hard evidence suggesting that the IR first approach is wrong; conversely I do have several clues that the IR first approach is effective (1) IR issues are a strong basis for WIR issues; (2) even if there are no books fully covering the IR-first approach, the research papers are accessible and understandable to students; using research papers has also the positive side effect of making the students acquainted with the scientific literature of the field; (3) an historical-like approach (as IR first is) is followed in several other disciplines; (4) accordingly to the results of a small survey, students do not feel unmotivated by having to wait the second half of the course for Web topics; and (5) lecturers seem to prefer the IR fist approach.

Therefore I will still use the IR first approach in the future. Anyway, I understand that for my personal teaching "style" this is the most natural approach (I am teaching introduction to programming in the same way, and during my university studies I was taught several computer science topics in the same way), which might not be true for all lecturers, and might change in the future. To mention at least a negative side of the IR first approach, I remark that it does not fit well with the students' presentations: since most of the talks are on WIR issues, these happen to be chosen quite late, toward the end of the term, and there is some organizational problem in finding an appropriate schedule before course end.

As a future development, I am considering to write a Wikibook (http://wikibooks.org) on IR, perhaps within the Wikiversity project (http://en.

wikibooks.org/wiki/Wikiversity). The book should be written collaboratively among teachers and students of (Web) IR courses, it should be freely available on the Web, it could also contain a collection of specific term projects and, in my opinion, it should be tailored to the IR first approach. Indeed, it should be a pure WIR book, assuming classical IR topics as prerequisite. No such book exists yet.

Appendix A. The Questionnaire

This questionnaire aims at providing to the lecturer useful data to improve the course. The questionnaire is fully anonymous and it is not used as an evaluation of the student.

Web Information Retrieval: Final Questionnaire The questionnaire is divided into two parts gathering, respectively, a-priori background knowledge and a-posteriori feelings and impressions on the course. Mark with a circle the numbers corresponding to your answers, remembering that:
  1 means *I strongly disagree*
  2 means *I partially disagree*
  3 means *I do not have a clear opinion*
  4 means *I partially agree*
  5 means *I strongly agree*

Part I

0) Academic year: ❐ 2004/05   ❐ 2005/06   ❐ 2006/07   ❐ 2007/08   ❐ 2008/09

1) Before the WIR course I already knew what a search engine is:

I strongly disagree   1   2   3   4   5   **I strongly agree**

2) Before course start, the number of search engines that I used was: ▭

3) Before course start I used the following search engines (write their names):

▭

4) Before course start, I already knew what an inverted index is:

I strongly disagree   1   2   3   4   5   **I strongly agree**

5) Before course start, I already knew what crawler is:

I strongly disagree   1   2   3   4   5   **I strongly agree**

Part II

6) I would have preferred more emphasis on Web related topics:

I strongly disagree   1   2   3   4   5   **I strongly agree**

7) The Web IR part is more interesting than IR part:

I strongly disagree   1   2   3   4   5   **I strongly agree**

8) The Web IR part is more difficult than IR part:

I strongly disagree   1   2   3   4   5   **I strongly agree**

9) The IR part is useful to better understand the Web IR part:

I strongly disagree   1   2   3   4   5   **I strongly agree**

10) The IR part is useful to understand the historical development of the field:

I strongly disagree   1   2   3   4   5   **I strongly agree**

11) Some topics should have been analyzed more in depth:

I strongly disagree   1   2   3   4   5   **I strongly agree**

12) Write down the topics that in your opinion should have been analyzed more in depth:

▭

13)   Some topics should have been analyzed less in depth:

I strongly disagree   1   2   3   4   5   **I strongly**
agree

14) Write down the topics that in your opinion should have been analyzed less in depth:

15) I would have preferred some further topics in the course:

I strongly disagree   1   2   3   4   5   **I strongly**
agree

16) Write down the further topics that you would have preferred:

17) Students' presentations have been interesting, useful, and understandable:

I strongly disagree   1   2   3   4   5   **I strongly**
agree

In the following two items, read a row (i.e., a pair of adjuncts) at a time and circle the number corresponding to the chosen answer (a circle for each row)

18) In your opinion, the IR part (the first part of the course) is:

	much	enough	some	none	some	enough	much	
interesting	1	2	3	4	5	6	7	boring
difficult	1	2	3	4	5	6	7	easy
important	1	2	3	4	5	6	7	unimportant
unpleasant	1	2	3	4	5	6	7	pleasant
simple	1	2	3	4	5	6	7	complex
not useful	1	2	3	4	5	6	7	useful

19) In your opinion, the Web IR part (the second part of the course) is:

	much	enough	some	none	some	enough	much	
interesting	1	2	3	4	5	6	7	boring
difficult	1	2	3	4	5	6	7	easy
important	1	2	3	4	5	6	7	unimportant
unpleasant	1	2	3	4	5	6	7	pleasant
simple	1	2	3	4	5	6	7	complex
not useful	1	2	3	4	5	6	7	useful

20) The course lasts 48 class hours. How many hours should it be, in your opinion?

21) Any other comments:

References

Albert R, Barabasi A-L (1999) Emergence of scaling in random networks. Science 286:509–512

Albert R, Jeong H, Barabasi A-L (1999) Internet: diameter of the world-wide web. Nature 401:130–131

Baeza-Yates R, Ribeiro-Neto B (1999) Modern information retrieval. ACM, New York

Barroso LA, Dean J, Hölzle U (2003) Web search for a planet: the Google cluster architecture. IEEE Micro 23(2):22–28

Belew RK (2000) Finding out about. Cambridge University Press, Cambridge, MA

Bharat K, Chang B-W, Henzinger M, Ruhl M (2001) Who links to whom: mining linkage between web sites. In: IEEE International Conference on Data Mining (ICDM '01), San Jose, CA, 29 Nov–2 Dec 2001

Blair DC (1990) Language and representation in information retrieval. Elsevier, New York

Brin S, Page L (1998) The anatomy of a large-scale hypertextual web search engine. WWW 7:107–117

Broder A, Kumar R, Maghoul F, Raghavan P, Rajagopalan S, Stata R, Tomkins A, Wiener J (2000) Graph structure in the web. Comput Netw 33(1–6):309–320

Chakrabarti S (2003) Mining the web. Morgan Kaufmann, San Francisco

Cho J, Garcia-Molina H (2000) The evolution of the web and implications for an incremental crawler. In: Proceedings of the 26th VLDB. http://rose.cs.ucla.edu/˜cho/papers/cho-evol.pdf

Croft WB, Metzler D, Strohman T (2009) Search engines – information retrieval in practice. Addison-Wesley, Harlow

Fetterly D, Manasse M, Najork M, Wiener JL (2004) A large-scale study of the evolution of web pages. Softw Pract Exp 34:213–237

Frakes WB, Baeza-Yates R (1992) Information retrieval: data structures and algorithms. Prentice-Hall, Englewood Cliffs, NJ

Grossman DA, Frieder O (2004) Information retrieval: algorithms and heuristics, 2nd edn. Springer, Heidelberg

Gulli A, Signorini A (2005) The indexable web is more than 11.5 billion pages. In: WWW14. http://www.cs.uiowa.edu/˜asignori/web-size/

IEEE & ACM (2001). The Joint Task Force on Computing Curricula – Computing curricula 2001: Computer Science – Final Report, 15 Dec 2001. http://acm.org/education/curric_vols/cc2001. pdf

Ingwersen P (1992) Information retrieval interaction. Taylor Graham, London

Ingwersen P, Järvelin K (2005) The TURN: integration of information seeking and retrieval in context. Springer, Heidelberg

Kleinberg J (1999) Authoritative sources in a hyperlinked environment. J ACM 46(5):604–632

Korfhage RR (1997) Information storage and retrieval. Wiley, New York

Lawrence S, Giles CL (1998) Searching the world wide web. Science 280:98–100

Lawrence S, Giles CL (1999) Accessibility of information on the web. Nature 400:107–109

Levene M (2006) An introduction to search engines and Web navigation. Addison-Wesley, Harlow

Liu B (2007) Web data mining – exploring hyperlinks, contents, and usage data. Springer, Heidelberg

Manning CD, Raghavan P, Schütze H (2008) Introduction to information retrieval. Cambridge University Press, Cambridge, MA

Marchionini G (1997) Information seeking in electronic environments. Cambridge University Press, Cambridge, MA

Mizzaro S (2007) Teaching of Web information retrieval: Web first or IR first? In: MacFarlane A, Fernández-Luna JM, Ounis I, Huete JF (eds) Proceedings of the first international workshop on teaching and learning in information retrieval (TLIR 2007). http://www.bcs.org/server.php? show=nav.00100v00500300100d001

Page L, Brin S, Motwani R, Winograd T (1998) The PageRank citation ranking: bringing order to the web. http://www-db.stanford.edu/~backrub/pageranksub.ps

Salton G (1989) Automatic text processing – the transformation, analysis, and retrieval of information by computer. Addison-Wesley, Harlow

Salton G, McGill MJ (1984) Introduction to modern Information retrieval. McGraw-Hill, London

van Rijsbergen CJ (1979) Information retrieval, 2nd edn. Butterworths, London

van Rijsbergen CJ (2004) The geometry of information retrieval. Cambridge University Press, Cambridge, MA

Witten IH, Moffat A, Bell TC (1999) Managing gigabytes – compressing and indexing documents and images, 2nd edn. Morgan Kaufmann, San Francisco

Chapter 11
Is a Relevant Piece of Information a Valid One? Teaching Critical Evaluation of Online Information

Josiane Mothe and Gilles Sahut

11.1 Introduction

With the digital information revolution, citizens are faced with the proliferation of information resources and ways to access them. Considering the Internet and the Web, Carr (2008) criticizes the impact of such media on the ability of people to concentrate and to reflect. He hypothesizes that human cognitive capabilities decrease when using the new technologies. On the other hand, Claburn (2008) claims that cognitive skills are improved using new technologies; basing his claim on a study at University of California that shows that searching the Web activates brain areas that are devoted to reasoning and decision making (Small et al. 2009). Indeed, media are not merely means of absorbing information but sources of reflection and thinking models (McLuhan 1964).

Several studies analyze the way people interact with the Web and virtual libraries. A study commissioned by the British Library and JISC (UCL 2008) analyzes searching behavior in virtual libraries. The authors found that users "spend as much time finding their bearings as actually viewing what they find." Additionally, this study shows that users do not spend time assessing authority; they trust in information by "dipping and cross-checking." When considering the Google generation (born after 1993), things are even worse. The study shows that young people "have a poor understanding of their information needs." As a result, they have difficulties in developing effective search strategies and in assessing the relevance of the retrieved information. Whatever the information, evaluating its quality is hard. The heterogeneity of Internet information makes the quality assessment process even harder.

J. Mothe (✉)

Institut Universitaire de Formation des Maîtres, Ecole Interne de l'Université de Toulouse le Mirail, Université de Toulouse le Miral, le Miral, France

Institut de Recherche en Informatique de Toulouse, CNRS-UMR5505, Cedex 9, France
e-mail: josiane.mothe@irit.fr

E. Efthimiadis et al. (eds.), *Teaching and Learning in Information Retrieval*,   153
The Information Retrieval Series 31, DOI 10.1007/978-3-642-22511-6_11,
© Springer-Verlag Berlin Heidelberg 2011

The academic culture may explain the behavior of the Google generation, which does not validate the information they find on the Internet. Formal education generally rests on textbooks. One of the special features of textbooks is the way they are validated at different stages: their authors are generally specialists in the book topic; textbooks have been reviewed either by peers or by editor boards; they are under the responsibility of a publication chair; they are chosen by the school, etc. and nevertheless mistakes still occur. The same kind of editorial process occurs in newspapers and more generally in the set of documents that a user will find in a library. Indeed, librarians select the documents that meet criteria that guarantee information quality; this selection occurs from a large number of documents that are published every month. Generally, books are removed from consideration for the library when self-published or edited by editors considered as nonreliable or expressing extremist political views. As a result, library users access information that has been filtered twice: before it is published by validation authorities and after it is published by librarians who select them. This process does not exclude some mistakes and bias occurs in books; in addition, because of their seriousness appearance, books can be used as vehicles of ideology.

The character of information production on the Internet is heterogeneous compared to the editorial process described above. Information literacy, a concept first introduced by Zurkowski (1974), thus becomes mandatory for people in their day to day life. Information literacy has been defined as the ability to "recognize when information is needed and have the ability to locate, evaluate, and use effectively the needed information" (ACRL 2000). Candy et al. (1994) identify information literacy as an essential element for lifelong learning. Indeed, citizens will not be more informed just because of an abundance of information and technology to access it; they need in addition to understand and to be able to use information effectively (Bundy 2004). In the case of self-education, the reader is responsible for validation of the information. Checking the validity of the information is essential. Teachers and trainers, as well as the authorities, should accompany trainees in this task of information quality assessment. Reference frames describe the skills an information literate user has but do not provide educational scenario to help teachers. This chapter offers a global view of related works in different disciplines and suggests a relation between theoretical concepts and practices.

In this chapter, we aim to point out the importance of information validity, specifically in the context of the Web, in which the quality information is variable. We provide a road map of useful criteria that should help users to ascertain the validity level of retrieved information and some pedagogical methods trainers could use to educate pupils and students. The chapter is organized as follows: Sect. 2 provides a general picture of the digital world and of the information evaluation issue. Section 3 presents elements of how Internet users evaluate information validity. Section 4 describes the educational goals and presents information validity in reference frames. Section 5 presents different studies and results and provides a taxonomy of criteria used to evaluate a piece of information. In Sect. 6 we discuss three methods that can be used to teach information validity. Finally, Sect. 7 provides some assessments and feedbacks.

11.2   Digital World, Web Users and the Information Evaluation Issue

Following the development of the Internet, information usage behavior evolved dramatically. Evaluating and selecting information became particularly complex tasks for online searchers.

First of all, people have been confronted with a very large number of information sources, which can contain contradictory or controversial information. The various levels of quality are partially due to self-publishing. Indeed, horizontal and decentralized communication constitutes one of the core principles of the Web. Beginning in the nineties, Internet users were publishing contents through personal or associative Web sites, or through forums and mailing lists. Since the middle of the following decade and the development of Web 2.0, the possibilities for people to publish content have greatly increased, with blogs, wikis, content sharing platforms, and social networks. Anyone can easily become an information producer. The counterpart of this freedom is that, when searching for information on the Web, Net users are confronted with information which has not been validated, that is to say not reviewed or subjected to a scientific or institutional authority before its publication. As a result, Internet users should now validate the information they use; validation is carried out downstream from its publication (Serres 2005).

The information validation task appears to be difficult and complex on the Internet. In the print world, document access can be done by means of a catalog. By consulting a catalog, users have access to a reference containing information on the resource: author, editor, publication date, etc. These elements make it possible to identify the origin of the information and thus to obtain a more precise idea of its degree of reliability. In addition, printed documents have a form and a physicality which allow the reader to easily recognize their nature and the kind of discourse that they convey (encyclopedia, newspaper, magazine, scientific magazine, etc.). The French historian Chartier (Chartier 2008) underlines that "a hierarchy of objects can more or less be used to indicate a hierarchy in the validity of the discourses." The digital world confuses these references. Computer screens became an aid to view any type of document or discourse. Internet users are thus confronted with a mix of different information types (Serres 2005). Thanks to the diversity of Web information, users have easy access to a plurality of sources in order to make their proper point of view on the question. However, information diversity renders more complex the task of identifying important document characteristics and evaluating the information within them, because clearly identifiable indications of these are frequently lacking.

The Internet encompasses different types of information objects. For example, blogs are usually maintained by a single person and contain either diaries or commentaries and news on a topic, whereas Wikipedia is a collaborative encyclopedia. However, the heterogeneity in terms of information objects is hidden on the Internet by a homogeneous way of searching and accessing information. Moreover, even when considering one type of object, the quality is variable (e.g. between scientific blogs and, say, more personal blogs). As another example, the encyclopedic aim of Wikipedia does not prevent it from being used as a propaganda tool. Indeed, information quality assessment is essential and even more important when considering information from the Internet.

11.3 Information Validity Assessment and Usage

Many studies consider the way users evaluate information. In the following, we do not claim to be exhaustive but rather aim at emphasizing some specific features in order to point out the need for citizens to be trained in evaluating information. Fogg et al. (2001) from Stanford University highlight that the general public considers primarily formal aspects (design, typography, colors, etc.) in judging the credibility of a site. On the other hand, resource characteristics (notoriety, statute, etc.) are taken very little into account.

Young people undervalue, even ignore, criteria concerning information validity. Hirsh (1999) presents a study of ten fifth-grade students (~10–11-year old) and shows that they very seldom quote the criterion of source authority to justify their document selection. The same conclusion was found in Boubée (2007) who observed and analyzed the behaviors of 15 primary school and high-school pupils while searching for information. When the trainees explain why they choose a given document, they refer only very seldom to criteria related to information validity or source reliability. When they do mention these criteria, the formulations typically remain vague. Grimes and Boening (2001), Brem et al. (2001), and Metzger et al. (2003) highlight that students evaluate Web sources only superficially. In their study, Le Bigot et al. (2007) corroborate these results. The 19-year-old students who participated to this study considered information coming from a personal blog as trustworthy as those emanating from a research center. In the same way, Walraven (2008) reports that students hardly evaluate results, information and sources. Thus, many studies report that evaluation skills are missing at the entire range of schooling levels.

Rieh and Hilligoss (2008) have a slightly different view. They show that students of secondary school are aware of the problems of information reliability and frequently compare several sources in order to check the information they have found. But the authors also underline the fact that the attention paid to information credibility depends on the type of search they conduce. When the search results involve other persons, young people tend to be more attentive to the source quality. Fink-Shamit and Bar-Ilan (2008) observed 77 individuals while performing information search tasks. The authors show that information quality assessment is composed of several elements such as content credibility, Web site credibility, supposed relevance and veracity assessment. Kiili et al. (2008) report the results of a study involving Finnish pupils aged 16–17 years. They point out the diversity of the skills and strategies they use to evaluate Web sources in an authentic learning task (writing an essay). The authors identify five evaluation profiles from the versatile evaluators and relevance orientated evaluators to the uncritical readers.

The authors conclude that students generally do not validate the source. Young Web users tend to privilege documents related to their search topic and newly published documents and are less aware than adults of qualitative criteria (authority, trustworthiness, etc.). Youth may be more prone to digital misinformation and less able to discern credible from noncredible sources (Flanagin and Metzger 2008).

On the other hand, Macedo-Rouet and Rouet (2008) studied how experts (in a given domain or in uses of document, such as historians or librarians) analyze and organize information. These users identify the explicit and implicit intentions of the authors and conceptualize a document as a pair composed of a source and contents. Not only do they consider the document content but also its author and the author's and source's objectives. They also succeed in forging relationships between sources, considering rhetorical associations (opposition, corroboration, etc.). The documentation expert (e.g. masters' students in library or information sciences) can more easily recognize the differences between good and bad quality documents. They use various criteria to evaluate information quality and use more criteria based on the source than do students in other disciplines; the latter can be considered as beginners in information studies (Macedo-Rouet et al. 2008).

Thus judgments of credibility used by experts are based on a process and on criteria more specific and more rigorous than those of the general public (Rouet 2006). Lessons related to librarianship skills and targeted at information quality assessment are likely to improve the competence of pupils and students.

11.4   Educational Goals for Information Quality Assessment

In this section we introduce the pedagogical objectives of teaching about information validity. Information quality assessment is considered to be the capacity to judge the quality of various pieces of information (Fitzgerald 1999).

Babu (2008) wrote an overview of the competency standards for information literacy; he shows that information quality assessment is a common issue. The *International Federation of Library Associations and Institutions* framework indicates that a qualified user must know how to evaluate information critically and competently. A qualified user "evaluates accuracy and relevance of the retrieved information." *Information literacy Standard, Indicators and School Libraries* indicates in a more precise way some specific skills related to information quality assessment. An information-literate user "determines accuracy, relevance and comprehensiveness," "distinguishes among facts, point of view and opinion," and "identifies inaccurate and misleading information." These skills can be supplemented by performance indicators. *Information Literacy Competency Standards for Higher Education* mentions that "the information literate student articulates and applies initial criteria for evaluating both the information and its sources"; he "validates understanding and interpretation of the information through discourse with other individuals, subject-area experts and/or practitioners."

Bundy (2004) edited the Australian and New Zealand Information Literacy Framework. Skills that are linked to information quality assessment are mentioned in a precise way, since according to this framework an information literate person is able to define and apply criteria for information quality assessment; this implies that an information literate person:

- Examines and compares information from various sources to evaluate reliability, validity, accuracy, authority, timeliness and point of view or bias
- Analyzes the structure and logic of supporting arguments or methods
- Recognizes and questions prejudice, deception or manipulation
- Recognizes the cultural, physical or other context within which the information was created and understands the impact of context on interpreting the information
- Recognizes and understands own biases and cultural context

These skills are also mentioned in almost identical terms in the *ALA* (American Library Association) and *ACRL* (Association of College and Research Libraries) published in 2000 (ACRL 2000) frameworks.

The French frameworks devoted to information literacy mention information quality assessment but with very few details. The FADBEN (Federation of Librarians of the French National Education System) framework published in 1997 mentions that high-school pupils should know how to select references with regard to some identified criteria (novelty, topicality, source, etc.) and how to analyze information in order to consider its subjectivity. The B2i (data-processing and Internet certificate for compulsory education) integrates information knowledge as well as data-processing technique skills. Pupil should have a critical and considered attitude with respect to the available digital information. A qualified person:

- Knows how to evaluate the subjectivity or partiality of a discourse
- Knows to distinguish a rational argument from an authority argument
- Learns how to identify, classify, organize hierarchically, criticize information, etc.

When analyzing these international guidelines, one can conclude that information quality assessment is universally regarded as an essential component of information literacy. We can also note that the guidelines and goals related to this skill are not equally detailed and do not consist of the same items in the different guidelines. Nevertheless, all guidelines mention critical analysis of the source using identified criteria either in an implicit or explicit way. Other skills relate to the informational contents and the discourse conveyed by the source (e.g. a literate person analyzes the structure and logic of supporting arguments or methods, knows how to evaluate the subjectivity or partiality of a discourse, etc.).

Theoretical approaches on how to teach information evaluation supplement the study of guidelines. Fitzgerald (1999) highlights the complex character of this task. According to her, components of evaluation include:

- Meta-cognition: it is defined as "knowledge or cognition that takes as its object or regulates any aspect of any cognitive endeavor" (Flavell 1981 referenced in Fitzgerald 1999).
- Source and information quality assessment are often associated with critical thinking. It is a core element in the media literacy programs of Anglo-Saxon countries (Piette 1996).
- Prior knowledge in a searched topic is an important component. However, it can also be a brake on learning new knowledge on the topic or to validate information that one will consider as true (Fitzgerald 1999).

11.5   Information Evaluation Criteria

As noted before, users can enumerate the criteria that justify their document selection. Researchers have also studied how searchers act and what should be the criteria an information literate user should use. Some lists of criteria have been derived from this and are available in the literature [see for example Barry and Schamber (1998), Boubée (2007)].

In the following, we propose a schema that presents the various evaluation criteria we consider as important for evaluating information. This schema takes into account previous works and guidelines previously mentioned in this chapter. Our goal is not to observe and report actual practice but rather to provide point of reference to teachers whose aim is to train users to be critical about information. Indeed, our experience as teacher trainers has shown us that teachers and librarians often face difficulties in conceiving teaching activities and distinguishing and treating on a hierarchical basis the evaluation criteria in order to teach them.

Indeed defining information quality is a complex and multifacetted issue. Numerous information quality frameworks that propose different criteria exist (Knight and Burn 2005). For example, the Université de Montréal suggests a grid that can be used to evaluate a Web page (Guertin et al. 2009). The authors consider three main classes of clues that can be used in order to evaluate the quality of a Web page. In the first part, the authors suggest considering the author of the page (Is he identified? What are the competences of the authors with regard to the page content? What is the publication date?, etc.) Secondly, they suggest considering the page content in terms of quality (clarity, objectivity, contradictory, citations, information noise such as ads) and finally the last part considers the importance of the page with regard to the objectives of the reader.

One difficulty when enumerating criteria is that there is no single terminology to designate these criteria. Information scientists and communication researchers

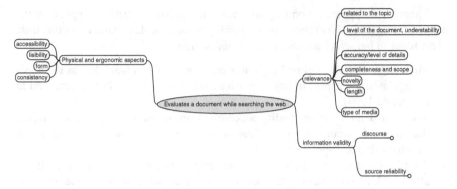

Fig. 11.1 Main criteria to evaluate document

often use different terms to denote close concepts such authority, credibility, reliability, trustworthiness, etc. (Savolainen 2007).

To try to solve these ambiguities and to facilitate the development of teaching sequences, we propose two diagrams that summarize and treat on a hierarchical basis the principal criteria of information quality assessment in the context of Web information retrieval.

Figure 11.1 provides a general picture of what document evaluation covers. We distinguish three main types of criteria. Physical and ergonomic aspects refer to criteria associated with the form of the document, its accessibility (including restricted access, price, software used to read it), its consistency (table of contents, delivers what it is supposed to, etc.), whereas relevance and validity are related to the information content. Indeed, like Rouet (2006) and Kiili et al. (2008), when considering information content, we distinguish information validity and information relevance. Document relevance refers to the fact that a document answers a user's information need in a given context (Mizzaro 1998). A document can be relevant, that is to say can appear to satisfy the user's information need, while containing errors, out-of-date data, or bias. A relevant document will address the research topic (*related to the topic criteria*); the user will be able to understand it and learn something from it (*level of the document, understandability*). According to the level of search, the user can also privilege the documents which treat various facets of the subject – this can also help him to specify his information need – or those which are precise enough (*accuracy/level of details and completeness and scope*). The document should contain up to date information (*novelty, topicality*). Of course, the length and type of media will be what the user is looking for e.g. video, music, etc. (*length, type of media*).

Figure 11.2 describes the information validity aspects (quality of the information content) in more detail. One generally considers as valid information which has been produced recently by an honest and qualified person in the field working from a disinterested stand point. Evaluating information validity consists of checking if the information meets these qualities (Sahut and Tricot 2010).

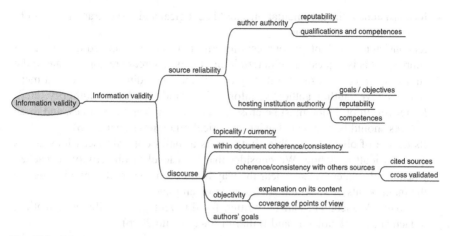

Fig. 11.2 Criteria related to information validity

Pupils must learn how to analyze the reliability of the source in order to be able to assess its credibility[1] on rational bases. That supposes that they can identify the source reliability. Source reliability depends not only on the author's authority but also on the institution's authority as well. The authority of the author depends on his reputability, his titles and functions, the quality and the number of his publications, his competences in the domain. In the same way, pupils and students have to be able to determine if information the author has published has been reviewed and validated prior to its publication and consider the intentions of the validating authority (for example the editor, the press agency, etc.) as well as the reputability, and the degree of expertise.

However, it is important not to systematically trust a validated document, merely because it has been validated in a particular context. Indeed, the competences and objectives of the institution or of the persons who have validated the information can sometimes be called in question. In such a case, it is mandatory to analyze the informational contents of the document in order to identify the kind of the discourse[2] (scientific, militant, encyclopedic, etc.)[3] and to evaluate the following aspects:

– Its topicality: the facts and data that are mentioned in the document should be valid at the time they are read.

---

[1] Like Macedo-Rouet and Rouet (2008) we consider that credibility is the subjective perception of the information receiver on its reliability.

[2] We considered that the discourse is a practical application of a language. Any discourse is subject to standards and organizational rules that exist in a given social group. In addition, any discourse testifies a transmitter's aim; the transmitter aims at producing an effect on the receiver (e.g. to cause a stir, persuade the reader or inform him) Mainguenau (2007).

[3] Some of these types of discourses can be declined into more specific types. For example, when they talk to general public, journalists use discourses that are codified according to quite particular types (reporting, editorial, news, etc.).

- Its consistency: the argumentation should be logical and no contradiction should occur within the document.
- Its consistency with other sources: this criterion can be evaluated through cited sources. This is a question of determining if these sources are appropriate to the subject covered for example if they are reliable according to the criteria mentioned above (author authority, information validation by an authority, etc.). Moreover, information must be cross-validated using various sources, and these sources should be connected using rhetorical relations (Rouet 2006).
- Its degree of objectivity. Objectivity refers to philosophical discussions and is quite difficult to define. We consider that high level of objectivity is reached when the document makes clear the way it has been constructed and it refers to the main points of view and studies on a given topic.
- Its goals. A document can be written for different goals: militant, scientific, didactical, etc. (Duplessis and Ballarini-Santonocito 2006).

Of course any criterion is subjective and can be applied differently according to the domain and the type of discourse of the document. For example, if the document topicality is a very important criterion for domains such as technologies, data become outdated slower in human sciences.

Text consistency can be evaluated differently according to whether the text is narrative, explanatory, descriptive, etc. Scientific discourses are at the same time coherent with other discourses but they are likely to bring something new, which is in rupture with the usual discourse.

In addition, we may note that these various criteria should be combined in order to assign an informational value to the document.

The examination of guidelines, didactic tools and teaching sequences in the field of information literacy makes it possible to identify competences that depend on information validity evaluation in order to:

- Evaluate the source reliability considering the competences of the author, his intentions, information topicality
- Differentiate the sources according to their level and their reliability degree
- Use various sources in order to compare and cross-validate information

Acquiring these competences supposes the understanding of certain concepts arising from the library and information sciences (author, editor, method of information creation, quotations, source, etc.) which allow one to better apprehend the conditions of information production and validation.

11.6 Teaching Validity

In this section, we present different ways to teach information validity to trainees. We considered pedagogical scenario from French databases (Edubases documentation, http://www.educnet.education.fr/bd/urtic/documentation/, Aivasat http://docs.

ac-toulouse.fr/aivasat/recherche.php), collaborative Web sites librarian teachers maintain (Docs pour docs http://docsdocs.free.fr/) as well as our proper experience.

We considered three different ways for a trainer to make trainees learning about information validity. They correspond to three different goals: awakening trainees, developing skills, and integrating skills in practice.

11.6.1 Awakening Students to the Information Validity Issue

The objective of this teaching is to show Internet users that some pieces of information seem valid while they are not. Teachers could search for real information that is already on the Web. However, some Web sites are built exactly to this purpose. For example, Teacher tap (http://eduscapes.com/tap/topic32.htm) lists misleading Web sites that can be "parodies, satire, hoaxes, or designed to show students the importance of questioning information found on the Web." Tic Tac doc does the same for resources in French (http://aristide.12.free.fr/spip.php?article84).

In order to illustrate this type of teaching approach, we report a teaching sequence carried out by Pierrat (2006) with 15- and 16-year-old pupils. Pupils are asked to answer questions about an animal called a "dahu" using some preselected sites. The types of questions they have to answer are: Which are the main characteristics of a dahu? Where does it live? Information pooling shows that the various visited sites are contradictory. This raises the crucial question: Does a dahu really exist? Pupils are then asked to consider various elements (author of the Web site, nature of the site, mention of the sources, etc.) which help them to evaluate the reliability of the sources using a grid. The main principle of this type of teaching activity is to develop a culture of doubt and a form of skepticism.

However, professionals of information and education do not completely agree with this teaching approach. Indeed it implies that some pages that contain errors and whimsical information are edited on the Web, sometimes on reliable sites (if only the other pages are considered). This teaching approach contributes to the bad quality of information available on the Web through misleading sites. And some teachers prefer to base their programs upon established and trustworthy information such as ipl2 (http://www.ipl.org/), which is the result of a merger of the Internet Public Library (IPL) and the Librarians' Internet Index (LII) or the Internet Scout Project (http://scout.cs.wisc.edu).

In addition, teaching practices that uses false information created for teaching purposes appear to lead to a binary representation of the quality of information (either true or false), which is undoubtedly one possibility for starting a training but which is reducing to train pupils with a task as complex as the information validity evaluation.

11.6.2 Developing Skills

The objective of this second pedagogic approach is to lead pupils to compare various sources using skill grids. The objectives of this teaching is first to provide skill grids and second, ways of using them. The role of the teacher is to preselect a certain number of documents on a hotly debated topic in order to confront pupils with discourses of various natures (institutional, scientific, media, militant, etc.). To analyze and to compare the preselected documents, it is possible either to give the students a grid of pre-established criteria or to help them building one.

Following a pooling of the analysis results of the various sites, the teacher can take again the various criteria and specify some of the concepts related to information validation. The purpose of this type of teaching activity is to lead pupils to characterize the various information sources, to identify the objectives of these sources and their degree of reliability. This type of activity refers in an implicit way to the Rouet' expert model of source uses (Rouet 2006) mentioned above.

However, Serres (2005) makes the point that some of the grids used for these teaching activities mix criteria related to the content and criteria related to the form. In order not to be too technical, he recommends teaching students some of the main concepts such as relevance, information quality, information organization, etc.

11.6.3 Based on Practice Skills

In this case, the objective of the pedagogical scenario is to place students in the role of information producer; authors who aim at providing valid information to Internet users.

This type of project is likely to improve information literacy because it is centered on the information production. Pupils can understand, in a concrete way, the various constraints that media production faces (temporal, technical, financial, linguistic, documentary, etc.) and the conditions under which choices are made. One interesting case is the development and correction of articles on collaborative encyclopedia resting on wiki technology (Wikipedia, Wikimini, etc.).[4] Students are first asked to analyze how the tool works and what the editorial rules are. They are then asked to locate articles that could be improved and to make the modifications they consider as necessary. The objective is to lead students to respect the constraints related to this mode of publication (sourcing, neutrality of the point of view, etc.) and thus to understand requirements for producing high quality pieces of information.

---

[4] In English, several projects are listed on Wikipedia:School and university projects http://en.wikipedia.org/wiki/Wikipedia:School_and_university_projects.

In French, a project description can be found on the following web page: Wikipedia:projets pédagogiques http://fr.wikipedia.org/wiki/Wikip%C3%A9dia:Projets_p%C3%A9dagogiques.

To conclude, we will mention different recommendations on teaching informa-tion validity:

- Acquiring evaluation skills implies a sufficient amount of time devoted to their teaching as well as regular practice. "Evaluating is much too difficult a process to be taught in one unit" (Fitzgerald 1999).
- Practicing debates that require formal argumentation is also likely to develop these skills (Fitzgerald 1999).
- It can be also relevant to lead pupils to browse the history and discussion pages of a Wikipedia article (Flanagin and Metzger 2008; Francke and Sundin 2009). That can result to a clearer identification of the various criteria of information quality assessment in collaborative encyclopedia. These criteria are then largely applicable to all types of sites, in their work in sociology of sciences (Callon and Latour 1990) proposes a specific activity for students at the university; this activity being complementary to the teaching activities we described above. The students are put in situation where they are asked to follow and analyze scientific controversies: they have to locate the various actors of the controversy, the relationships that link them, the arguments considered in the debate. This type of activity makes it possible to go further than a binary approach of information evaluation (true/false). The advantage of this activity is that it locates information in the social domain and makes people become aware of the temporal and conflicting character of information and knowledge.

11.7   Assessment and Feedback

Several authors report that it is difficult to improve students' information evaluation practices. Boisvert (2002) shows that skills used to evaluate resource credibility increase very slowly during schooling.

Studies take into account the practice and show the difficulty in teaching students information evaluation skills, which are truly effective. In higher educa-tion, Manuel (2005) observes that the first-year students can be able, after a training, to quote evaluation criteria such as authority and credibility, scope, coverage, relevance, bias, accuracy, currency, navigability, commercialism. However she also points out that they face real difficulties in applying these criteria to the documents they find. Mothe (2010) shows that even if students acknowledge they learnt some skills they think they will not change their practices.

The central problem seems to be the durable integration of information evalua-tion skills and their transfer from a learning situation to other situations. Walraven (2008) tested two educational programs on students. The first program is called "the high road program" and aims at developing meta-cognitive skills. In this program, teachers draw the attention of students to the various steps in a validation process and to the way these steps can be used flexibly in different situations. The second one is called "the rich representation theory" and it aims at helping students to acquire deep knowledge of concepts associated with the key concept of evaluation. For that, students are required by teachers to discuss the evaluation criteria of some sites and use mind mapping in order to represent them. Walraven (2008) shows that these two programs help the transfer of the information evaluation skills.

11.8 Conclusion

In this chapter, we analyzed various frameworks in order to elaborate a synthetic approach of the skills linked to information evaluation: we distinguished skills associated with source analysis and skills associated with discourse analysis.

We also clarify criteria that can be used to evaluate information from a teaching perspective: a first level considers three main classes: physical and ergonomic aspects, relevance and information validity. Considering the information validity, the criteria as directly associated with the skills we mentioned above.

Finally, we depicted three teaching models associated with these skills:

- Awakening students to the information validity issue by providing trainees with pages that contain either errors or controversial information (eventually built by teachers themselves).
- Developing skills by using skill grids and some chosen pages.
- Based on practice by placing trainees in the role of information producer.

Considering the difficulty the students face to apply the concepts they learn, whatever the model the teacher chooses, it is essential to devote enough time to practical application. In addition, as teachers training school teachers, we think that teachers continuing education is a key component of information literacy.

References

ACRL (2000) Information literacy competency standards for higher education. Association of College & Research Libraries, Chicago, IL

Babu R (2008) Information literacy – competency standards and performance indicators: an overview. J Libr Inf Technol 28(2):56–65

Barry CL, Schamber L (1998) Users' criterias for relevance evaluation: a cross study comparison. Inf Process Manag 24(2/3):219–236

Boisvert J (2002) Pensée critique et sciences humaines – étude sur l'évolution de la pensée critique des élèves du programme de sciences humaines au collégial. Research report, Cégep

Boubée N (2007) Des pratiques documentaires ordinaires: Analyse de l'activité de recherche d'information des élèves du secondaire. PhD thesis, Université de Toulouse Le Mirail

Brem SR, Russel S, Weems L (2001) Science on the web: student evaluations of scientific arguments. Discourse Process 32:191–213

Bundy A (2004) Australian and New Zealand information literacy framework, principles, standards and practices, 2nd edn. Library Publications, University of South Australia, Mt. Gambier

Callon M, Latour B (1990) La science telle qu'elle se fait, Paris, éditions La Découverte

Candy P, Crebert G, O'Leary J (1994) Developing lifelong learners through undergraduate education. AGPS, Canberra

Carr N (2008) Is Google making us stupid? The Atlantic 302(1):56–58, 60, 62–63

Chartier R (2008) Le livre: Son passé, son avenir. La Vie des idées.fr, 29 Septembre 2008

Claburn T (2008) Is Google making us smarter? Information Week articleID = 211200721

Duplessis P, Ballarini-Santonocito I (2006) Véridicité. In: Dictionnaire des concepts info-documentaires. http://www.savoirscdi.cndp.fr/index.php?id=432. Accessed 21 June 2010

FADBEN (1997) Référentiel: Compétences en information-documentation. Fédération des enseignants documentalistes de l'Education nationale, Médiadoc, 28p

Fink-Shamit N, Bar-Ilan J (2008) Information quality assessment on the Web- an expression of behaviour. Inf Res 13(4):paper 357

Fitzgerald MA (1999) Evaluating information: an information literacy challenge, vol 2. School Library Media Research, Chicago, IL

Flanagin A, Metzger M (2008) In: Flanagin A, Metzger M (eds) Digital media and youth: Unparalleled opportunity and unprecedented responsibility. The MIT Press, Cambridge

Flavell JH (1981) Cognitive monitoring. In: Dickson W (ed) Children's oral communication skills. Academic, New York

Fogg BJ et al (2001) What makes websites credible? A report on a large quantitative study. CHI 3:61–68

Francke H, Sundin O (2009) In search of credibility: Pupils' information practices in learning environments. Inf Res 14:4

Grimes DJ, Boening CH (2001) Worries with the Web: a look at student use of Web resources. Coll Res Libr 62:11–22

Guertin et al (2009) Chercher pour trouver. www.ebsi.umontreal.ca/jetrouve/

Hirsh SG (1999) Children's relevance criteria and information seeking on electronic resources. J Am Soc Inf Sci 50(14):1265–1283

Kiili C, Laurinen L, Marttunen M (2008) Students evaluating internet sources: from versatile evaluators to uncritical readers. J Educ Comput Res 39(1):75–95

Knight SA, Burn JM (2005) Developing a framework for assessing information quality on the World Wide Web. Inf Sci 8:159–172

Le Bigot L, Rouet JF, Coutieras A, Goumi A (2007) Comment mieux évaluer les informations issues de sources multiples? In: Proceedings EIAH'07, Lausanne

Macedo-Rouet M, Rouet J-F (2008) Qui dit quoi ? L'évaluation des sources, une compétence d'avenir. Usages, usagers et compétences informationnelles au 21e siècle. Hermes

Mainguenau D (2007) Analyser les textes de communication. Armand Colin, Paris

Manuel K (2005) What do first-year students know about information research? And what can we teach them? National Conference of the Association of College and Research Libraries, Chicago, IL, pp 401–417

McLuhan M (1964) Understanding media, the extensions of man. McGraw-Hill, New York

Metzger MJ, Flanagin AJ, Zwarun L (2003) College student Web use, perceptions of information credibility, and verification behaviour. Comput Educ 41:271–290

Mizzaro S (1998) How many relevances in information retrieval. Interact Comput 10:303–320

Mothe J (2010) Teaching information validity – Case study, Internal report, IRIT/RR-2010-21-FR

Pierrat B (2006) Chasser le dahu au bahut. Médialog 60:4–9

Piette J (1996) Education aux médias et fonction critique. L'Harmattan, Paris

Rieh SY, Hilligoss B (2008) College students' credibility judgements in the information-seeking process. In: Digital media youth and credibility. The MIT Press, Cambridge, pp 49–72

Rouet JF (2006) The skills of document use: from text comprehension to Web based learning. Lawrence Erlbaum Associates, Mahwah

Rouet M, Rouet JF, Zampa V, Bouin E (2008) L'information sur Internet: Le jugement de crédibilité des usagers. In: SFSIC, article 132

Sahut G, Tricot A (2010) Dictionnaire des concepts et des notions. In Rivano P et al (eds) Aide à la
    Validation du Socle commun – Académie de Toulouse
Savolainen R (2007) Media credibility and cognitive authority. The case of seeking orienting
    information. Inf Res 12(3):319
Serres A (2005) Evaluation de l'information sur Internet: Le défi de la formation [Evaluating
    information from the Internet]. Bull Bibliothèques de France 6:38–44
Small G, Moody T, Siddarth P, Bookheimer S (2009) Your brain on Google: patterns of cerebral
    activation during internet searching. Am J Geriatr Psychiatr 17(2):116–126
UCL (2008) Information behaviour of the researcher of the future.
Walraven A (2008) Becoming a critical websearcher: effects of instruction to foster transfer. PhD
    thesis. Arhnem, Openuniversiteit Nederland
Zurkowski PG (1974) The information environment: relationships and priorities. National Com-
    mission on Libraries and Information Science, Washington DC

Chapter 12
Training Students to Evaluate Search Engines

Mark Sanderson and Amy Warner

12.1 Other Things to Teach

It would appear that there are two classic expectations about the sorts of students that will result from information retrieval courses. In Computer Science (CS), students who go on to use the skills they learn will either implement IR systems or they will research novel techniques which will eventually be of interest to developers of IR systems. Within courses taught in Information Schools (IS), there is an expectation that students will learn how search engines work and so in their eventual place of employment they will be effective managers of information and/or know how to query for data expertly. However, it is increasingly clear that there is an emerging set of skills that need to be taught in both types of department.

Ever increasing numbers of organisations offer search of their information for either internal or external use, using common commercial search solutions set in their default configuration. There is a growing realisation amongst the organisations that these standard settings are not producing the ideal searching system and that adjustment and customisation could provide a substantially improved service. However, exactly how such customisation can be done is poorly understood in most organisations.

White (2006) suggested that such improvements will be brought about by a multi-disciplinary search team composed of both CS and IS trained people monitoring and manipulating the performance of the engine for an organisation. We have started exercises within our IR course to address the training needs for the IS people in White's suggested teams. To this end, we created a course that teaches both how information retrieval systems work and the range of possible ways (from IR research) that the systems could be improved. As the only way that improvements and customisations can be assessed is through evaluation, this topic was a key

M. Sanderson (✉)
School of CS & IT, RMIT University, Melbourne, VIC, Australia
e-mail: mark.sanderson@rmit.edu.au

E. Efthimiadis et al. (eds.), *Teaching and Learning in Information Retrieval*,
The Information Retrieval Series 31, DOI 10.1007/978-3-642-22511-6_12,
© Springer-Verlag Berlin Heidelberg 2011

component of the course delivered both through lectures and coursework. The coursework on evaluation is what is described in this chapter.

It was decided that a problem led teaching approach would be taken with the coursework with students set two different evaluations:

1. The students were instructed to find a Web-based search engine, which they had to assess, reporting on its qualities as well as detailing ways in which it could be improved.
2. The students collectively conducted a test collection-like measurement of the effectiveness of two search engines, which were indexing the same information. Here, the work was conducted in collaboration with an information provider.

These two evaluations are now described in more detail. The work described here was carried out while the author was working at the Information School at the University of Sheffield, UK.

12.2   First Evaluation: Assessing a Search Engine

The inspiration for this style of coursework was taken from the work of Heuwing et al. (2009) who assessed a wide range of publicly accessible company-based extranet search engines across a range of evaluation criteria. The broad finding was that most of the engines were poorer than a Google search restricted to the company's public Web pages (commonly known as a *site search*). However, it was clear from the study that it was possible to optimise a locally run search engine to outperform Google. This work showed the generally poor state of locally run search services on the Web, while at the same time demonstrating the improvement to search quality that local knowledge of information and users can bring about. It was decided, therefore to set coursework where the students were given the task to seek out and assess a poorly performing search engine and recommend ways in which it could be improved.

12.2.1 Education Goals and Objectives

The educational goals of the exercise were to get students to assess and suggest improvements for a search engine that they had found. The educational objectives of the exercise were that at the end of the coursework students would be able to:

- Find a suitable search engine to study in their coursework.
- Identify the general characteristics/qualities of the users of the selected search engine.
- Determine the needs of those users.
- Assess the ability of the search engine to meet those needs.

• Apply a relevant sub-set of the course's lecture material so as to meet the identified needs.

An additional objective of the work was to demonstrate to the students that there was great potential for improving established search services and that with the knowledge gained during the course that they were potentially in a position to provide those improvements.

12.2.2   Practicalities of the Exercise

A structure was provided to the students to help them complete the work successfully. In order to maximise the students' chances of finding a search engine in need of improvement, they were told to focus on candidate engines from relatively small organisations. They were told to avoid organisations where search was their core business (e.g. Google, Bing, YouTube, etc.) as it was unlikely that students would be able to come up with valuable suggestions for improvements. The students were asked to demonstrate their understanding of the search engine audience by constructing a set of queries, which they considered might typically be submitted to their chosen system.

Using Broder's two main categories of queries (Broder 2002), they were asked to detail which were navigational (queries aimed at locating a home page within the site) and which were informational (queries seeking documents containing relevant information). The students were asked to demonstrate the workings of the search site, the content of search results and how they were laid out. Finally, the students were asked to describe which ideas from course materials or even independently found research papers could be used to potentially improve the search engine.

12.2.3   The Running of the Exercise

This exercise was run at the University of Sheffield for 3 years in a course taken each year by both undergraduate and Masters level students. Such is the range of search sites available on the net, across the 90 or so students who have taken this exercise, only a small handful of sites were assessed more than once. Highlights from the exercises run so far include:

– A detailed critique of the UK Government's DirectGov search engine[1] using both an extensive literature review and multiple examples of queries that fail to find any relevant item. Along with suggestions on how the search engine could be improved.

---

[1] In more recent years, the quality of this search engine has been much improved.

- An examination of the search engine of a UK regional newspaper, where the students conducting the evaluation, upon finding an extensive audio interview archive on the newspaper Web site, suggested the addition of speech recognition technology to provide transcripts which could be searched.
- A student while trying to locate the sort of searches conducted on a UK University Web site used the Alexa service[2] to research typical queries used.
- Finally, an examination of the search engines behind a Pakistani newspaper, which published its articles simultaneously in Urdu and English. Different search engines were used for the two languages and the student used this situation to contrast the features of the two engines by issuing the same query (translated to the correct language) to both engines. The value of spell correction or stemming present in one search engine but not the other could be shown in this situation.

Students reported their work back through a 10-min presentation to the class and in a written report.

12.3   Second Evaluation: Test Collection Evaluation

Test collections have long been a standard way in which a searching system can be evaluated. The three classic components of a document collection, a set of queries (also known as topics), accompanied with a set of relevance judgements (also known as qrels) have their origins in work dating back to the early 1950s (Thorne 1955; Gull 1956). Used in conjunction with an evaluation measure, the test collection has been a classic form of evaluation since that early work. Even in the past 10 years where the rise of the query log analysis has taken a greater role in assessing search effectiveness, it is clear that test collections still form a core part of the evaluation processes of major search companies; see White and Morris (2007) and Chapelle et al. (2009) for brief descriptions of test collections used in Microsoft and Yahoo! respectively.

It was decided to engage the students in building a component of a test collection for a search engine as part of their coursework. At this time, the UK Government's archive, TNA (The National Archives) approached the author asking if it would be possible to run a student project to assess the effectiveness of their publicly facing search engine[3] and, as Heuwing et al. (2009) had done, contrast it with Google site search. In the past, the department had run Masters student projects on measuring search output, the most notable of which had resulted in the creation of a well-used test collection (Davies 1983). However, the outcomes of such

---

[2] http://www.alexa.com/.

[3] http://www.nationalarchives.gov.uk/.

projects were entirely dependent on the skills of a single student. Therefore, a more fault tolerant less risky approach was considered.

Analysing search logs from TNA, the most popular queries to the search engine were identified for use in the test collection; more detail is provided in the "Queries" section. As building relevance assessments for such a collection can be a time consuming process it was decided to partition the gathering of assessments across the students taking the course. The students were each given a set of queries against which they were asked to assess the relevance of the top n documents returned by the TNA search engine and Google site search. The students were given different sets of queries and by working in a "crowdsourcing fashion" they were hopefully able to assess a sufficient number of queries to produce a statistically meaningful evaluation.

12.3.1 Educational Goals and Objectives

The educational goals of the exercise were to engage students in an actual comparison of two search engines. Students would conduct the evaluation and write a report on their experiences of the two search engines as well as their view on which was the better engine. Thus the educational objectives were that at the end of the exercise the students would be able to:

- Conduct a test collection-like evaluation comparing two search engines
- Compute an evaluation measure over a set of results
- Conduct a broader evaluation of the two systems taking into account a wide range of qualities of the search engine
- Describe how hard it can be to judge the relevance of documents

As with the earlier exercise, an additional objective of this exercise was to show students the potential for improving the quality of search systems, and a real world example of the importance of a search engine.

12.3.2 Running the Exercise

As with any coursework, it was important to ensure that students were clear on what they had to do. As the plan was to use outputs from each student in a formal comparison of search engines, the importance of the clarity of instructions to students was even stronger. It was important to gather data that enabled the course lecturer to check the information that students returned. Several iterations of the exercise were run, each introducing a new element that reduced the chance of error and speeded up the use of the student generated evaluation data.

Here we describe the four main components of the exercise, how students worked with or generated those components and how the exercise has evolved over its multiple running.

12.3.2.1 Search Engines

The exercise involved comparing two search engines which indexed the same collection. The first engine was TNA's search tool available in the top right hand corner of all the pages on its Web site, the second was Google searching over just TNA Web pages, invoked with the command "site:www.nationalarchives.gov.uk" typed into the search box in addition to any entered query, see Fig. 12.1.

Monitoring of outputs from the students indicated that most successfully followed the instructions to search on these two Web sites. However, a number were found to have issued different queries or they did not use the site restriction on Google correctly. In an attempt to reduce these errors, a more managed system was created with a standard Web-based form into which the students entered their query and choose from a popup menu which search engine the query was to be sent to, see Fig. 12.2.

Use of this form in the most recent running of the exercise reduced the number of errors in the data provided by students.

12.3.2.2 Queries

The queries that the students ran against the search engines were manually selected from query logs drawn from the TNA search engine. The queries chosen were the most popular queries submitted to the engine. Only the text of each query was preserved in the log, therefore a TNA staff member familiar with the content of the collections selected, studied and augmented a sub-set of popular queries with a written description detailing the searcher's probable information need. After an initial analysis of the logs, it was discovered that there were both informational and navigational queries being submitted to the TNA system, from the categories of Broder (2002), therefore queries were also tagged as either navigational or informational. Determination of these two types were made by the TNA staff member based on their knowledge of the internal structure of the TNA Web site, and the data TNA held. For navigational queries, there were certain home pages known to be good starting points for types of search, such as family history or census queries.

In total, 48 queries – 24 informational, 24 navigational – were selected; each student was given 5–6 to run on both search engines. The queries were given to at least two students so that if one student was found to have made a mistake, hopefully the topic would still be assessed correctly by the other.

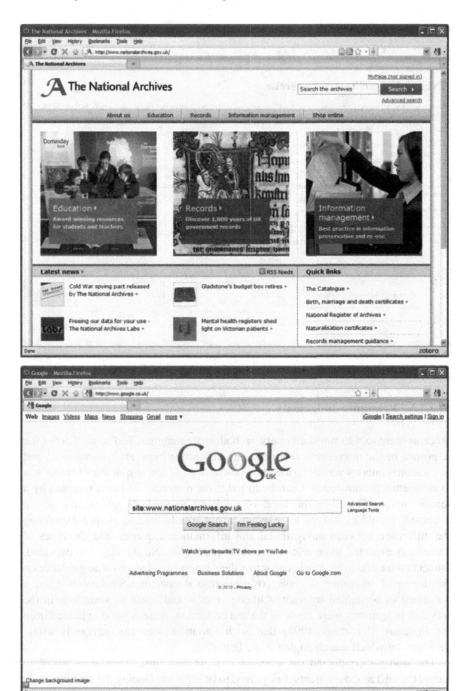

Fig. 12.1 Screenshots of the two search engines to be compared

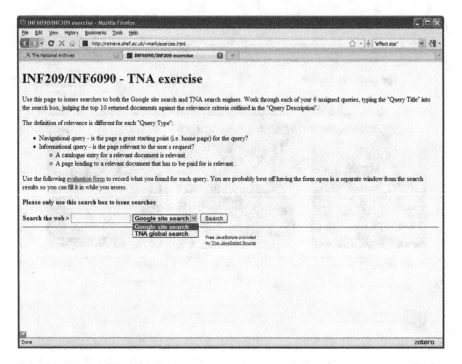

Fig. 12.2 Customised query entry form

12.3.2.3 Relevance Judgments

Students were told to run each query on both search engines and to note down the relevance of the documents returned. The difference between informational and navigational queries was described to students. Part of the aim of the exercise was to show students how hard it can be to judge the relevance of items returned by a search engine. Therefore the level of guidance to students on exactly how a document should be judged as relevant or not was limited to simply explaining the difference between navigational and informational queries and the types of documents expected to be relevant to each query type. No training was provided. Students were told to be consistent across their judgments, but given no guidance on the degree of relevance or topic coverage in a document necessary to cause a document to be judged relevant. Although this would result in variations in the way that judgements were made in the test collection, there is good evidence from the literature (Voorhees 1998) that such variation does not adversely affect decisions on which search engine is the better.

The students conducted the exercise in their own time. They were asked to record the URLs of documents they judged to be relevant. Getting the students to do this was found to help the course lecturer monitor for any mistakes made by students. In the initial running of the exercise students were told to email results to the course coordinator, in subsequent running of the exercise, an online form was created to ensure that data returned was structured and complete. The level of detail gathered in the form was increased over time.

In the current version (see Fig. 12.3), the students enter their name, the title of the query, indicate the query type, and detail the degree of relevance for each of the top 10 results for both search engines on that query. A large text entry box is provided where the students copy the URL of any relevant or partially relevant documents found.

12.4 Evaluation Measure

The evaluation measure, precision at rank 10, was initially used chosen because of its long standing popularity. As degrees of relevance were being gathered, Discounted Cumulative Gain (DCG) measured at rank 10 (Järvelin and Kekäläinen 2000) was also calculated. Using the most recent relevance judgement form, the measures could be computed automatically. In addition, statistical significance and power analysis tests were conducted to determine the importance of comparisons made between the two search engines' outputs.

12.4.1 Feeding Results Back to Students

The first two times the exercise was run, the results from the students were collated by the course instructor and a brief summary of the comparisons between the systems was fed back to students in the next lecture. However, it was realized that more could be done with this part of the coursework. In the last two runs of the exercise, a longer feedback session was held. Here a spreadsheet of all the data from the students was displayed in a lecture and the details of the way in which the data was manipulated to produce a scientific result were demonstrated live to the students.

This included showing how the results from the students were checked for errors with mistaken input removed from the calculations. Then the scores for the same query from multiple students were merged before an overall score for the two search engines was calculated and compared. Students were shown the comparisons as well as details of statistical significance tests that were run to determine the probability of the differences observed being due to chance. Splitting the queries by type (i.e. navigational/informational) and re-computing the comparisons was also done as were comparisons with results from previous runs of the experiment.

The chief priority of the work was to construct an experimental design that students would be able to conduct correctly and complete, without being over burdened with unnecessary procedure. However, taking a simplistic approach meant there were flaws in the experimental methodology:

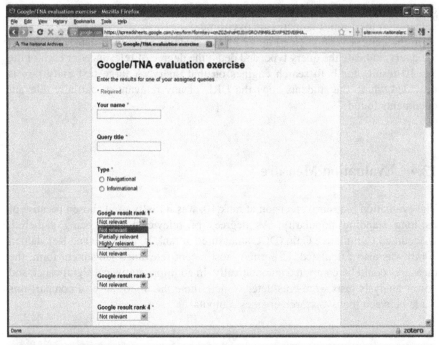

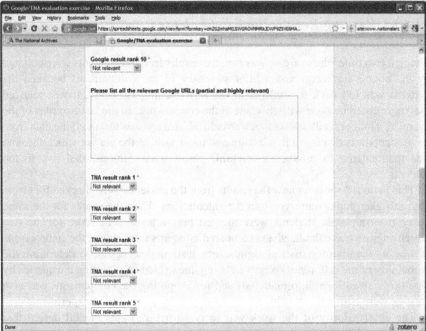

Fig. 12.3 Screenshots of the online form used by students to record the relevance of search results

- There was no control on the order in which students assessed the two search engines. Order effects are a well-known problem in experimentation involving people (Hogarth and Einhorn 1992).
- Students can see which search engine produced which result. Their likely familiarity with Google might influence their relevance judgements on documents returned by that search engine; there is experimental evidence of such a bias towards the Google brand (Jansen et al. 2009).

However, the flaws were made a feature of the exercise; in the feedback session, students were asked to critique the design of the experiment and suggest improvements. In the first running of this feedback session, students pointed out the potential problems of familiarity with the Google brand and their judgements as well as issues with order effects. They also suggested potential problems with their own consistency of assessment and their lack of familiarity with some of the topics behind the selected queries. This facilitated discussion of relevant research on topics such as assessor consistency (Voorhees 1998) and assessor expertise (Bailey et al. 2008).

12.4.2   Execution of the Exercise

The exercise was run four times in total across two modes of delivery. Twice as an exercise given to students to conduct in their own time returning results by a deadline; twice as a 1-h exercise run live in class, while instructors were present to answer any questions. The exercise was given to second year undergraduate students and taught Masters' students as well as to PhD students attending an information retrieval summer school. All four times the exercise was run success- fully to conclusion producing statistically significant meaningful results, which confirmed the validity of this crowd sourced approach to evaluation. As it is unlikely that students will have encountered such an exercise like this elsewhere, the instructions and procedures need to be explained clearly in order to ensure that it runs smoothly. It was also clear that the job of judging relevance is a repetitive somewhat tedious task, so ensuring that the student do not have to undertake a large number of judgements is also important.

It was found that across each of the four runs of the exercise, a consistent picture emerged of one of the compared engines outperforming the other. Differences between the two were statistically significant and different results were found for the two query types: informational and navigational. One of the search engines was found to be particularly good at navigational queries, while the difference between the engines for informational queries was smaller. Running the exercise multiple times with different groups of students provided a form of internal validation. More recently the results derived from one of the student-based exercises (same queries, same collection) were repeated using a group of paid assessors. The results of the search engine comparisons from this experiment were again consistent with the results from the student-based exercise, which leads us to be more confident than the student-based exercise not only provided a learning experience for the students but also generated valuable research outputs for search engine owners.

12.4.3 Impact of the Exercise

A clear peripheral benefit of running the exercise was the ability to develop a relationship with a large organisation, in our case TNA, for which search is an important service. The organisation was able to get, for free, a series of sufficiently rigorous experiments comparing their search engine with another. In the case of TNA, the findings of the first two running of the exercises were found to agree with internal tests run by the organisation. Consequently, the results fed into decisions made by the search engine team on how to develop their services further.

The impact for the students was seeing that they were active participants in research. An introductory lecture from TNA was given to the students about the practical running of a search engine. Students saw the importance of their work when TNA staff attended the meeting showing the results of the exercise. This relationship between TNA and the department led to a number of closer ties between the two, including a small funded research project to explore evaluation further.

A formal request for feedback from students revealed that both kinds of search engine evaluations were viewed as one of the best parts of the information retrieval course.

12.5 Conclusions and Potential Extensions

The motivation for both forms of evaluation exercise described here were derived from a realisation that there is a large relatively well-established group of search engine users who are neither researchers nor developers, but rather information providers. These are people who have bought in a search system, are provided with many options to customise, change or improve their search services, but do not necessarily know how to go about such alterations. While the course content is relatively standard for an information studies department, the exercises are specifically targeted at enabling students to develop skills to help them assess the quality of a search engine and at the same time conduct different forms of evaluation including a conventional test collection like assessment. The evaluations have proved to be the most popular part of the course and have enabled the development of links with an organisation that is keen to get access to such skills.

In planning for future versions of the exercises we examined the pedagogical literature on project-based learning. The idea of engaging students in learning centred on projects is long standing (Kilpatrick 1918). However, as Barron et al.

(1998) point out, the level of adoption of such an approach is relatively low; they suggest four principles that should underlie successful project-based learning. We list them here; detail what is currently done to achieve these principles in our exercise and what is planned to be done in the future:

1. *Learning-appropriate goals*: Barron et al. state that it is not sufficient to set goals to ensure the student achieves the project outcomes, it is also necessary to set goals for learning also. In both exercises, so-called "additional objectives" were set, which could be viewed as learning-appropriate goals. However, no form of summative assessment of these objectives was carried out. Future versions of the exercises will conduct such evaluation.

2. *Scaffolds that support both student and teacher learning*: Barron et al. state it is necessary to structure exercises to ensure that students address all stated objectives. In early versions of the exercise there was little provision of such scaffolds. Over time, the definition of the two exercises became more structured providing the structure Barron et al. require. However, in the first exercise the evaluations conducted by the students are relatively ad hoc, what is needed is a more methodical way of considering how well an engine is successfully providing services to users.

3. *Frequent opportunities for formative self-assessment and revision*: While conducting exercises, Barron et al. state students should be able to assess their progress and revise their project if necessary. Particularly with the second exercise, it was found that students often requested help from the course tutor to check that they were "doing things right". Explicit provision of formative self-assessment – such as example queries and relevance judgements – will be provided in revised versions of the exercise.

4. *Social organisations that promote participation and result in a sense of agency*: The first exercise arranged students in groups to jointly conduct the work, which it was hoped would improve participation; in the second exercise visits by TNA staff to the class was hoped to encourage a sense of agency in the students. In future versions of the exercises; however, the extent to which these arrangements succeeded will be examined through student feedback.

There are also a number of IR specific improvements that could be made. The current requirement for students in the first exercise to examine only the search engines of potentially weaker searching systems is perhaps rather limiting. Even state of the art search engines have plenty of opportunities to be improved; therefore, allowing students the possibility to assess any type of search engine will be examined in future.

With the second exercise, the primary aim for improvement is to consider how to refine the experimental procedure to remove biases in the measurement of the two search engines. For example, were students likely to be biased in judging the quality of Google search results? While the IR community has a well-established method for assessing the effectiveness of a search engine using test collections, there is less of a commonly agreed standard for evaluating the other aspects of the engines, which is an aspect to be better understood for this exercise. In addition, given the success of involving search providers in the second exercise, seeking information providers interested in being involved in having their system assessed in the first exercise is another hopeful extension of the course.

Acknowledgments The author is grateful to TNA for allowing their search engine be used in the evaluation exercise. He also wishes to thank the reviewers of this chapter for their invaluable comments. Finally, many thanks to the students who took part in the exercises and whose innovation, feedback, and comments made running the IR course such a joy.

References

Bailey P, Craswell N, Soboroff I, Thomas P, de Vries AP, Yilmaz E (2008) Relevance assessment: are judges exchangeable and does it matter. In: Proceedings of the 31st annual international ACM SIGIR conference on research and development in information retrieval. ACM, New York, pp 667–674

Barron BJS, Schwartz DL, Vye NJ, Moore A, Petrosino A, Zech L, Bransford JD (1998) Doing with understanding: lessons from research on problem-and project-based learning. J Learn Sci 7(3):271–311

Broder A (2002) A taxonomy of web search. SIGIR Forum 36(2):3–10. doi:10.1145/792550.792552

Chapelle O, Metlzer D, Zhang Y, Grinspan P (2009) Expected reciprocal rank for graded relevance. In: Proceeding of the 18th ACM conference on information and knowledge management. ACM, New York, pp 621–630

Davies A (1983) A document test collection for use in information retrieval research, Dissertation. Department of Information Studies, University of Sheffield, Sheffield

Gull CD (1956) Seven years of work on the organization of materials in the special library. Am Document 7(4):320–329. doi:10.1002/asi.5090070408

Heuwing B, Mandl T, Womser-Hacker C, Braschler M, Herget J, Schäuble P, Stucker J (2009) Evaluation der Suchfunktion deutscher Unternehmenswebsites. In: Wissensorganisation 09: "Wissen – Wissenschaft – Organisation" 12. Tagung der Deutschen ISKO (International Society for Knowledge Organization), Bonn

Hogarth RM, Einhorn HJ (1992) Order effects in belief updating: the belief-adjustment model. Cogn Psychol 24(1):1–55. doi:10.1016/0010-0285(92)90002-J

Jansen BJ, Zhang M, Schultz CD (2009) Brand and its effect on user perception of search engine performance. J Am Soc Inf Sci Technol 60(8):1572–1595

Järvelin K, Kekäläinen J (2000) IR evaluation methods for retrieving highly relevant documents. In: Proceedings of the 23rd annual international ACM SIGIR conference on research and development in information retrieval. ACM, New York, pp 41–48

Kilpatrick W (1918) The project method. Teach Coll Record 19(4):319–335

Thorne R (1955) The efficiency of subject catalogues and the cost of information searches. J Document 11:130–148

Voorhees EM (1998) Variations in relevance judgments and the measurement of retrieval effectiveness. In: Proceedings of the 21st annual international ACM SIGIR conference on research and development in information retrieval. ACM, New York, pp 315–323

White M (2006) Making search work: implementing Web, intranet and enterprise search. Facet, London

White RW, Morris D (2007) Investigating the querying and browsing behavior of advanced search engine users. In: Proceedings of the 30th annual international ACM SIGIR conference on Research and development in information retrieval. ACM, New York, pp 255–262

Chapter 13
Teaching Information Retrieval Through Problem-Based Learning

Clare Thornley

13.1 Introduction and Structure of Chapter

I argue that information retrieval (IR) is a fascinating subject with the potential to appeal to and inspire a far wider student body than the computer and information science students which are its current main audience. It has direct practical application to most people as the prevalence and importance of IR systems in daily life makes it useful to understand how they work and how to use them. It can also be a creative introduction to many fundamental philosophical and scientific problems (Thornley 2008). The things that are problematic for IR, storing, representing, and communicating information, as well as accurately assessing whether we have been successful in this enterprise, raise central issues of meaning, knowledge, and the research process which transcend particular subjects. IR provides, in my view, an almost unique opportunity to demonstrate these, often abstract, issues in the tangible form of the workings of an IR system. So IR has the potential to improve both the theoretical and conceptual tools available to our students as well as practical and technical skills in using and developing IR systems. The goal of the chapter is to introduce a teaching perspective on IR which focuses on IR as a series of problems and draws connections from other disciplines about how these problems can be tackled and also shows how IR can provide insights into the problems of other disciplines. I am not only interested in, for example, how philosophy can help IR (as seen in the work of Blair 1990, 2006) but also how IR can help philosophy and other subjects.

Problem-based learning (PBL), or teaching IR as a series of problems to be investigated and tackled, is one way to improve its accessibility and relevance to more students. In the spirit of the problem based approach I start by outlining some of the problems or difficulties in teaching IR and then go onto explore solutions.

C. Thornley (✉)
School of Information and Library Studies, University College Dublin, Dublin, Ireland
e-mail: Clare.thornley@ucd.ie

E. Efthimiadis et al. (eds.), *Teaching and Learning in Information Retrieval*,
The Information Retrieval Series 31, DOI 10.1007/978-3-642-22511-6_13,
© Springer-Verlag Berlin Heidelberg 2011

The main challenges in IR are the disparate and diverse nature of both the learners and the subject. I then go onto to discuss what PBL is and how it can be used to tackle these challenges.

The first section discusses the educational philosophy behind PBL and the particular goals and objectives of teaching IR in this way. This then leads onto a discussion in Sects. 13.3 and 13.4 about the implications of this for understanding the learners of IR and also IR as a subject, followed by Sect. 13.5, which discusses a number of specific teaching exercises, and, finally, Sect. 13.6 which examines the feedback and assessment from students.

13.2 Educational Philosophy

PBL has to be understood within a broader education philosophy, as discussed by Barrett (2005), rather than simply as series of techniques. This section discusses what I am trying to achieve in terms of educational goals and objectives in this approach to IR teaching and, perhaps more importantly, why. Any educational goal has to be understood within a broader approach or philosophy of learning: what is the purpose of education in the first place? Within this philosophy what is the purpose of education in IR? My own philosophy of education is based partly on my academic background in philosophy and also my research into IR theory (Thornley 2005; Thornley and Gibb 2007, 2009). My aim is to help students develop effective strategies for analyzing and tackling difficult problems and to understand how these problems relate to wider theoretical issues in IR and beyond. I want them to have both a conceptual framework to "make sense" of problems and a number of techniques or approaches to tackling problems. I also want them to be "comfortable" with or able to tolerate problems which steadfastly resist complete solutions. Finally I want to inspire and develop the potential of new researchers by introducing problem analysis and indicating some of the theoretical and methodological issues that arise in original research. Ideally, for some of these students, this will enable them to develop new techniques and new models, not taught by me at all, that they can then use to progress knowledge. This educational philosophy can apply across any subject and, quite possibly, at any educational level. In the next two sections I discuss PBL and how it can be used to meet the educational goals and objectives of teaching IR within a university setting.

13.2.1 Problem-Based Learning

What is PBL? Defining "PBL" can lead one, in a similar way to a definition of "evidence-based practice" to the "as opposed to what?" question. If learning does not help us solve problems (in the broadest sense) then are we really learning anything at all? In summary PBL is an approach which starts with a problem and then leads to solutions (as far as possible developed by students) rather than the traditional method of providing facts and solutions and then, finally, testing the students' ability to use these to solve problems through assessment. So the ability to tackle problems is in most learning somewhere, but in PBL it is brought further to the front of the learning process.

I would argue, following Barrett (2005), that PBL has been in existence since the evolution of humans. The ability to identify, analyze, and create solutions to problems, whether at the basic level of how to survive against predators on the savannah or, more abstractly, how to solve the problem of relativity, is an essential part of what it is to be a human and help explain the success of the species. The ability to think abstractly, to take one problem and solution and see how it might help solve a different but related problem in a different context, is a very important intellectual ability. Finally, and of particular relevance to IR, the ability, with the development of recorded knowledge, to collect, build upon, and share solutions to problems enables the growth of knowledge and technological progress. Thus PBL is nothing new at all.

It is, however, seen as relatively new within the context of higher education, although, in fact, it is clearly used in the teaching technique of Socrates (circa 469–399 BC), who presents problems or dilemmas and invites his students to discuss them until some kind of agreement or solution is reached. "In 'Theaitetos' (Plato, trans. Warrington, 1961) for example," the group of friends begin a debate on the nature of knowledge.

> Socr: Well, that is just what puzzles me; I cannot satisfy myself as to what exactly knowledge is. Can we answer that question? What do you all say? Which of us is going to speak first? Everyone who misses shall play "sit down and be donkey," as children say when they play ball; anyone who gets through without missing shall be our king and shall be entitled to make us answer any question he likes to ask. Why the silence? I hope; Theodoros, that my love of argument is not making me rude; I only want to start a conversation so that we shall feel at home with one another like friends. [146]

This quotation actually provides a fairly complete description of this approach to learning. It starts with a puzzle or a question, it relates to prior knowledge (come on you all know this children's game), it recognizes silence (rather than instantly filling it with input from the teacher) and gently encourages participation by a emphasizing the similarities (feel at home with) rather than a rigid divide between teacher and learner.

13.2.2   Educational Goals and Objectives

An educational goal is generally understood as a broad overall ambition of a particular program, course, or lesson. An educational objective is the small specific steps that need to be achieved in order to meet that goal. Different teaching techniques or methods can then be used to try and meet these goals and objectives. Within IR my overall educational goal is to elicit a deep understanding of the fundamental concepts of IR, realize that the relationship between these concepts is problematic, and provide some tools for overcoming this at a level appropriate to the particular student. I approach this goal through a number of more specific objectives, achieved using various methods to be discussed, throughout the course.

The nature of any educational goal and our likelihood of achieving it depend on what we are teaching and whom we are teaching it to. Ideally we want some kind of congruence between subject and learner, as discussed by Jones (2009), in the context of IR. I propose that in IR, as also discussed by others (Bawden et al. 2007), the variety within the student group is wide and also that there is a wide variety of approaches to IR. This diversity has to be dealt with both in terms of the learner and the subject and can make congruence difficult. It can, however, also be used as an advantageous tool. My own experience of teaching IR is in two different contexts. I will discuss these briefly to provide a background to a more detailed discussion of the teaching approaches used, and also to show the connections, despite the different educational level, of both different groups of students.

13.3 Learners

The underlying theme of students taking IR courses is normally the lack of an underlying theme. Diversity of academic background and motivation are common, and if the trend for modularization increases, it is likely to become more so. University College Dublin (UCD) has a modularized undergraduate program which means that students can take a substantial number of modules outside their primary degree subject (a total of 12 modules are taken each year over two semesters). If we wish to use these new degree structures to extend the teaching of IR outside of the information and computer sciences, then we will need some approaches and techniques to deal with an even more diverse range of students. This section describes the profile of the students at UCD taking the two IR courses, one at undergraduate level and one at postgraduate level, discussed in this chapter.

13.3.1 Undergraduate

The undergraduate (primarily second years) "information retrieval and organization" module has approximately 40–50 students. It contains both some students (a minority) undertaking an undergraduate information studies (in which case it is a core subject) degree (often in combination with another major subject) and the rest of the students (the majority) are taking the subject as an "elective" with UCD's modular degree system. This means that they most likely have done no previous information studies or computer science courses and they can, and do, come from within the entire range of degree subjects taught within the university. Thus in one class there will be a mixture of arts, science, professional (e.g. physiotherapists), business, and humanities students. The particular challenges in teaching this class are the very disparate nature of their academic "cultures" or "norms" and also the very disparate nature of prior knowledge and skills which they bring to the class. It is not possible, for example, to assume any particular level of mathematical or logical ability from the more arts-based students. In terms of those from a more scientific background the ability to read conceptual papers or write discursively on theoretical questions cannot be assumed. Finally, they have many different motivations for doing the course and different views on how important or otherwise they perceive it to be in terms of their final degree subject. There is general challenge, not particularly linked to IR, in that if students take a large number of unrelated modules it can result in less synthesized learning. In terms of previous literature on teaching IR, this course would seem to have some similarities with the undergraduate course at Dublin City University discussed by Jones (2009), who also used a problem-based approach, with the important difference that the students at UCD could have no prior knowledge (or more specifically no prior teaching) on computer or information studies before beginning this IR course.

13.3.2 Postgraduate

The other class is a postgraduate module of the Master of Information and Library Studies program. This class, of approximately 20 students, is an elective taking place in the second semester, and comprises a wide range of students. There is a variety of ages as some students are returning to education to retrain after many years in the work place, some have just finished their undergraduate degree, and some also are doing the masters degree part time while working. In a similar way to the undergraduate class they have very different academic backgrounds ranging from the science to the arts, although the majority comes from an arts or humanities background rather than science. Thus in some way the challenges are similar, one cannot assume much shared previous knowledge or a unified academic approach. These are lessened, to an extent, in so far as everyone has successfully completed one degree so a level of competence can be assumed. There is also more sustained and unified motivation within the class as they all wish to get a professional qualification.

An important difference with the postgraduate course is that it is part of professional qualification, thus one is not only trying to teach a particular subject, in this case IR, but one is trying to instill or teach how "to be" a successful information manager or librarian with IR as one part of this overall goal. Crucially, I am trying to get them to "think like" a good information manager or librarian. This issue, and how to address it educationally, has been discussed within the context of professional education in a number of different subjects. Atherton (2008), for example, discusses the problem of getting students to understand central or threshold concepts which will enable them to think in the ways necessary to be successful in their subject. In terms of library and information science I would argue that we need practitioners who can recognize problems and analyze them in terms of what information, in what form and to whom, would be the best way to progress toward solution.

So to summarize there are a number of educational challenges in terms of the learners on these courses. The common theme is one of diversity and difference: different levels of previous knowledge; different academic backgrounds; different ages (not always in favor of the youngest as a memory of command line searching can be an advantage for older students); different ambitions (at least in terms of undergraduates). These all make it unlikely that the traditional model of primarily using lectures describing subject content to teach will work for most students. This diversity, although not straightforward, can be productive when students are asked to bring examples in from their own academic or professional experience in terms of IR.

13.4 Subject

In addition to the diversity of the learners there is also the difficulty that information science (or studies, the two terms in themselves, tell a story), and perhaps particularly IR, is a subject which resists a unified agreed analysis of its central problems and approaches. This can be seen in the early text books, Salton and McGill (1983, p. 431) claim in their "future directions in IR" final chapter.

> "Many insights relating to the IR problem are obtainable by studying the elements of related areas such as decision theory, artificial intelligence, software engineering, information theory, combinatorial mathematics, linear algebra, computational linguistics, pattern recognition, scene analysis, and logic. Viable solutions to the information problem will eventually be found by combining results derived from these various disciplines."

Modern IR students and indeed lecturers might find this subject list slightly daunting. It is, however, still the case that many different disciplines can be seen as relevant to progress in IR. Blair (1990, 2006) argues that Wittgenstein's (1953) work on the philosophy of language should be central to our understanding of IR and claims that IR's difficulties are partly because it has no clear view of its central questions.

> "IR is a difficult area in which to work because it is often unclear what the fundamental issues or problems of the field are. In short, it is not so much a question of finding the right answers but of, even more fundamentally, asking the right questions." (Blair 1990, p. 1)

This has also been discussed in other textbooks, such as Ellis' (1996) book "Progress and Problems in Information Retrieval," which cites as a motivation for the book a desire to provide some conceptual cohesion of the field. Thus within IR there is a wide variety of possible approaches and disciplines which can be seen as pertinent to IR but no clear agreement as to which are the most important. In teaching, particularly at an undergraduate level, we do not want to overwhelm our students with too much choice or variety or, however, to present a picture of unity which does not exist. I have found that focusing on IR as a problem, rather than as a subject, can, to an extent, create a more coherent story line for students. We need to get them to ask the "right questions" and to understand the wider context from which they may get some answers.

What exactly, however, does it mean to present IR as a problem? I argue that this can be seen as an, at least, two-stage process. First, IR in a broad sense can be understood as a solution or an approach to the problem of access to stored information. This "solution" then itself raises the problem of what is the best way to go about this. IR is therefore both a solution to a problem and a problem of how to improve the solution. It is an attempt to solve a problem, in the broadest sense how to both store and provide access to the accumulated knowledge of humanity, and, in a more specific sense, how to represent documents so that a user who would find them relevant can retrieve them. What kind of problem is this or perhaps, more accurately, what kinds of problems does it consist of? Both of these problems have philosophical and technical levels and both of them are fundamental problems to do with what is distinctive about humanity. Hence both of them will relate to theoretical issues discussed in other disciplines. They will also relate directly to the experience of all students as, at some point, they will have used an IR system, and they can all see evidence of accumulated knowledge around them. These linkages can be used as "ways in" to students from a range of different disciplines.

13.5 Teaching Methods: Examples and Discussion of the Problem-Based Approach

This section provides some examples of specific techniques and approaches used in class. The order in which they are or should be tackled has no clear answer and I have tried a number of different sequences, all with different strengths and difficulties. Generally in PBL one should start with the problem but in IR it can be difficult to know which problem is the best one to begin with. I used a similar approach in both the under- and postgraduate courses although pace and level were adapted to the students. All of these techniques are clearly only starting points for discussion and are used in combination with other teaching methods.

13.5.1 Stage One: Why It Matters?

In terms of teaching I start with a "why it matters" overview to show how the effective storage of information over time is important. Why is it important that we solve the problem of accessing to information and take serious efforts to improve it? I use examples, normally from the recent news, of what can go wrong when information is not retrieved accurately and quickly. This is, perhaps, more important for undergraduates, as one would hope that those committed to a postgraduate

library and information course, would already be convinced of this. There is a
difficulty with this stage of the course which I have not yet completely managed to
solve. It is, I think, to do with the potentially self-important impression of standing
up and saying "this is why my subject is terribly important." This will appeal to
students who are already interested in the issues, it can just put off students, who
have not reflected or thought about the subject at all. The use of better examples
may help here with perhaps more variety of current and historical issues. On
reflection, for the next undergraduate intake I may move straight onto stage two
which starts with the student's immediate experience and then tries to abstract out
from that as the course develops.

13.5.2 Stage Two: What Is It Like to Use an IR System?

This stage, linked in strongly with the problem-based approach in terms of
acknowledging and starting with prior knowledge (Barrett 2005), starts with
student's existing knowledge of IR systems. The objective is to get them to think
about what an IR system is, think about how effective they thought it was, and start
thinking about how they would improve it. It is also an effective way of assessing
the current level of understanding and knowledge of IR among the students. This
particular exercise is only part of this stage but is a good illustration of using active
learning to stimulate the production of problems from the students which can then
be used as examples to introduce some the central problems of IR.

The exercise requires them, as an individual initially, to write down an IR system
(this definition is deliberately left vague and wide) they have used recently, state
whether they found what they were looking for and suggest, if appropriate, anything
they would change to make the system "better." After they have done this they then
compare their examples with one or two other students and briefly discuss their
findings. This discussion is then brought out and a selection of examples are
discussed and reflected upon with guidance from the lecturer.

The outcome of this exercise is, first, a wide variety of different examples are
presented to the class so they start to see the range of different systems that can be
seen as IR systems. Second, at least so far with this exercise, a significant minority
of people have failed to find what they are looking for. This introduces the idea that
despite "Google" and some of its associated hype perhaps IR is not always totally
straightforward. Third, some of the suggestions about how it might have been
improved begin to show that students are starting to look critically at the IR systems
they use. Finally, and perhaps, most importantly, I use some of the examples and
ask how they can be certain that they did find exactly the information they were
looking for? How can they know they did not miss something important? The
suggested "improvements" from students are also normally excellent material as
some focus on interface issues and some more on what is retrieved. Thus one can
discuss the distinction between "ease of use" and effectiveness of an IR system.

At the end of the exercise the students have been introduced to a range of different IR systems and they have realized that they all do not work well all of the time. They have also began to understand that it is very hard to be sure how effective or otherwise an IR system actually is and have started to think about what would improve a particular IR system for them. The examples provided can be also be used to illustrate wider problems in IR in terms of defining one's information need and related query, correctly identifying relevance, the ways in which documents are presented (abstract, full text, title etc.). This exercise does involve a significant ability to cede control to students, as discussed with reference to PBL (Barrett 2005), as one is relying on the fact that the examples give enough material to illustrate the learning objectives one is trying to achieve.

13.5.3   Stage 3: What Is It Like to Be an IR System?

The philosophy behind this stage is that it is important that students understand how IR systems work (Johnson 2008) even if they will only ever be IR users not system designers. One way to improve understanding of something is to have experience of being that thing. By this stage students have hopefully moved on from the unreflective use of IR systems and are now starting to question both how they use them and how effective the systems themselves may be. This exercise is used to introduce them to how IR systems tackle these problems as a starting point for covering different meaning representation techniques, queries, and relevance. This exercise, inspired loosely by Nagel's (1979) essay "What is it like to be a bat?," where he argues that if you wish to understand something you need to be able to say what is it like "to be" that thing, aims to provide the students with experience of "acting out" being different part of an IR system. Clearly, and also in respect to Nagel who argued fiercely for the important and unique nature of consciousness, the IR system the students "act out" involves humans and is not an automated system. Indeed the differences between a "human" IR system and an "automated" one are part of the learning objective of this exercise. This exercise is preceded by using Salton and McGill's (1983) definition of an IR systems as a query, a set of documents, and some mechanism for determining which (if any) of the documents are relevant to the query. The learning objective is to show the multiple ways in which one document can be "represented," the multiple ways in which one information need can be represented in a query, and the multiple ways in which a judgment about relevance between a document and a query can be made.

The exercise requires multiple copies of one document and one information need in this case couched as relatively straightforward issue "how can I improve my swimming?" (clearly it could be any other activity). The document is a newspaper article about the importance of practice in achieving mastery of any field (for best demonstration of the point of exercise it is best if it does not actually include the activity described in the information need). Initially the class is split into two groups, one are given the document, the others the information need. The students then work as individuals and are asked to pick ten words that they think best represent the document or the information need, and, to pick one word which they would put first. This is then brought to class level discussion and analysis led by the lecturer comparing and reflecting upon the results.

The first comparison is between the document groups: how similar were there lists of words they chose and were any of their "main" words the same. There are clearly a wide range of differences here and this shows students how one document can be interpreted in a number of different ways. The request for one "main" word is also used in the sense of where would you shelve this document and this can be used to show differences between indexing a physical document and indexing an electronic document regarding single or multiple access points. The second aspect of the comparison is between their approaches to the exercise: how did they choose the words? Normally this is fascinating in its variety and can be used to, for example, illustrate the distinction between assigned and derived indexing depending on if they referred to previous knowledge. Some students actually sometimes count words (often instinctively or through prior knowledge not counting "stop words") and also use document structure (e.g. title, first paragraph etc.) or meta-data (source, author, date etc.). Thus in one short exercise they can be introduced to the basics of a number of different approaches to document representation, and, as they have actually done it, rather than just been told about, it tends to be learned at a deep rather than a surface level (Biggs and Tang 2007, Chap. 2).

The second comparison is between the query groups: how similar were there lists of words and were any of the main words the same? This includes a discussion about how they approached the exercise and any background knowledge they brought to the query. It can also discuss if, and how, they tried to combine or structure the words in their query.

The third and final comparison pairs up each document student with a query student, and they discuss whether the document was, in fact, relevant to the query. So far there has been very wide, and often forceful, disagreement on this. I try and lead this discussion into looking at the reasons, including interests, age, competitiveness (do they want to be a leisure or Olympic swimmer?) of the user. In this particular example age is an excellent context example as after a certain, relatively young age, it is simply not possible to put in the hours of practice suggested before one would become too old to compete, and hence there is narrow window of relevance. They then also count how many words were shared by the document list and the query list and are asked to decide whether the query would have, in fact, found the document. Thus, immediately, they see that the existence of shared words between a document and a query is not the same as relevance.

13.5.4   Stage 4: Theoretical Context and Conceptual Framework

This stage of the course has the educational goal of enabling students to see theories of meaning, information, and communication as tentative solutions to problems.

I do not start with a description of different theories and then relate them to IR. I find it better to start with what is problematic about these concepts and then move onto to some different theories which try to "make sense" of or explain how these concepts work. In this way it is possible to demonstrate, rather than just to say, that a theoretical understanding of meaning, information, and communication as problems can clarify problems in IR. As such the aim is to put philosophy to work rather than just describe it and show that "philosophy is not a theory but an activity" (Wittgenstein 1922, 4.112).

13.5.4.1 Meaning

This is concept, which in a similar way to IR systems, most people may think they understand but, nevertheless, they have not really thought about it too much. The aim here is to encourage reflection on how meaning then works in ordinary life to provide a framework for understanding different approaches to meaning representation in IR. I ask students to provide their own answers to a number of questions about meaning focusing on: "how does a word mean something?"; "how can I know someone else shares my understanding of what a word means?" The first question normally results in a number of "because it stands for or refers to something" answers. The limitations of this and counter examples can then be discussed to show how it does not always work that way. The second question is more interesting in many cases and more clearly immediately relevant to IR for some of the students. Discussion of context, socialization, and checking with the person talking are often mentioned. This can lead onto a discussion about the extent, or otherwise, in which these kinds of tools for checking shared understanding of meaning are available in IR systems. In particular, for example, it becomes more difficult, as Blair discusses (1990, 2006), to check if the IR system is using the same words as the user to describe the content of a document even if query and document may, in fact, be about the same thing. The aim is to show that meaning, which we normally take for granted, is, on reflection, both complex and problematic. These complexities also tend to become more difficult to solve in IR than in "face to face" communication. It also provides a context for teaching vocabulary control as one approach to improving "communication." After this exercise and discussion I cover a fairly simplified version of some theories of meaning mainly focusing on the lexical, semantic, syntactic, and pragmatic levels of meaning and also, to provide one more approach, the distinction between content and context. Techniques of meaning representation, including more recent developments such as IR in context, can then be taught by relating them specifically to one of the levels of meaning and analyzed in terms of which problem of meaning they are trying to solve. It is also a useful reflection tool on the exercises they have done on "being" an IR system.

13.5.4.2 Information

In my view the relationship and the difference between meaning and information are crucial to developing a deep understanding of the essential problem of IR (Thornley and Gibb 2009). This has also been discussed by Ingwersen (1992) and Ingwersen and Jarvelin (2005) who argue that an accurate representation of a document's meaning does not necessarily mean that it will inform the user in terms of changing their knowledge state. I emphasize that meaning is often to do with reproduction of a message while information is about a message that changes something. This can then be used as an introduction to the problem of relevance, a document needs to be similar enough to be on the same topic as the query but also different enough to actually provide new knowledge. It also highlights the problem of failing to recognize a relevant document due to lack of understanding.

I aim to teach this as tension which has no complete solution. Decisions on how to manage this "matching" process must be made depending on the particular type of IR scenario involved. This then links into the tension between recall and precision, in what scenarios is one more important than the other and why? Students are asked to think of examples and different scenarios where different approaches might be taken and to justify their decisions. This can be used as a starting point to discuss both system design (in what contexts should design enable precision over recall?) and also search design and approach (in what contexts should a searcher focus on recall or precision?). The difference and also the relationship between meaning (is this document "about" my query) and information (does this document change what I know about my query topic) provide a conceptual map in which students can place IR.

13.5.4.3 Communication

Communication is itself a solution to a problem; the problem of the limited knowledge and understanding of any one individual. Communication, as enabled by the written word and, more recently, by the development of information communication technologies, is a solution to this problem on an almost (but not completely) global scale. It is now possible to communicate both across distance (space) and also time in that we can access documents which were produced in the past. This historical nature of IR, highlighted by Buckland (1991), is important to the effective teaching of IR as it puts IR in a meaningful context in the pursuit of human progress. It also, however, increases the chances of miscommunication because as the historical distance between the document creation and the user increases the chances of them using different ways to describe the subject matter are likely to increase.

In teaching this I ask students to find examples of "failed" IR either from their own experience, or from history or from the current news. They then bring these examples to class and each one is discussed in terms of what "went wrong" with the communication process between the document and the user and what were the effects of the IR failure. This is then explicitly linked to theories of meaning in terms of which level of meaning failed, lexical, syntax (in these cases was the document unclear or input incorrectly resulting in nonretrieval), semantics (did people fail to understand it), or pragmatics (was their social or political reasons why it was not used or acted upon even though it was retrieved). Finally this leads into a discussion about how these failures could have been prevented in terms of IR. A good discussion of an historical example of this discussing the initial lack of impact of Mendel's paper on genetics can be found in Bawden's (2004) paper on lost and forgotten documents.

13.6   Student Assessment and Evaluation

Traditionally the purpose of assessment is to find out how well the students have met the learning objectives of the course. Student evaluation can be seen as an opportunity for students to comment on their experience of the process. Despite providing some useful indicators of quality both are flawed instruments as they provide a "snapshot" perspective and cannot really indicate how the learning outcomes or experience may impact in the longer term.

13.6.1   Assessment

Ideally the assessment of any course should provide a way of accurately testing the attainment of its learning objectives. Within PBL, as discussed by Barrett (2005), the assessment should reflect the underlying philosophy of deep understanding and self-directed learning. Within a university setting, however, one often inherits or is obliged to fit in with existing models of assessment and can have limited flexibility. I use fairly traditional modes of assessment: a written assignment; a group project and presentation; a class test. I explain that the essay and group project are to test their analysis of the problems of IR and the test is to assess the knowledge of possible solutions. In the essay and group project I offer the students a large degree of flexibility in how they interpret and tackle the questions set. I also provide clear instructions that whatever approach they take they must explicitly outline the scope and approach at the beginning of their work. The written assignment was to write a position paper on whether they thought IR was a communication process and why. The group project required an investigation into the role of IR in a range of different organizational contexts e.g. health, law, politics. Their remit, as an "information team" was to identify the problems which these different areas were dealing with e.g. in a hospital one problem (among others) is to how to provide the best treatment, identify the role of information in addressing this problem and critically evaluate how current IR solutions were contributing to solving the problem with suggestions for improvement. The aim was to provide some experience of "thinking like" an information professional in terms of why information matters to my organization and how am I going to convince people of this. The class presentation was not part of the undergraduate assessment and was replaced by presentations and discussion in tutorials. The class test is a way of testing knowledge and understanding of IR techniques and is fairly factual in its format. These were all covered after the central problems and issues had been taught so that they could be seen as potential solutions to a problem rather than simply a list of techniques.

How effective were these assessment techniques? In summary they seem to allow strong students the opportunity to excel while weaker students, or possibly those just less familiar with the approach, tend to flounder. The stronger students were initially anxious about the freedom to interpret the question but then went on to do some interesting work. Some of the weaker students never seem to grasp how to tackle a question and submitted or presented very descriptive work. This can be a general difficulty with the problem-based approach to learning as it does require independent thinking and the confidence to try out different approaches. I do not have a clear solution and I also do not know if, even for the weaker students, it provided a useful starting point which they may be able to develop in the future.

13.6.2   Evaluation

Student evaluation is comprised of a mixture of student surveys and focus groups, and feedback was very varied and often contradictory. Some students were very enthusiastic about the course whereas others complained of feeling lost and disorientated. The perceived lack of guidance in assessment was frightening for some students whereas others found it liberating. The theoretical context was found interesting by about half the students and they complained about the difficulty of technical content and the rest had exactly the opposite complaint. These mixed messages make it hard to draw firm conclusions about the impact of this teaching approach. I have noticed over time, however, that the students who thrive in the undergraduate course have progressed to get good final degrees and also to move into our masters programs. On discussion with colleagues adopting similar teaching approaches this trend has also been noted. This suggests that for stronger students this kind of teaching may improve their research and original thinking skills.

13.7   Conclusions

In the same way that is difficult to design an IR system which will please all of the people all of the time it is difficult to design an IR course which well effectively teach all students at all stages. This problem-based approach is one way into a complex and important subject which, inevitably, will work better for some students rather than others. It does, however, in my view provide academic substance in terms of theory, academic training in terms of problem analysis, and technical knowledge in terms of how IR systems work and how to get the best results from them. It can overcome some of the challenges of diversity within the student group and the subject and has the potential to develop interest in the subject to a wider range of students.

References

Atherton JS (2008) Doceo: introduction to threshold concepts. http://www.doceo.co.uk/tools/threshold.htm. Accessed 15 Oct 2010

Barrett T (2005) Understanding problem based learning. In: Barrett T, Mac Labhrainn I, Fallon H (eds) Handbook of enquiry problem based learning. Galway CELT. Released under creative commons license. http://www.nuigalway.ie/celt/pblbook. Accessed 15 Oct 2010

Bawden D (2004) Forgotten and undiscovered knowledge.'J Document 60(6):595–596

Bawden D, Bates J, Steinerovu J, Vakkari P, Vilnar P (2007) Information retrieval curricula: contexts and perspectives. In: First international workshop on teaching and learning of information retrieval, London, UK, 10 Jan 2007. http://www.bcs.org/server.php?show=conWebDoc.8777. Accessed 15 Oct 2010

Biggs J, Tang C (2007) Teaching for quality learning at university. Oxford University Press, Oxford

Blair DC (1990) Language and representation in information retrieval. Elsevier Science, Amsterdam

Blair DC (2006) Wittgenstein, language and information: "Back to the rough ground!" Springer, NewYork

Buckland MK (1991) Information and information systems. Greenwood, New York

Ellis D (1996) Progress and problems in information retrieval. Library Association, London

Ingwersen P (1992) Information retrieval interaction. Taylor Graham, London

Ingwersen P, Jarvelin K (2005) The turn: integration of information seeking and retrieval in context. Springer, Dordrecht

Johnson F (2008) On the relation of search and engines. In: Second international workshop on teaching and learning of information retrieval (TLIR 2008). London, UK, 18 Oct 2008. http://www.bcs.org/server.php?show=conWebDoc.22355. Accessed 15 Oct 2010

Jones GJF (2009) An inquiry-based learning approach to teaching information retrieval. Inf Retr 12(2):148–161

Nagel T (1979) What is it like to be bat? In: Mortal questions. Cambridge University Press, Cambridge, MA

Plato T (1961) Parmenides and other dialogues (Translated by J. Warrington). J. M. Dent, London

Salton G, McGill MJ (1983) Introduction to modern information retrieval. McGraw-Hill International, Tokyo

Thornley C (2005) A dialectical model of information retrieval: exploring a contradiction in terms, PhD thesis, University of Strathclyde, Glasgow. http://personal.cis.strath.ac.uk/~ir/research_students/diglib.html. Accessed 15 Oct 2010

Thornley C (2008) Teaching information retrieval as a philosophical problem. In: Second international workshop on teaching and learning of information retrieval (TLIR 2008). London, UK, 18 Oct 2008. http://www.bcs.org/server.php?show=conWebDoc.22354. Accessed 15 Oct 2010

Thornley C, Gibb F (2007) A dialectical approach to information retrieval. J Document 63(5): 755–764
Thornley C, Gibb F (2009) Meaning in philosophy and meaning in information retrieval (IR). J Document 65(1):133–150
Wittgenstein L (1922) Tractatus logico philosophicus. Routledge, London
Wittgenstein L (1953) Philosophical investigations. Blackwells, Oxford

Chapter 14
Educational Resource Development for Information Retrieval in a Digital Libraries Context

Seungwon Yang, Sanghee Oh, Barbara M. Wildemuth, Jeffrey P. Pomerantz, and Edward Fox

14.1 Teaching Information Retrieval Within the Context of a Digital Libraries Course/Curriculum

Information retrieval (IR) modules are critical components of a digital library (DL); indeed, IR is a core technology undergirding DLs. Both the histories and the current status of the two types of systems are inextricably linked. The collections of resources in DLs can be useful and meaningful to users only when they are accessed and retrieved and satisfy needs. For these reasons, educational resources related to IR play a key role in the recent development of a curriculum for graduate-level digital libraries education.

In this chapter, we describe educational goals and the development and field testing of several course modules on IR topics. They were developed as part of a multiyear project focused on the development of materials for DL education, but can easily be incorporated in IR courses or similar courses on related topics. After providing an overview of the DL curriculum framework and the role of the IR modules within that framework, the procedures used to develop and field test the modules are described, with particular emphasis on the IR-related modules. This chapter concludes with a description of the way in which these materials are being made available to educators.

14.2 Educational Goals

The overall goal in teaching and learning IR in a DL context is to have learners gain knowledge of both fundamental principles and practical skills based on lecture notes, reading materials, exercises, class activities, demos, and class projects. Those

S. Yang (✉)

Department of Computer Science, Virginia Tech, Blacksburg, VA, USA

e-mail: seungwon@vt.edu

E. Efthimiadis et al. (eds.), *Teaching and Learning in Information Retrieval*,
The Information Retrieval Series 31, DOI 10.1007/978-3-642-22511-6_14,
© Springer-Verlag Berlin Heidelberg 2011

are included in the educational modules, which are explained in the following sections. In order to satisfy the overall goal, each educational module in our project includes a list of learning objectives, and then has additional information corresponding with the objectives. For example, the learning objectives of the "Image Retrieval" module in our curriculum are stated as:

At the end of the module, students will be able to:

- Explain the basics of image retrieval and its needs in digital libraries.
- Explain the different image retrieval types.
- Classify content-based image retrieval based on various features and differentiate between the techniques being used.
- Explain the various image retrieval systems in existence and evaluation strategies.

The learning objectives of the "Image Retrieval" module indicate that the module covers various features, techniques, and systems related to image retrieval as well as a description of the basics of image retrieval. In order to accomplish its goal, the module provides an appropriate body of knowledge with a list of essential resources required to learn the module, as well as learning activities including in-class exercises. We expect that our approach will ensure that learners have a balance between theoretical and technical knowledge necessary to satisfy the needs of the DL profession.

14.3   The Context: The Digital Library Curriculum Development Project

Digital libraries (DLs) have been developed and studied both in Computer Science (CS) and Library and Information Science (LIS), with each discipline taking a rather different perspective on DLs although there has been a degree of commonality (Ma et al. 2006, 2007). CS has focused on developing and integrating various technologies to create efficient and effective DL systems that can address different user needs (Pomerantz et al. 2007). Research and development in LIS has centered on understanding the users of DL systems, as well as providing and designing enhanced services (Pomerantz et al. 2006a; Tammaro 2007).

As an effort to unite the system-oriented and service-oriented DL emphases of the two disciplines in order to better support needs of DL professionals (Choi and Rasmussen 2006; Lee et al. 2007; Mostafa et al. 2005), the CS Department at Virginia Tech and the School of Information and Library Science (SILS) at the University of North Carolina at Chapel Hill have been collaboratively developing a DL curriculum useful to both disciplines (with NSF funding January 2006–December 2009, and informally thereafter). The design approach for the DL curriculum was to create multiple short educational modules, so that each module could be taught individually and/or several of them could be flexibly combined to form a DL course or a complete curriculum (Pomerantz et al. 2006b).

Figure 14.1 presents the DL curriculum framework developed by this project. It consists of 47 modules grouped into ten core topics. To emphasize the IR-core modules included in the curriculum, they are highlighted. The availability of high-quality educational modules will allow instructors to enhance their existing courses with minimal effort. For example, an IR course, which had been focused more on textual IR, could be enhanced with a module, 7-a (1) Image retrieval, to provide strategies (e.g., content-based image retrieval) and methodologies to deal with an image dataset.

The IR-core modules are distributed throughout the DL curriculum. To construct effective and efficient DLs, an understanding of users' information needs and searching behaviors is necessary; further, user interaction with the services provided by the DL should be understood (see modules 6-a, 6-b, and 9-c). DL collections are created, shared, organized, and preserved to suit the diverse needs of users (modules 3-c, 3-f, 4-b, 7-a, 7-a (1), 7-d, 8-b). Appropriate recommendation of resources and allowing personalized search/browse features provide a more productive and satisfactory experience for the users (modules 7-c, 7-g). DL user communities are formed to share and maintain high-quality information in their specific fields of study (module 7-d). These IR-core modules in the DL curriculum demonstrate the significant overlap between IR and DL education.

14.4   The Process of Module Development, Evaluation, and Field-Testing

14.4.1   Module Development

The DL educational module structure resembles that of a small-scale syllabus. Compared to a syllabus, which is designed for use during a semester, each module will be taught in one or two class sessions with additional out-of-class hours for group learning activities, exercises, and readings.

Table 14.1 shows the template used for module development. The Scope describes what is to be included in a module. There is a strong mapping among the Learning objectives, Body of knowledge, Resources, Exercises and Learning activities, and Evaluation of learning objective achievement. The 5S theory (streams, structures, societies, scenarios, spaces) explains five perspectives on a minimal DL system (Goncalves et al. 2004), each of which may apply to a particular module. The Body of knowledge section resembles lecture notes related to both theory and practice. This section consists of multiple topics and corresponding explanations that are important in the module so that topics could be taught selectively. A list of Resources is provided with each module, identifying readings and other materials useful to the students and the instructor. Most resources listed in that section are freely available from the open Web. Exercises and learning activities facilitate deeper understanding of the lesson. It is designed to

FRAMEWORK FOR A DIGITAL LIBRARY CURRICULUM[1]

CORE TOPICS	MODULES	
1	Overview	1-a (10-c): Conceptual frameworks, models, theories, definitions	1-b: History of digital libraries and library automation
2	Digital Objects	2-a: Text resources 2-b: Multimedia 2-b (1): Images	2-c (8-d): File formats, transformation, migration
3	Collection Development	3-a: Collection development/selection policies 3-b: Digitization	3-c: Harvesting 3-d: Document and e-publishing/presentation markup 3-e (7-e): Web (push) Publishing 3-f (7-f): Crawling
4	Info/ Knowledge Organization	4-a: Information architecture (e.g., hypertext, hypermedia) 4-b: Metadata 4-c: Ontologies, classification, categorization	4-d: Subject description, vocabulary control, thesauri, terminologies 4-e: Object description and organization for a specific domain
5	Architecture (agents, mediators)	5-a: Architecture overviews 5-b: Application software 5-c: Identifiers, handles, DOI, PURL	5-d: Protocols 5-e: Interoperability 5-f: Security
6	User Behavior/ Interactions	6-a: Info needs, relevance 6-b: Online info seeking behavior and search strategy	6-c: Sharing, networking, interchange (e.g., social) 6-d: Interaction design, usability assessment 6-e: Info summarization and visualization
7	Services	7-a: Indexing and searching 7-a (1): Image retrieval 7-b: Reference services 7-c: Recommender systems	7-d: Routing, community filtering 7-e (3-e): Web (push) Publishing 7-f (3-f): Crawling 7-g: Personalization
8	Preservation	8-a: Preservation 8-b: Web archiving	8-c: Sustainability 8-d (2-c): File formats, transformation, migration
9	Management and Evaluation	9-a: Project management 9-b: DL case studies 9-c: DL evaluation, user studies 9-d: Bibliometrics, Webometrics	9-e: Intellectual property 9-f: Cost/economic issues 9-g: Social issues
10	DL education and research	10-a: Future of DLs 10-b: Education for digital librarians	10-c (1-a): Conceptual framework, theories, definitions 10-d: DL research initiatives

Fig. 14.1 Digital Library Curriculum Framework (IR-core modules are *highlighted*)

engage and motivate students with group presentations/discussions, software demos, class projects, scenario-based analysis exercises, etc. Each module concludes with a glossary and a list of additional useful Web links.

The project team used two different approaches for module development (1) module development initiated by a project member, and (2) a group of graduate

Table 14.1 Educational module template

- Module name
- Scope
- Learning objectives
- 5S characteristics of the module
- Level of effort needed (In-class and out-of-class time needed for students)
- Relationships with other modules (Pre- and postrequisite modules listed)
- Prerequisite knowledge/skills required (Completion optional)
- Introductory remedial instruction (Completion optional)
- Body of knowledge (Theory + practice; an outline that will be used as the basis for lectures)
- Resources (Reading materials and other educational resources for both students and instructors)
- Exercises/learning activities
- Evaluation of learning objective achievement (e.g., grading criteria)
- Glossary
- Additional useful links
- Contributors (authors and reviewers of the module)

students participated in initial module development under the supervision of a project team member (a DL expert) in graduate-level IR or DL classes. For the first approach, project team members either worked on their own (e.g., 1-b History of DL and library automation by Pomerantz) or collaborated with another expert in the field in some cases (e.g., 9-e Intellectual property by Weiss and Wildemuth). This approach is beneficial in that the expertise of a project member, who has projects and teaching experience in DL, is reflected in the module.

The benefit of the second approach is that multiple modules can be developed more quickly with little degradation in quality. A project member (a DL expert) works closely with graduate student teams or individual graduate students, from the beginning, to help with defining the module's scope and with selecting topics. Once a draft of a module is developed by graduate students, the project team members review, update, and distribute the draft modules for further review and refinement. Meanwhile, the graduate students involved learn a great deal, and gain experience with activities that are valuable if in the future they are involved in education or training.

14.4.2   Evaluation

In addition to developing the curriculum framework and developing educational modules, the project has undertaken the evaluation of the modules (Yang et al. 2007). They are reviewed by the project team members first. Once updated, the modules are posted on a wiki (http://curric.dlib.vt.edu/wiki) for DL expert review. A group of DL experts are invited to review them and leave comments on modules. For each module, three or more experts provide comments related to five areas:

- Objectives: Are the objectives appropriate for the topic?
- Body of knowledge: Does the module address all areas of the topic that need to be addressed?

- Readings: Are the readings the best and most appropriate for the topic?
- Learning activities: Are the activities appropriate for the topic?
- Logistics: Is it feasible to teach the module as it is currently constructed?

This use of a wiki for evaluation allowed asynchronous communication among the evaluators. They could read other evaluators' comments for the same module and express their (dis)agreement on the wiki discussion page, as well as add their own evaluation comments (Oh et al. 2009). Based on the reviewers' comments, the modules were revised prior to their evaluation in the field.

14.4.3   Field Testing

After the initial review and revision, each module was made available for field testing (Wildemuth et al. 2008). The module field testing incorporated instructors' perceptions (through one-on-one interviews), students' perceptions (through Web-based surveys related to course content and student effort/learning), and student outcomes (when they had completed exercises or assignments related to the module). During three semesters (spring 2008, fall 2008, and spring 2009), 44 field tests of individual modules were conducted. One or more modules were implemented at each of 15 universities in four different countries (mostly in the USA). A brief report was prepared for each field test, summarizing the results from that implementation.

The list of student survey items is shown in Table 14.2. A total of nine modules were tested by 12–75 students (average: 37.6) in 2–7 classes (average 4.2). Survey items were rated between 2.82 and 3.83 on average using a Likert-like scale between 1: strongly disagree and 5: strongly agree. The fact that 14 items out of 17 were scored in the upper three ratings showed that most sections of the tested modules were satisfactory to students. Results from some of the early field tests have already been reported (Wildemuth et al. 2009). In general, the survey results were positive.

14.5   IR Module Development and Integrated IR Course

14.5.1   IR Module Development

As mentioned earlier, there is a significant amount of overlap between IR and DL education. Table 14.3 lists a total of 23 IR modules from the DL curriculum framework, which comprises 47 modules. In other words, approximately 50% of the DL educational modules consist of IR modules. At the time of this writing (spring 2010), 15 IR modules have been developed and eight more module development activities are planned.

Table 14.2 Ratings for student survey (1: strongly disagree – 5: strongly agree)

Survey items	Mean	SD
Clearly outlined objectives and outcomes were provided (McGorry 2003)	3.83	0.38
The module was well-organized (Neal 2004)	3.76	0.4
The amount of work required for this module was appropriate (Neal 2004)	3.64	0.34
The assigned readings helped me better understand the subject matter (Neal 2004)	3.68	0.42
Given the module's objectives, the learning activities and/or assignments were appropriate (Neal 2004)	2.97	0.61
The learning activities and/or assignments required thinking and understanding (Snare 2000)	3.02	0.61
The learning activities and/or assignments were stimulating (Flashlight evaluation handbook)	2.85	0.59
Assignments for this module helped me understand what will be expected of me as a professional (Flashlight evaluation handbook)	2.82	0.69
I learned useful professional skills from this module (Snare 2000)	3.56	0.26
I know significantly more about this subject than before I took this module (Neal 2004)	3.7	0.34
Class lectures added to my understanding of the subject (Snare 2000)	3.52	0.28
I gained a good understanding of the basic concepts related to this subject (McGorry 2003)	3.71	0.41
I learned to interrelate important issues related to this subject (McGorry 2003)	3.31	0.77
This module stimulated me to think critically about the subject matter (Neal 2004)	3.24	0.74
I feel that this learning module served my needs well (McGorry 2003)	3.27	0.75
I was very satisfied with this learning module (McGorry 2003)	3.19	0.78
Overall, considering its content, design, and structure, this module was effective (Neal 2004)	3.38	0.80

IR modules are marked either "Core" or "Related" in Table 14.3 after examination of their descriptions. All IR-core modules, with the exception of 3-c Harvesting, are ready to be used in classes. Project team members developed four modules: 4-b Metadata; 6-a Info needs, relevance; 6-b Online info seeking behavior and search strategy; and 9-c DL evaluation, user studies. The other seven modules have been developed by either individual graduate students or graduate student teams as part of their IR or DL class at Virginia Tech, under the guidance of at least one project team member. These modules were evaluated by other graduate module developers and then updated further. They include: 3-f/7-f Crawling; 7-a Indexing and searching; 7-a(1) Image retrieval; 7-c Recommender systems; 7-d Routing; 7-g Personalization; and 8-b Web archiving. The graduate module developers presented their modules at mid-semester and as their final project report. The mid-semester and final versions of their modules were reviewed and updated by the DL curriculum project members.

IR-related modules are the ones that include some IR-related topics in their Body of knowledge section as well as their main topics. Those modules might be taught in a way that supports learning IR-core modules. For example, learning IR-related modules such as 2-a Text resources, 2-b Multimedia, and 2-b(1) Images as background knowledge, before studying IR-core modules such as 7-a Indexing and

Table 14.3 IR-core and related modules in DL curriculum framework

No.	Module name	Description	Relevance
3-c[a]	Harvesting	The technical and political methods to automatically collect online resources from the extant Web sites or other online databases that are accessible to the public will be covered	Core
3-f/7-f	Crawling	Technical methods to crawl online information that are represented in diverse formats are introduced	Core
4-b	Metadata	This module outlines metadata concepts in representing and organizing digital objects into collections. Intellectual, structural, administrative, and technical approaches to create, maintain, and update metadata are described	Core
6-a	Info needs, relevance	Aspects of user's information needs and how it might affect the user's interactions with the DL are discussed. Relevance judgments, and their relationship to the user's information needs, are also discussed	Core
6-b	Online info seeking behavior and search strategy	This module covers the theories, models, and practices related to online information seeking behaviors in different settings of digital libraries	Core
7-a	Indexing and searching	This module covers the general principles of information retrieval (IR) models, indexing methods, and the working of search engines applicable to digital libraries	Core
7-a(1)	Image retrieval	The module covers a basic explanation of image retrieval, various techniques used, and its working in existing systems.	Core
7-c	Recommender systems	This module addresses the concepts underlying Recommender Systems, along with the different design approaches, recommenders in current use, and challenges	Core
7-d	Routing	An overview of models and practices of routing, which leads to better search result quality in DLs, is presented	Core
7-g	Personalization	The approaches, effects, limitations, and challenges of personalization standards are addressed	Core
8-b	Web archiving	This module covers the general ideas, approaches, problems, and needs of Web archiving to build a static and long term collection consisting of Web pages	Core
9-c	DL evaluation, user studies	This module focuses on methods for evaluating the outcomes, impacts, or benefits of a digital library, including cost/benefit analyses. It also includes methods that are useful for general user studies	Core

(continued)

Table 14.3 (continued)

No.	Module name	Description	Relevance
2-a[a]	Text resources	The technical structures and standard formats of text resources are addressed	Related
2-b[a]	Multimedia	The standard data formats and technical structures of multimedia resources of image, music, and map databases as well as text-oriented resources will be introduced	Related
2-b(1)[a]	Images	As a sub-module of 2-b Multimedia, this module focuses on technologies related to image processing.	Related
2-c/8-d	File formats, transformation, migration	This module covers the principles and application of the transformation and migration processes for the preservation of digital content. Key issues surrounding preservation strategies are highlighted	Related
3-d[a]	Document and e-publishing/ presentation markup	XML is the most well-known markup for digital resources in DLs. This module will explain the major components of XML, and their functions and applications will be introduced	Related
3-e/7-e	Web (push) publishing	This module covers the general principles of Web publishing and the various paradigms that can be used for storing and retrieving content within digital libraries	Related
4-c[a]	Ontology, classification, categorization	Various approaches to building ontology/ classification/categorization schema of genres and file formats in DLs will be discussed	Related
4-d[a]	Subject description, vocabulary control, thesauri, terminologies	Approaches to develop subjects or domains of DLs are presented. Vocabulary control mechanisms for DL collections and their applications in DLs will be addressed	Related
5-c[a]	Identifiers, handles, DOI, PURL	Resources are accessed through identifiers, handles, etc. Technologies to provide persistent access to resources are addressed	Related
5-d	Protocols	The concepts, development, and implementation of protocols used in DL systems are addressed. Roles of protocols in IR and Service Oriented Architecture (SOA) are also covered	Related
9-e	Intellectual property	This module defines the purpose of copyright and copyright protection of DL resources, and discusses the controversial issues related to privacy. It will also deal with technical methods to protect the authorship of resource creators	Related

[a]Not developed yet

searching and 7-a(1) Image retrieval, may help students understand the topics at a deeper level. In contrast to a near "complete" development of IR-core modules, four out of 11 IR-related modules have been developed at the time of this writing.

Table 14.4 Comments from module developers (graduate students)

	Comments
Success factors	• Keep meeting schedules
	• Frequent group communication
	• Existing modules as guidelines
	• Multiple reviews for content organization
	• Support from the instructor (e.g., scope)
	• Good reference books and papers
	• Exhaustive literature search
Challenges	• Finding good resources
	• Creating the scope, structure
	• Decision on topics to include or omit.
	• Unfamiliar topics
Suggestion for future developers	• Use time wisely: start early
	• Collaborate from day one
	• Find as many references as possible to support topics
	• The given structure of the body of knowledge is not always the best way to present the module in class. Think about better ways to present a module
	• Hold each other accountable
	• Think of yourself as a designer/implementer
Concluding remarks	• Module development was a good teaching/learning activity
	• Guidance in scope decision and access to resources is essential

The module development methodology, which involved graduate students (generally in teams) under the guidance of a project team member, has been successful, and we expect that it will be successful in helping us to develop additional IR modules and add them into the curriculum framework. Considering that this methodology will be used continuously, it will be beneficial to present feedback from the graduate developer teams so that the future developers could avoid unnecessary obstacles and develop modules more efficiently. Their comments are summarized in Table 14.4. The students emphasized the importance of guidance in scope decision, topic selection, and finding resources.

14.5.2 Integrated IR Course

After extensive analysis of the DL literature (Pomerantz et al. 2006a; Pomerantz et al. 2007), modules have been identified based on the principle of the highest cohesion within a module, and lowest coupling between modules, to allow maximum flexibility in their usage (Pressman 2009). Thus, IR modules in Table 14.3 can be combined to create an integrated IR course for both CS and LIS classes. One or multiple modules could be plugged into an existing IR course to enhance it with new topics and engaging learning activities, etc.

For example, a new IR course might utilize modules in the following sequence. First, some of the IR-related modules can be taught to provide background

Table 14.5 Modules in an example IR course

Sequence	Modules
I	• IR-related
	− 2-a Text resources
	− 2-b Multimedia
	− 2-b(1) Images
	− 5-d Protocols
	− 9-e Intellectual property
II	• IR-core (LIS perspective)
	− 6-a Info needs, relevance
	− 6-b Online info seeking behavior and search strategy
	− 4-b Metadata
	− 3-c Harvesting
	− 9-c DL evaluation, user studies
III	• IR-core (CS perspective, fundamental)
	− 3-f/7-f Crawling
	− 7-a Indexing and searching
IV	• IR-core (CS perspective, application)
	− 7-a(1) Image retrieval
	− 7-c Recommender systems
	− 7-d Routing
	− 7-g Personalization
	− 8-b Web archiving

information (see sequence I in Table 14.5). IR-related portions of the modules should be emphasized (e.g., OAI-PMH is highlighted when teaching 5-d Protocols). Second, IR-core modules that have an LIS perspective can be adapted to emphasize models, theories, and user behaviors as well as knowledge about metadata and harvesting (see sequence II in Table 14.5). Further, retrieval evaluation is emphasized in 9-c. Third, IR-core modules with a CS perspective are taught, focusing on fundamental technical solutions for IR (see sequence III in Table 14.5). Then, other IR-core modules with a CS perspective are taught (see sequence IV in Table 14.5).

Depending on the instructor's preference, modules or topics in a module can be omitted or strengthened further, supported by additional class activities and projects developed by the instructor herself. Considering that each module is designed to be taught in one or two classes (e.g., approximately teaching one module per week), the course discussed above might be taught throughout an academic semester.

14.6 IR Module Distribution and Plan for Project Sustainability

The project team is using two different venues to publish DL curriculum modules for broad dissemination and refinement by the members of the community: the main project Web site and Wikiversity.org. Each is described below including notes about its strengths and weaknesses.

14.6.1 DL Curriculum Development Project Web Site

The developed and reviewed modules are posted on the project's main Web site (DL Curriculum Development Project homepage) for use and reference purposes. Along with the modules, other information is provided in the main Web site such as older versions of the modules, the DL module framework, the module template, publications, and a list of advisory board members for the project. These materials constitute one of the computing education-related collections of the Ensemble project (http://www.computingportal.org), a Pathways project that is part of the NSF-funded National Science Digital Library (http://www.nsdl.org).

14.6.2 Wikiversity.org

Technologies in DL systems (including IR technologies) change rapidly; learning about them should be incorporated into the DL curriculum. Posting the DL modules to a public wiki site allows community members to constantly upgrade them with newer information. Our choice was to use Wikiversity.org since DL modules are to be used as learning resources. The "Digital Libraries" link displays the DL curriculum framework (DL Curriculum Project at Wikiversity.org). Uploaded modules are being added in the wiki format for easy editing. A link to our Wikiversity.org page has been added to an article, "Digital Library," in Wikipedia, as a cross-reference. It is our hope that modules will continue to be revised by community members who are interested, and will be used by them and many others to enhance their CS/LIS courses.

14.7 Summary

Over a 4-year NSF-funded project period, the DL curriculum project group developed educational modules. A significant overlap between IR and DL topics was found; therefore, IR education can be enhanced by focusing on the IR modules (both core and related modules) in the DL curriculum framework. Team-based module development was effective in creating multiple high-quality modules with support from the instructors and the project members. By the end of 2009, a total of 11 IR-related modules have been developed and posted on the project Web site, as well as made available in Wikiversity.org. It is our practice (including through the end of 2010) and vision that they will be continuously upgraded and used, ensuring that they are satisfying the needs of the IR education community.

Acknowledgments This material is based upon work supported by the National Science Foundation under Grant No. IIS-0535057 (to Virginia Tech) and IIS-0535060 (to the University of

North Carolina at Chapel Hill). Any opinions, findings, and conclusions or recommendations expressed in this material are those of the authors and do not necessarily reflect the views of the National Science Foundation.

References

Choi Y, Rasmussen E (2006) What do digital librarians do. In: Proceedings of the 6th ACM/IEEE-CS joint conference on digital libraries (JCDL '06), Chapel Hill, NC, USA, 11–15 June 2006. ACM, New York, pp 187–188. doi:http://doi.acm.org/10.1145/1141753.1141789

DL Curriculum Development Project homepage. http://curric.dlib.vt.edu. Accessed Oct 2010

DL Curriculum Project at Wikiversity.org. http://en.wikiversity.org/wiki/Digital_Libraries. Accessed Oct 2010

Flashlight evaluation handbook. http://www.tltgroup.org/Flashlight/Handbook/TOC.htm. Accessed Oct 2010

Goncalves M, Fox E, Watson L, Kipp N (2004) Streams, structures, spaces, scenarios, societies (5 S): a formal model for digital. ACM Trans Inf Syst 22(2):270–312

Lee CA, Tibbo HR, Schaefer JC (2007) Defining what digital curators do and what they need to know: the Digccurr project. In: Proceedings of the 7th ACM/IEEE-CS joint conference on digital libraries (JCDL '07), Vancouver, BC, Canada, 18–23 June 2007. ACM, New York, pp 49–50. doi: http://doi.acm.org/10.1145/1255175.1255183

Ma Y, Clegg W, O'Brien A (2006) Digital library education: the current status. In: Proceedings of the 6th ACM/IEEE-CS Joint Conference on Digital Libraries (JCDL '06), Chapel Hill, NC, USA, 11–15 June 2006. ACM, New York, pp 165–174. doi: http://doi.acm.org/10.1145/1141753.1141786

Ma Y, O'Brien A, Clegg W (2007) Digital library education: some international course structure comparisons. In: Proceedings of the 7th ACM/IEEE-CS joint conference on digital libraries (JCLD '07). Vancouver, BC, Canada, 18–23 June 2007. ACM, New York, p 490. doi: http://doi.acm.org/10.1145/1255175.1255289

McGorry SY (2003) Measuring quality in online programs. Internet High Educ 6:159–177

Mostafa J, Brancolini K, Smith LC, Mischo W (2005) Developing a digital library education program. In: Proceedings of the 5th ACM/IEEE-CS joint conference on digital libraries, (JCDL '05), Denver, CO, USA, 07–11 June 2005, 427–427. ACM, New York. doi: http://doi.acm.org/10.1145/1065385.1065533

Neal E (2004). Course evaluation questionnaire (Developed for use in the University of North Carolina School of Nursing). University of North Carolina, Chapel Hill

Oh S, Wildemuth BM, Pomerantz J, Yang S, Fox EA (2009) Using a wiki as a platform for formative evaluation. A poster in Proceedings of ASIST 2009, 6–11 Nov 2009, Vancouver, BC, Canada

Pomerantz J, Oh S, Yang S, Fox EA, Wildemuth BM (2006) The core: digital library education in library and information science programs. D-Lib Mag 12:11. http://www.dlib.org/dlib/november06/pomerantz/11pomerantz.html

Pomerantz J, Wildemuth BM, Yang S, Fox EA (2006) Curriculum development for digital libraries. In: Proceedings of the 6th ACM/IEEE-CS joint conference on digital libraries (JCDL '06), 11–15 June 2006, Chapel Hill, NC, pp 175–184. doi:http://doi.acm.org/10.1145/1141753.1141787

Pomerantz J, Oh S, Wildemuth BM, Yang S, Fox EA (2007) Digital library education in computer science programs. In: Proceedings of the 7th ACM/IEEE-CS joint conference on digital libraries (JCLD '07), 18–23 June 2007, Vancouver, British Columbia, Canada, pp 177–178. http://doi.acm.org/10.1145/1255175.1255208

Pressman RS (2009) Software engineering: a practitioner's approach, 7th edn. McGraw-Hill, London

Snare CE (2000) An alternative end-of-semester questionnaire. Polit Sci Polit 33:823–825

Tammaro AM (2007) A curriculum for digital librarians: a reflection on the European debate. New Libr World 108(5/6):229–246

Wildemuth BM, Pomerantz J, Oh S, Yang S, Fox EA (2008) A digital libraries curriculum: Expert review and field testing. D-Lib Mag 14:7–8. doi:10.1045/july2008-inbrief

Wildemuth BM, Pomerantz J, Oh S, Yang S, Fox EA (2009) The variety of ways in which instructors implement a modular digital library curriculum. Poster at the 9th ACM/IEEE-CS Joint Conference on Digital Libraries (JCDL '09)

Yang S, Wildemuth BM, Kim S, Murthy U, Pomerantz JP, Oh S, Fox EA (2007) Further development of a digital library curriculum: evaluation approaches and new tools. Springer, Heidelberg. LNCS 4822:434–443. In: Proceedings of the 10th international conference on Asian digital libraries, ICADL 2007, 10–13 Dec 2007, Hanoi, Vietnam. doi: 10.1007/978-3-540-77094-7_55

Subject Index

E. Efthimiadis et al. (eds.), *Teaching and Learning in Information Retrieval*,
The Information Retrieval Series 31, DOI 10.1007/978-3-642-22511-6
© Springer-Verlag Berlin Heidelberg 2011

Printed in the United States
By Bookmasters